Daughters of Desire

In memory of my mother, Athia Bano Kabir.

With love to my sisters:
Shireen Bano and Anees Khan, whose
mothering ran out, for their inspiration
and the example of their courage.

Nasreen Munni Kabir, Priya Bano Kumar
and Nargis Hafeez, sisters who are
other mothers to me.

Daughters of Desire

Lesbian Representations in Film

Shameem Kabir

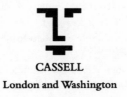

CASSELL

London and Washington

Cassell
Wellington House
125 Strand
London WC2R 0BB

PO Box 605
Herndon
VA 20172

First published 1998

British Library Cataloguing-in-Publication Data
A catalogue record for this book is available from the British Library.

Library of Congress Cataloging-in-Publication Data
Kabir, Shameem, 1954–
    Daughters of desire: lesbian representations in film / Shameem Kabir.
        p.   cm.
    Includes bibliographical references and index.
    ISBN 0-304-33381-6 (hardcover). — 0-304-33382-4 (paperback)
    Lesbianism in motion pictures.   I. Title.
PN1995.9.L48K23   1997
791.43'6538'068843—dc21   97–16279
                                                                      CIP

ISBN 0-304-33381-6 (hardback)
        0-304-33382-4 (paperback)

Thin Ice is available on video from Dangerous to Know, 17a Newman Street, London W1P 3HB.

When Night Is Falling is available on video from Tartan Video, 79 Wardour Street, London W1V 3TH.

Designed and typeset by Ben Cracknell Studios
Printed and bound in Great Britain by Biddles Ltd, Guildford and King's Lynn

Contents

Acknowledgements

With thanks:

To Jane Greenwood, my brilliant editor, who commissioned this book and talked me through it.

To my previous editors, Liz Gibbs, Lucy Whitman, Patricia Duncker and Suzanne Raitt, and my first publisher, Lilian Mohin.

To friends, Heather Price, Kate Mackintosh, Liz Gibbs, Lucy Whitman, Rosa Ainley, for reading first drafts.

To early friends from Château Mont-Choisi for the riotous times we had: Cynthia Edmundson, Jane Schwartz, Lucretia King-Hedinger, Nadia Alatas, Pag Sampatissiri, and especially Mariana Schackne Hoyt.

To college and BA friends: Celine Castellino, Deryn Phillips, Jackie Nicholls, Janet Ostrey, Katie Doitch, Krys Swift, Lindis Lane, Liz Payne, Lyndie Brimstone, Maggie Kaye, Sharon Piggott, Suzanne Bosworth, Valya Alexander and Wendy Wheeler, for our inspiring conversations in the canteen and elsewhere.

To friends from the MA: Heather Price, Nina Hartman and Tina Papoulias, especially with thanks for our social studies socials, where we would meet to discuss reading and issues, and spend the evening in uproarious laughter.

To friends for believing in me: Ali Courtney, Annie B from New York, Barry Scott, Ben Trainin, Bev Thorpe, Bob Robert, Caroline Bevan, Caroline Montanaro, Erica Torchen, Farrah Ali, Feroz Zaidi, Frances Connelly, Haldane Grace, Helen Bishop, Jacqueline Geering, Jeanne Brodie, Joyce Chester, Juliette Kay, Karen Ventsel, Kate Elander, Liz Elander, Margaret Monod, Munir Ata-Ullah, Nishabda Malik, Nita Scott, Peter Chappell, Rosie Guy, Sandy Chapman, Sarah Child, Shaila Shah, Sue Evans, Talat Majid Dar, Tom Langham, Tony Chidgey,

Urvashi Butalia, Val Stein, Yoshi Tobari, Younas Umer, and especially Florence Hamilton.

To teachers and lecturers, for their encouragement and inspiration: Ann Seller, Brigit Mitchell, Chris Richards, Chris Rolfe, Elizabeth Blackwell, Elizabeth Cowie, Elizabeth Watson, Jacqui Halson, Jan Montefiore, Janet Sayers, Jenny Mulrennan, Jill Davis, John Thieme, Lucy Bland, Lucy Gent, Mary Evans, Nigel Alexander, Paul McSorley, Pete Messent, Sue Lees, Trevor Griffiths.

To colleagues from work, past and present: Amelia Fairney, Auri de Stacpoole, Behroze Gandhy, Carole Spedding, Charlotte Cole, Cheryl Farthing, Christine Mark, Christopher Hird, Claire Beavan, Devon Howse, El Glinoer, Emma D'Almeida, Gaby Young, Helen Williams, Helen Windrath, Jacky Belfon, Jane Dibblin, Jayne Egerton, Jo Rabiger, Karen McCarthy, Karol Davies, Katie Sampson, Katie Yant, Kirsty Dunseath, Laurie Critchley, Liz Foody, Mandy Merck, Margaret Doyle, Martin Roche, Mary Hemming, Nicole Hillson, Pascale Carrington, Paula McFarlane, Penny Johnson, Phil Woodward, Pratibha Parmar, Richard Kwietniowski, Ros Lyle, Sarah Edwards, Sarah Wasley, Shauna Brown, Shobu Kapoor, Sue Chambers, Sue Copas, Susan Ardill, Yasmin Keyani, Yvonne Metherell, and especially Kathy Gale.

To the Economic and Social Research Council for granting me an award to study for an MA in Women's Studies.

To staff at the library of the University of North London, the British Library, Rachel Williams at Routledge, Rupert Snell, and especially Barbara Laplace for help with books.

To advisors on the way: Fiona Sanders, Liz Badger, Sally Marstrand and Terry Rooney.

To family, for always caring: Hafeez, Zeeba, Gagu, Zehra, Omar, Jamil, Murad, Salman, Kert, Zulfi, Allessandra, Rupert and Naveed. To the little ones: Farrukh, Amina, Minah, Alex, Jasira and Benji. And to my father, for having been such a gentle man, Dr Syed Ahmed Kabir.

To my fictive family, Barbara Laplace, Gill Price and Lucy Whitman, especially Barbara for all her concrete help towards this book, with love, and to Gill, for all her support.

And to reiterate my love and gratitude to my sisters, Nargis Hafeez, Priya Bano Kumar and Nasreen Munni Kabir, all mothers to me, without whose love and support none of this would have been possible.

Filmography

At First Sight (*Coup de Foudre*, aka *Entre Nous*), 1983, Diane Kurys
Bagdad Café, 1988, Percy Adlon
Claire of the Moon, 1992, Nicole Conn
The Color Purple, 1985, Steven Spielberg
Desperately Seeking Susan, 1985, Susan Seidelman
Fire, 1996, Deepa Mehta
Fried Green Tomatoes, 1991, Jon Avnet
Go Fish, 1994, Rose Troche
The Hunger, 1983, Tony Scott
The Killing of Sister George, 1968, Robert Aldrich
Lianna, 1983, John Sayles
Maidens in Uniform (Mädchen in Uniform), 1931, Leontine Sagan
Maidens in Uniform (Mädchen in Uniform), 1958, Geza von Radvanyi
Nocturne, 1990, Joy Chamberlain
November Moon (Novembermond), 1984, Alexandra von Grote
Personal Best, 1982, Robert Towne
Queen Christina, 1933, Rouben Mamoulian
Rebecca, 1940, Alfred Hitchcock
Salmonberries, 1991, Percy Adlon
Thelma and Louise, 1991, Ridley Scott
Thin Ice, 1995, Fiona Cunningham Reid
When Night Is Falling, 1995, Patricia Rozema

Introduction: Desire, Dyke-Icons, Mothers and Others Matter

My hope is that our lives will declare
this meeting
open

June Jordan[1]

'Call me Marlon', he said, and so it was, albeit briefly at the age of twelve, that I came to be on first-name terms with Marlon Brando. He had met my mother in America and she invited him to visit us when in London. He did so when his work brought him here for the filming of *A Countess from Hong Kong*, directed by Charlie Chaplin at Pinewood Studios. We met on several occasions, and he was extraordinarily kind to me. One evening he showed me a coin-disappearing trick which completely mystified me. He then empowered me by showing me how it was done. I spent all that evening practising.

On one occasion he arranged for a car to take two of my sisters and me to Pinewood so we could sit in on the shoot. Chaplin did not look at all as I had expected. Sophia Loren was there, playing the title role, and several hours were spent filming the same scene, with her repeating lines such as 'This marriage is just a formality' over and over. I thought this was a bit tedious. But I was still in awe.

On another occasion, Brando invited us to a house to watch an old Chaplin movie. We arrived late at the private screening, and I scrambled on the floor in front of a sofa. At the end of the film I turned round to see Sean Connery seated on the sofa. As a then fan of James Bond and enamoured of *Marnie*, I was suitably star-struck. But not uncool, I hope.

I begin anecdotally, less for the purpose of dropping names and more to indicate the sense of awe I felt at seeing these acting giants at close quarters. For me, Hollywood was peopled with geniuses. The visit to Pinewood stays with me.

Coming from an Asian family where we were all obsessed with music and especially cinema, Indian, Hollywood and European, I was fascinated with film from an early age. Those first sightings into the workings of cinema, with its labour and its machinery, made me realize the construction behind the magic. I came to see the film text as a fabrication, produced from the tissues of illusion. I arrived at a position where I evolved a spectatorial response which was critical but engaged, consciously able to enjoy the pleasures of the text, though often at a racial remove. Years later, after a long spell of being a serious cinema addict, of working in television on film, and of studying texts on film theory for pleasure, I have developed this split position of conscious consumption. This spectatorial position involves engagement and enjoyment, assessment and analysis, and challenge and contestation, where I can extract pleasure from the text while being aware of its contradictions and while simultaneously supplying resistant readings. I explore the configurations of this split position of spectatorship in this book, and I also discuss the investment of film in narrative and desire, while suggesting ways to incorporate the pleasures of the mainstream within practices which are alert to alternative political positionings.

One reason I went to the cinema was to make sense of my sexuality in relation to issues of masculinities and femininities. With the imagings of women, I often preferred to experience desire *for* them rather than *as* them, as my identifications with the masculine position made me complicit with the values and operations of objectification. With the imagings of men, I saw their vulnerabilities despite their apparent power. I saw their emotional engagements as a testimony to their relational capacities, even though these often took an exclusively sexual trajectory. I saw that these men were attempting to resist the more commonplace enculturations of masculine behaviours. But they too were capable of rape. I am thinking of *Gone with the Wind*, as well as the suggested and equivalent rapes in *A Streetcar Named Desire* and *Marnie*. No matter how delicately implied or thankfully left off-screen, these rapes confirmed that an assertion of masculinity can sometimes be an expression of aggression against the woman. Just as my desire for women involved a problematic objectification, so my identifications with the masculine position became increasingly troublesome. This took place in the context of an increased incidence of violence in the cinema which I found to be completely alienating. When this violence, often directed at the figure of the woman, came to dominate the screen, I lost most of my interest in mainstream cinema. Coinciding with a switch to video, I became determined to consume only the smallest fraction of this sickening output. Selection led me to focus on women-centred films, including lesbian films, of course.

The first lesbian film I saw was at the age of thirteen, on television. *The Loudest Whisper* (aka *The Children's Hour*) gave me the first hint that I was not alone in having lesbian desires. I was devastated when the character played by Shirley MacLaine hangs herself because she realizes she desires the woman played by Audrey Hepburn. I desperately wanted to see a reworking of this lesbian desire. I needed images that would rewrite the lesbian without the tragedy. Naïvely, I sought out other images of MacLaine and Hepburn specifically, looking desperately for some suggestion that lesbian desire was OK. From *The Yellow Rolls-Royce* to *Gambit* to *The Apartment*, from *My Fair Lady* to *How to Steal a Million* to *Charade*, I watched for some sign of lesbian desire. There was none. But so began my search for the lesbian subtext. And now I celebrate some of the explicit imagings of our desire, as mainstream cinema finally wakes up to the fact of lesbian desire and recognizes audience fascination with, or even just interest in, them. After years of being starved of representations of us, or of receiving images of ourselves as perverts and monsters who must be punished and destroyed, we are finally at a juncture where lesbian desire is being rewritten to inspire respect, where it invites a reworking of paradigms that have formerly only defined sexual dissidence as pathological.

Of course there have been dyke-icons for lesbian spectators for years without explicit imagings or openly out identities, where a combination of reading lesbian and of grapevine gossip has fuelled our ability to spectate with a lesbian look. The present interest in imagings of lesbian desire has enabled a movement from the margins to the mainstream, where lesbian desire is no longer unspeakable but spoken, no longer to be killed off but celebrated, no longer about pathologization but about oppositional choices and healthy preferences. We need to maximize what the mainstream can offer us, while remaining alert to representations that are not respectful, but distorting, sensational, or even abusive in their treatment of lesbian desire. We need to resist such imagings, while celebrating those which convey the dignity and courage of lesbian identities, which also convey our complexities and our capacities for mergence. Lesbian desire can rewrite how desire is both constituted and enacted. By that I mean it can supply a model of desire for non-lesbian identities as well, where a politicization around concepts of mastery and control can rewrite how we function as subjects in a phallocentric order, so as to resist and reformulate that order. In this book I discuss the phallicization of desire, which has been appropriated by phallocentric definitions that need to be dismantled. I attempt to expose the fraudulence of the phallus, and I make some speculative suggestions about the structuration of an alternative symbolic order.

My position as an Asian lesbian feminist has enabled me to negotiate race, sexuality and gender in other, dissident and alternative terms. As an Asian who now identifies as black, as a lesbian who is proud to be out, and as a feminist whose vision involves inclusion, I have arrived at a politics which seeks the eradication of systems of violence, hatred and domination. This has happened in gradual stages, where my present political positioning is in contrast to earlier positions.

For many years I psychically passed as white, and this has allowed me to read white logic from the inside. I came to do this because I never internalized feelings of racial inferiority at being Asian, so for years I refused to recognize how racism impacted on me. My pride at being Asian without absorbing ascriptions of racial inferiority was a result of having spent my formative years in different parts of the Indian subcontinent, where to be Asian was normal, not different or other, but part of a culture that mirrored my Asianness. After arriving in London, before the bitter winter of 1963 which saw the death of Sylvia Plath and the emergence of the Beatles, I had to renegotiate language and culture, diet and dress, schools and peers, and so on. Without knowing it at the time, but based on those experiences, I later realized that because culture was constructed, because identities were in flux, because language was shifting, and desire was often repressed into the unknowable of the unconscious, anything was possible and everything had to be fought for in the context of slippage, fragility, uncertainty and loss. Rather than accept ascriptions of cultural and racial inferiority, I was proud to be Asian, but this was not an 'othered' identity, because I passed psychically as white in refusing to acknowledge race and racism. Although I have been physically attacked and verbally abused for being black, although I have received racist treatment, unconscious or overt, from some friends as well as former partners, although both my education and my employ-ment have sometimes been subjected to cultural pathologization and discriminatory practices, for many years I preferred to pass as white. I thought I was being different in doing this. I was especially proud that I had not incorporated a self-hatred at having black skin, which is a common response to internalizations of racism. I was the other who was the same.

I also went through a thankfully brief phase of thinking that women were superior to men. I did this from a position of ignorance, again thinking this was different. When I read more feminist work, I realized there was nothing different or revolutionary about this view, but that in fact it aligned with a reactionary politics, including inverse sexism. It was as a closet lesbian that I felt self-hatred the most, where I moved between imagings of myself as degenerate, pathological, sick. The process of my politicization has moved from the reactionary to the radical, with liberalism thrown in as a transitional phase. As a black subject I have moved from passing psychically as white and refusing to acknowledge racism to a position where I now know we have to dethrone white logic which still clings to notions of supremacism. As a feminist I have moved from the essentialist to the constructionist position, where I reject archaic notions of inferiority and strive for the equality of all social subjectivities that would characterize a just social order. And as a lesbian, too, I have moved from the position of having internalized homophobia in the form of self-loathing, to where I now feel worthy and happy at having a lesbian identity. I explore some of the theory behind a lesbian identity, which is historically a recent phenomenon as an identity, although of course the incidence of lesbian activity is probably transhistorical and crosscultural.

The phenomenon of passing psychically correlates to passing actually in an adopted identity. It is always the disadvantaged group that aspires to membership of the dominant group. By passing psychically as white, I was internalizing the values of assimilation and integration to a ridiculous degree, where my whitewashing made me blend into the background of polite white circles. In retrospect, my response seems on a par with the logic of supremacism, where it was easier to conform to prevailing ideologies than to challenge them. Passing therefore becomes a strategy for negotiating the dominant culture. For example, there are still many lesbians and gays who have so internalized homophobia that they prefer to repress their sexualities, passing psychically as straight even to themselves because they cannot confront the repercussions of a lesbian or gay identity. There are also women who psychically see themselves as men, wanting to function like masculinist men rather than change how these men function. There is also the phenomenon of the lesbian who wants to pass as a man, and this for me is the ultimate in contradictions, not as accommodating but as confused. It is in my opinion to mask the retrograde to pass itself off as revolutionary, and that is what the cult of the phallus is about. Lesbians have always been defined in terms of phallocentric desires. There is nothing radical about wanting to adopt the phallus. On the contrary, I find it is retrogressive, playing with the very terms we need to reformulate. Given that work is being done to expose the behaviours of some masculinities as aggressive and abusive, where it is the adulation of the phallus that is at fault, to want to pass psychically as a man is a sorry step on the road to a new symbolic order.

To arrive at a new symbolic order I think we have to rewrite the mother. We need a reverence for the mother, not out of gratitude for her self-sacrifice, not as lip-service appreciation of her labour, but as a respect for her as a separate subject, whose autonomy and agency have too often been suppressed. The mother must be seen as a subject of desire, whose desire is self-determined and not dependent on phallic identifications. Only such reformulations can refigure the mother to enable a recognition of the other. A conceptualization of the mother as other allows social subjectivity a model of alternative structurations, where her autonomous desire encourages alterity and individuation, agency and independence. The mother as other, as the m/other, enables our respect for her while facilitating recognitions of ourselves as individuated, as well as enabling identifications with others, ranging from mutual respect to the capacity for mergence with the other. The relation with the figure of the mother as other can dictate the capacity for relational contact, respect and recognition. If we do not recognize the other as valuable, this may have less to do with their positioning and more with our own relational in-capacities. The model of the m/other allows both mergence and individuation, both engagement and a maintenance of boundaries. I believe it is only by reformulating the status of the mother away from its systematic derogation that we can appreciate the other, but I am not in favour of regressed identifications with the mother. Instead, I would want to emphasize her subjectivity as separate and autonomous. Although the mother is often reduced to the function of maternity, which in turn is often seen as invested in heterosexual desires and phallic identifications, the right of the mother to express her agency in the choice of her desires and identifications must be respected. Although I argue that lesbian desire can dismantle phallocentrism by providing counter-paradigms for the embodiment of desire away from heterosexual models, nevertheless I think it is the mother's desire as self-determined that can provide a revised blueprint for female desire. Whether that desire is lesbian or heterosexual would be secondary, although I imagine it is the lesbian desire that would speak more fluently of alterity and dissidence, contestation and challenge.

My previous occupation of certain reactionary positions has enabled me to read the logic of the oppressor from the inside, where I have had to resist the seductions of power and control that oppressive practices apparently promise. Resisting the values of mastery for mutuality, of power for parity, I feel privileged to have tentatively escaped a mindset that thrives on domination and dispossession. Because I can guess how the oppressor thinks, I am able to expose the fraudulent pretensions behind the façade, where corruption and deception are at the heart of the social fabric. This social sickness is most evident in the treatment of the black subject. Rather than acknowledge that black subjectivity informs white subjectivity, that white subjects are just as racially constituted as are black subjects, white logic would have us believe that white is right, black is bad, and that such social constructions of racial categories are natural.

White subjects have remained largely resistant to recognizing the equal subjectivity of black subjects. The dominance of white cultural imperialism rests on presenting and perceiving itself as the racial norm, without recognizing the abnormalization in the way black subjects are perceived. Racism pathologizes the black subject. We are said to be abnormal in our behaviour as it has been defined by the norm of white supremacism, which we can never measure up to except as lacking. Because of white resistance to self-awareness as well as a resistance to the facts of black subjectivity, I go into some detail on the historical constructions of race and racism in the context of slavery and colonialism, in the hope that this material is taken more as a relevant reminder than a guilt-evoking reproach that white subjectivity still has much to learn about the black subject.

One way for white subjects to readdress the issues at stake is for them to rewrite their sometimes unconscious racism, just as directly racist subjects need to rethink their identities in terms of their own disorders, where they project their undesirable behaviours onto the black subject. In terms of active strategies, readdressing the issues of race and racism needs the acknowledgement of the equally valid and valuable subjectivity of the black subject. There is little evidence of our subjectivity being accorded the status it deserves. While some of us are given a voice, sometimes for reasons of tokenism, where some white subjects invite our inclusion so that they can be seen to be addressing black under-representation, we are the fortunate few who cannot truly represent anyone but ourselves. What would be more helpful would be the address to an equal black subjectivity on a large scale, as a cultural identity and political force, where the urgency of racism needs to be acknowledged by rewriting black history, black culture, black politics, black identities, ultimately by rereading us on our own terms.

I am not a scholar, nor an academic. Although I make certain assertions, although they are based on convictions informed by my identity, although I have written them after much thought and reading, I offer them not as an authority, but in the spirit of sharing, speculating, daring. I am aware that some of what I attempt may not work for some readers, given that I am negotiating two different media in the book, the verbal and the visual. For instance, I delight in a detailed retailing of the films, although narrative as analysis is unusual in a book of film criticism. I hope my emphasis on content and character are not seen as outmoded or ignorant of issues of form and the means of textual production. I am convinced that 'character' is a telling mode of cultural commentary, just as content allows us to explore cultural preoccupations. A more serious objection could be that the juxtaposition of passages of narrative with discussions of theoretical issues is sometimes jarring. Although I personally find that the material is integrated organically, some readers may be jolted by this juxtaposition. This is part of a larger writing project to take risks and to attempt new syntheses. I apologize if this has an alienating effect. I am also aware I have covered only a fraction of the material potentially available for research purposes, and I especially regret having had to omit discussions on issues of language in relation to discourse. This will have to wait for a future project.

This book has given me a forum not only for exploring the work of diverse authors from different disciplines, but also for conveying the necessity for a serious reconsideration of how the social order is founded on fraudulent values. There is an urgent need for social transformation, beginning with a revision of the past, activating change in the present, and questing for a global alteration of the social order if we are to avert in the future the horrors that constitute much of human history so far. For this we would need another system of sociality, where subjects have actual and not abstract rights to equal subjectivities, and where black and white subjects, men and women, lesbians and gays, can accommodate the plurality of positionings that we all necessarily occupy, in a politics of inclusion and a feminine economy of exchange and not exploitation. The theory is in place and, on this level, solutions are already in speculative play, where the rewriting of black subjectivities, the reworking of gender and the resistance to oppressive and abusive systems are all underway, in the form of contestation and the enactment of alternative practices. How we are to move beyond resistance to an active articulation of another social order remains the priority, and I believe it is not enough merely to challenge the dominant order but that we must engage in actually changing it.

As we move into the new millennium, if we do not accord each other recognition in an ethics of respect, if we do not take responsibility for social transformation beginning with our personal relationships, if we do not revise the structure of the social order away from perverted values of oppression and domination, if we do not celebrate our capacity for the relational but persist with aggression and violence, we will be playing our lives with a dangerous hand characterized by the destructiveness of a death-dealing order. Many a turn-of-the-century ethos evokes proclamations of alarmist anxieties, and this is evident more so on the turn of a new millennium. At this critical juncture of human history, we need to aspire to a new epoch and another system of sociality. More of the same will not do. We must change to survive. Nothing less than the future and this planet are at stake.

On a more optimistic note, we need to celebrate our survival so far, to commemorate and acknowledge that our lives are in mutual process, where we engage in a perpetual dialogue which is about language as communication and not command, where all subjects can locate workable identities in a politics of inclusion. Surely this is what we would want.

A final dedication, to the daughters of desire who have gone before us, many nameless: 'Our mothers and grandmothers, some of them: moving to music not yet written. And they waited.'[2]

London, December 1996

Notes

1. June Jordan, 'Metarhetoric (1976), quoted by Adrienne Rich (1979: 279).

2. Alice Walker, *In Search of Our Mothers' Gardens* (1983b: 232).

PART ONE

Desire

Lesbian Desire on the Screen

The Mother as Other: *The Hunger*

> *Women's cinema must embody the working through of desire: such an objective demands the use of the entertainment film.*
>
> Claire Johnston[1]

This discussion of *The Hunger* will traverse film theory in relation to fetishism and the look, in which I favour a move away from objectification while acknowledging the pleasures of scopophilia. I analyse the film in detail in order to demonstrate its use of avant-garde devices in the service of mainstream entertainment, a synthesis I endorse. And I discuss the position of the mother as she has been traditionally situated, as an object of the desire of others. I suggest that we see the mother as other, in terms of her equal subjectivity as an other in her own right, the author of her own destinations and the subject of her own desires.

Lesbian desire is now being imaged more frequently on the screen. We are at a juncture of new articulations after over a hundred years during which white Western feminisms and lesbian identities have found a voice. Conjoining with a century of cinema, and building on a hundred years of psychoanalysis, we have the theoretical paradigms in place to effect the articulation of a different social order. This is especially so in the context of a reworking of black subjectivity as valuable, thereby discarding the racist discourses that have dehumanized and demonized us. I think that the black lesbian, who is multiply positioned as other, can benefit from her alterity by contesting and challenging the dominant order. Such a positioning is not about alienation or negation, but about interrogation with engagement. Therefore I favour those strategies, on the screen and otherwise, which allow for both resistance and engagement, both protest and pleasure. A brief overview of film theory, drawing especially on the work of Laura Mulvey, will confirm the possibilities we have for playing with filmic forms, whereby we can rewrite some of the masculinist operations in film languages to achieve alternative positionings of pleasure.

Mulvey deploys psychoanalytic theory 'as a political weapon' to demonstrate 'the way the unconscious of patriarchal society has structured film form' (Mulvey, 1975: 57). She argues that 'mainstream film coded the erotic into the language of the dominant patriarchal order' and she is in favour of 'daring to break with normal pleasurable expectations in order to conceive a new language of desire' (*ibid.*: 59).

It was with the aim of effecting this break that feminists in the 1970s attempted to challenge the languages of mainstream film. Film theorist Claire Johnston suggested a 'counter-cinema' to oppose the practices of Hollywood, but she also recognized the necessity for the pleasures of 'the entertainment film' that Hollywood has so skilfully packaged for global consumption (Johnston, 1973: 217). Johnston proposed a strategy of reading against the grain, and she was alert to Hollywood director Dorothy Arzner's use of 'the device of *making-strange*' (Johnston, 1975: 41; original emphasis). She cited the Russian Formalist attention to *ostranenie*, the device of denaturalization and defamiliarization (*ibid.*: 41; cf. Jefferson, 1984: 19). By rendering strange or denaturalizing the status of representations as apparently real and natural, the text can be seen as a site of internal contradictions and ideological tensions. This of course implies the occupation of active positions of spectatorship.

B. Ruby Rich was in favour of not denying the power of women spectators as 'active producers of meaning' (1978: 278). Women's active positions are confirmed by more recent studies on spectating (Mayne, 1993; Jackie Stacey, 1994). The position of active spectating can counter attempts to co-opt our voices. With the emergence of the 'women's film' in the 1970s, there was a feeling that progressive strategies would merely be defused through their incorporation within the larger hegemonic order (Brunsdon, 1987: 119–20). Elizabeth Cowie argues that 'the problem of recuperation is a red herring' because it 'denies the moments of productivity' in the circulation of images (Cowie, 1979: 112, 111). This means 'the film-as-process is denied' (*ibid.*: 111) because the act of spectating contains positions of active contestation as well as conformity, where these positions unfold both independently and correspondingly with the text in a play with process. As text and spectator meet, meanings are generated in the realm of social interactions, so that social meanings are 'to be understood as practices and processes', not as 'static objects' (Kuhn, 1988: 6). Therefore, our active spectating positions as women can allow us to extract pleasure from texts which apparently leave us little agency to express desire as subjects of desire.

Mulvey's early work first concentrated on the issues of spectating positions figured as masculine. On examining the pleasures that the cinema offers, Mulvey identified scopophilia, the pleasure in looking, as being connected to the 'pleasure in using another person as an object of sexual stimulation through sight', where it is 'a function of the sexual instincts' (Mulvey, 1975: 61). Additionally, the spectator's 'fascination with likeness and recognition', an 'identification with the image seen', is a function of ego libido (*ibid*.: 60–1). Mulvey posits a male spectator who enjoys the pleasure of scopophilia, of seeing 'the female form displayed for his enjoyment', and who enjoys the pleasure of identifications, where the spectator is merged with the male protagonist (*ibid*.: 63). She suggests that identifications enable the spectator to control and possess the woman through the temporary mergence with a male protagonist whose power is often signified by a look that carries agency (*ibid*.: 63). Mulvey connects voyeurism and narrative to a sadistic impulse involving the possession of the woman, so that 'by means of identification with him, through participation in his power, the spectator can indirectly possess her too' (*ibid*.: 64).

Of course voyeurism is inescapable in cinema. But I would argue that it can be reworked to move away from a controlling of the woman to a position of celebrating her, through a variant on voyeurism, that of fetishism. Mulvey is clear that the key issue involves the concept of castration, where the woman signifies lack and reminds the man of the threat of his own castration (Mulvey, 1975: 64). Mulvey locates two ways for the male unconscious to escape its castration anxiety, either by controlling the woman, or by worshipping her (*ibid*.). The first connects voyeurism with sadism, the second connects fetishism with scopophilia. When the male spectator is reminded of his own structuration in lack by the figure of the woman who signifies lack in her absence of a penis, the metaphor of castration describes the sense of threat to male potency. The male can reassert his potency through the processes of voyeurism and/or he can defuse the threat through the processes of fetishism. As voyeurism connects with sadism, the voyeuristic position is to identify with the male who controls the woman, whether by punishment or reward or both. Fetishism, which disavows the castration of the woman and seeks to idolize her, can connect with scopophilia, so that 'fetishistic scopophilia' is a position where 'the erotic instinct is focused on the look alone' (*ibid*.).

I find that voyeurism consists of watching as an act of omnipotent surveillance, whereas fetishism consists of looking, and being satisfied with the seen as a source of pleasure without subjecting the scene to controlling demands. John Ellis locates in fetishism 'the opposite tendency to that of voyeurism', where 'fetishistic looking implies the direct acknowledgment and participation of the object viewed' (Ellis, 1982: 47). Fetishistic scopophilia involves 'the abolition of looking itself', in which we bridge 'the gulf that separates viewer and object' (*ibid*.). For the fetishistic look, the woman does not signify threat because we have fetishized her beauty. Here, instead of the woman being held at a distance and subjected to a controlling gaze, the woman is close, and her beauty is the subject of our idealization and idolatry. This can involve mutuality and not control, where the reverence for the woman can be not just about objectification but celebration, not just reification but respect.

I am therefore arguing in favour of fetishistic scopophilia, where we resist the separation of a controlling gaze dominated by voyeurism as sadistic, and where instead we develop the pleasures of visual beauty dependent on a mergence between our look of reverence and the on-screen spectacle of beauty. This is to rework castration, by disavowing that the woman is lacking except in a symbolic sense, and it also involves the reworking of fetishization, where we divest the processes of fetishism from their usually phallic associations. The lesbian position can be specifically advantaged in being able to resist sadism in favour of celebration, and in asserting the fracturations of fetishism as a possible escape from the phallus.

This is to rework desire away from masculine trajectories. Mulvey's identification of the look of the camera(man), of the male protagonist and of the implied male spectator seemed to cancel the place of the woman (Mulvey, 1975: 68). By inference, the woman is only representable as the object of male desire. As E. Ann Kaplan says of this, because the woman lacks the phallus and cannot be a subject, 'she is the recipient of male desire, the passive recipient of his gaze' (Kaplan, 1984: 327). She cannot be a subject of desire because of her objectification in the discourse of male definitions, and hence 'her desire is to be desired' (*ibid*.). Therefore, the woman spectator can identify with the woman on screen in a position of wanting to be desired. Mulvey outlined in a later essay that the woman spectator could identify across gender in the masculine position as a subject of desire in a 'transvestite' position, caught uncomfortably 'between "passive" femininity and regressive "masculinity"' (Mulvey, 1981: 74). Or, as Cowie suggests, the woman could do both simultaneously, that is, be in a position of wanting to be desired as well as identify across gender with an active male desire. This multiplicity of positions is available to all subjects, where 'the gender of the character is not a necessary determinant of identification' (Cowie, 1980: 135). However, what the woman spectator cannot usually do is identify with the woman on screen as an active subject of desire, because the woman does not ordinarily carry the agency associated with the male gaze. Jacqueline Rose refers, in another context, to 'the impossibility of subject *and* desire' for the woman (Rose, 1986: 46; original emphasis), and this apparent impossibility has much to do with the phallicization of desire and its rigid appropriation within masculinist definitions.

It is the lesbian position that can deliver oppositional locations of desire, where we are both subjects of non-phallocentric desire as well as in possession of agency in the form of evoking a return of desire. It is in this reciprocity of desire that plenitude can be refigured, not as phallocentric but as fragmented, where our celebration of the woman involves respect and reverence, not sadism and control.

Turning to the look as central in cinema, Mulvey states 'It is the place of the look that defines cinema', and her work, in film theory and practice, explores 'the possibility of varying it and exposing it' (Mulvey, 1975: 67). With this aim in mind, I follow the differentiation between the look as the function of the eye, and the gaze as a function of the phallocentric (Evans and Gamman, 1995: 16). Caroline Evans and Lorraine Gamman refer to Foucault's concept of the 'panopticon' as an all-seeing eye, where a controlling gaze can be cast at any time on a vast number of subjects who cannot look back. As they point out, this form of surveillance crystallizes the alignment of power with knowledge (*ibid.*: 15). Mary Ann Doane *et al.* also confirm that Foucault's analysis of the panopticon demonstrates 'the collaboration between power and the gaze' (Doane *et al.*, 1984: 13). Here, the properties of the visual are harnessed for the purposes of control. In a similar scopic mode, Lola Young refers to the 'imperial "I/eye"' of the colonial explorer (Young, 1996: 122), which I understand as the power of naming through a visual classification of the other. Homi Bhabha alludes 'to the problematic of seeing/being seen', where 'the *surveillance* of colonial power' functions 'in relation to the regime of the *scopic drive*' (Bhabha, 1983: 322; original emphases). This confirms the connections between power and surveillance, and how surveillance sustains power.

Annette Kuhn characterizes voyeurism by the spectator's look in which 'the circuit of pleasure will never be broken by a returned look' (Kuhn, 1985: 28), and it is on this 'return' that I wish to focus. In addition to the looks of the camera, protagonist and spectator that Mulvey identified, Paul Willemen has located 'the fourth look', where 'the viewer *imagines*' that his/her look at pornographic images is being returned (Creed, 1992:

132; original emphasis). Willemen argues that this imagined fourth look 'is the look of woman', which reassures the male spectator that the woman looking back at his looking signifies her submission to his gaze (*ibid.*: 133). I would like to appropriate from this the possibility of reworking the return of the look, where the spectator sees the 'object' not as objectified but as the other. Instead of inviting readings of submission, complicity and guilt, the object seen can evoke the right to respect. Of course the object cannot look back in the cinema. Therefore we need to imagine the return of the look, as with Willemen's 'fourth look', but see it as signifying not submission but resistance. This is to look with responsibility, to be aware of the dubious politics of some positionings. Evans and Gamman posit the model of a mutual gaze by referring to cultural practices such as cruising, where there can be reciprocity in the exchange of eroticized looks (Evans and Gamman, 1995: 15). In this model we have the possibility of responsibility precisely because there is a mutual relation or relaying of looks which can move beyond initial objectifications. As Young argues, returning the look can activate its 'potential to be de-colonized' (Young, 1996: 152).

Constance Penley parallels filmic practices with the processes of fetishism as 'an inscription of the look on the body of the mother', and she suggests that we 'begin to consider the possibilities and consequences of the mother returning the look' (Penley, 1989: 28). This has raised objections, including from Stephen Heath, who sees this as an inversion and not a transformation of unequal regimes of looking (Heath, 1978: 86). Penley clarifies how she was referring to the Oedipus scenario as a tripartite structure that includes 'the presence or agency of the mother and the father' where 'the look of the child onto the body of the mother' involves positions which should not be confined to masculine identifications. Wanting to break from this 'too-simple model', Penley favours later feminist theories for their work on 'the multiple possibilities of identification in film spectatorship' (Penley, 1989: 28). I think what is helpful in her formulation of 'the mother returning the look' is the possibility of disinvesting the gaze of its impulse towards objectification.

Barbara Creed suggests 'a fifth look', which is to look away from the screen, especially common in the horror film, where 'not-looking' allows the spectator to withhold identifications so as to 'reconstitute the "self" which is threatened with disintegration' (Creed, 1993: 29). Here, 'not-looking' allows the interruption of narrative flow and spectator identifications. This is to relocate the look in the realm of 'self-consciousness', a position where the self is aware of its unique subjectivity as well as alert to and conscious of the external conditions always in attendance on a text. Rose refers to work where the problem 'of "seeing oneself seeing oneself"' involves 'the risks inherent in recentring the spectator's look' (Rose, 1986: 212). This can entail 'a filmic practice in which one watches oneself watching' (Gidal, quoted by Penley, 1989: 10). Such practices enable the spectator to activate the processes of intelligibility, which are a source of pleasure. By this I mean that when we consciously produce meaning to enable us to read a text, intelligibility as a process can become a self-conscious strategy. This is pleasurable, especially if the inter-pretations we provide are confirmed by the text, whereby we feel satisfaction at making competent readings. This process is more pronounced when there is a gap in the meaning. Consider how a joke is received, how sometimes we have to supply readings to get its meaning on additional layers, and how pleased we can feel if we have been clever in accessing these additional meanings. In a parallel mode, reading a film text activates pleasure in the processes of intelligibility, of consciously producing meaning.

The work which has begun to challenge mainstream filmic languages involves what Mulvey describes as a project 'to free the look of the camera into its materiality in time and space and the look of the audience into dialectics, passionate detachment' (Mulvey, 1975: 68). I see this project as most productive when exposing and denaturalizing the practices of mainstream cinema, thereby reaching distanciation and demystification, but still maintaining, in 'passionate detachment', the ability to engage with the text in split positionings of spectatorship.

About the so-called lesbian gaze, Evans and Gamman suggest that there is no 'essential' model of it, and that we 'bring different cultural com-petences' to lesbian spectating (Evans and Gamman, 1995: 35). Of course we also bring political positionings, and I want to emphasize that certain politicizations around power and control as mastery make some of us uncomfortable with the gaze as surveillance, as serving the functions of the phallus through voyeurism. I for one prefer the pleasures of fetishistic scopophilia, where we celebrate the beauty of the woman without wanting to control or punish her. Elizabeth Grosz makes the point that 'vision is not, cannot be, masculine', and that though it may serve the production of 'patriarchal power relations', this is not inevitable (Grosz, quoted by Evans and Gamman, 1995: 16).

I take the view that if we relinquish the impulse to want to control the other, and we instead see the other in a mutual dialogue with the self, we will be able to reduce objectification and increase engagement. Our looks will therefore carry more respect and responsibility than can be granted under the operations of voyeurism and sadism and the operations of the gaze as serving phallocentric functions of surveillance. Opening up the look away from the singular, seeing the viewer as engaged in a 'continual construction of looks', Cowie suggests a model of process, productivity, and plurality in the activity of spectating (Cowie, 1980: 137).

For me, pleasure is produced when I can engage in the consumption of a product while remaining aware of how it is constructed. *The Hunger* gives me pleasure even while I remain resistant to its main generic form, the horror film. I will retail the narrative of the film in some detail. The first half will be in conjunction with a discussion of the avant-garde techniques it deploys, and the second half will be in terms of its lesbian content.

The Hunger begins with a credit to MGM, so it is immediately identified as originating in Hollywood. There are sound effects of an audience as music begins to a blank black screen, then the first image is of a male figure . . . in a cage? We are not sure. The figure suggests something non-human. The names of the actors – Catherine Deneuve, David Bowie, and Susan Sarandon – are intercut with this male figure in a cage moving to music, then on the left of the screen we get a glimpse of part of a guitar. Suddenly we realize this is a 'stage-cage', that this is a performance. The film's title appears on-screen at that point of realization, in bold black capitals. Shots of a disco, with Bowie and Deneuve wearing dark glasses, and strobe lights flashing intermittently, are intercut with the 'stage-cage' and shots of what is later established as a monkey.

What this beginning signifies for me is that the notion of 'performance' is made explicit, so that as spectators we are immediately aware of the film as a visual product to be consumed consciously. Of course the presence of a film's opening credits always has this distancing effect, but in this case the punk band's performance in the stage-cage at the disco frames the direction of our look as inquiring, a questing for meaning. Because we have had to supply meaning in gradual unfolding stages, the process of wanting to make sense is activated in our gaze.

The smoking of cigarettes is a recurrent activity in the film, signifying desire, appetite, hunger, as well as distress. As Deneuve and Bowie look around the disco, smoking, they see a heterosexual couple dancing. They obviously scrutinize the couple with the aim of picking them up, something the couple are also aware of. Meanwhile the punk band's vocalist sings a song with the hook 'undead, undead, undead'. Bowie and the man signal to each other, and there is a cut to the four of them in a car. They arrive at a remote house. The notion of performance continues as the young woman dances in front of a screen for the visual pleasure of the others. The two couples split into separate rooms, Deneuve and the man, Bowie and the woman. The scene begins with sex and ends with murder as Deneuve and Bowie kill their victims. This is intercut with shots of a mad monkey, and images of blood and torn flesh, but they are cut so fast that we cannot be sure of what we are seeing, although it emerges that the monkey has attacked its partner.

Cut to Sarandon with a female colleague. Sarandon says 'Oh, my God!' when she sees the ravaged corpse of the dead monkey. Cut to Deneuve and Bowie in their car, smoking cigarettes, feeling good after a murder, then to Sarandon smoking, feeling distressed. Two different value systems are quickly established. Deneuve and Bowie drive up to their New York residence, which turns out to be a massive house.

This opening sequence of the film is highly disturbing. On one hand we are excluded at first from knowing what is going on. The film's strength lies in the editing, in both its revelation and its refusal to reveal. The murder scene, for instance, suggests rather than shows what happens. And what is shown is gradually revealed, a layering of our knowledge as it unfolds intermittently, so we go from unknowing to knowing to unknowing.

There begins a deliberate intercutting between Bowie who is suffering from insomnia, and the monkey who is the subject of a research centre's investigation. The research team is composed of Sarandon, her lover Tom, the woman we saw earlier with her, and a black male doctor. They discuss the monkey murdering its partner. The way the account of the monkey's manic state and lack of sleep is intercut with Bowie suggests that there is a direct synchronization between the two behaviours. Sarandon wants to monitor the monkey with video equipment. In a romantic interlude, a hallucination or memory that Bowie has, Deneuve appears to him in what could be a wedding veil. She kisses him, declaring 'Forever and ever.'

This sequence establishes an art-house feel to the film, not quite the same as an avant-garde practice, but still oppositional or at least different in style from Hollywood, carrying a slow and textured pace reminiscent of some European cinema. A lot of attention is paid to spectacle, from watching the research team watch the monkey to the self-reflexive decision to get in video equipment to monitor the monkey. The strategies are self-reflexive and self-referential, reflecting and referring to cinematic codes that have an established place in the relaying of images. Here, however, the effect is to make us conscious that we are consuming images, partly achieved through devices that distance us by making us aware of our spectatorship.

Cut to a close-up of part of a disfigured face being relayed on a television screen, with Deneuve watching a programme in which Sarandon is being interviewed about a book she has written about premature ageing. Is Deneuve interested in the content of the interview? Or in Sarandon? As it transpires, she is interested in both. Bowie appears, looking the worse for wear. He has realized he is ageing rapidly and that something is seriously wrong with his body.

Cut to a copy of Sarandon's book being bought by Deneuve. She looks up at a video circuit screen to see Sarandon signing copies upstairs. Deneuve goes upstairs and this is carefully established in conventional spatial and temporal terms. In a sudden disjuncture in space and time, Deneuve is apparently on the other side of the room when Sarandon suddenly feels she is being addressed; then without any movement Deneuve is standing close to her. Deneuve says she would like to talk to her, Sarandon says yes, she would like that, and their first meeting is left with a look from Sarandon of enquiry, attraction, anticipation. This contact between the two women may well suggest the stirrings of lesbian desire, even though it is within phallocentric terms, in that both women are 'phallic mothers', both with the power to be and to have what they want to possess. For now, because of Deneuve's prior visual 'knowledge' of Sarandon, relayed to her on television and video screens before she actually meets Sarandon, she is the more powerful of the two women. And from the first moment of contact, power between the two women is an issue.

Meanwhile Bowie continues to age rapidly: his hair is falling out in handfuls, he is understandably distressed. It emerges that this has happened before to Deneuve's previous partners, including women. Bowie goes to the sleep research centre to meet Sarandon, who assumes from his manner that he is disturbed and does not believe he is ageing rapidly. She manages to evade him by telling him to wait in the patients' lounge where she leaves him for several hours. While he waits, Sarandon and her colleagues watch a video replay of the monkey's ageing, and there is a direct synchronization between the monkey as it ages 'at a rate of five years per minute' and Bowie in the waiting room, also ageing dramatically. The video screen flashes with disturbed signals as the monkey's life signs start terminating, with special effects of its skeleton disintegrating. This synchronization gives us a double imaging, where one level of action visualizes for us what is happening on another level of action. It also prefigures the film's conclusion.

When Sarandon realizes Bowie was genuine in coming to her about premature ageing, she wants to talk to him but he leaves. When Deneuve next sees him he has aged beyond recognition. He wants to die, but it is apparently impossible for the undead to die. Deneuve puts his still-breathing body in a coffin, next to the coffins of her other previous lovers.

This moment belongs to the horror genre, with premature burial coming directly out of Edgar Allan Poe. This burial of Bowie is effectively a removal of the male partner, and allows the film to follow another direction, the lesbian content that has been figured in the look of desire between Deneuve and Sarandon.

Sarandon has traced Bowie's residence and comes to Deneuve's house, where a shot of her on the video security screen again shows that Deneuve has more power because she can see Sarandon while Sarandon cannot see her. Sarandon identifies herself as a doctor from the centre, Deneuve says 'I know', and opens the door. Sarandon recognizes her immediately. This is their second meeting. Sarandon says, 'Oh, hello', and electronic sound effects signal her desire. This moment of recognition, following that first look of desire in the bookshop, conveys a thrill as Sarandon now has contact with Deneuve, she knows her name, where she lives, she has a reason of sorts to be there. In terms of narrative logic, we feel we have arrived at a moment of justifiable anticipation.

Sarandon tells Deneuve that they get a lot of cranks at the hospital and that she didn't believe Bowie. This is intercut with Sarandon's quick glance at the ankh hanging at Deneuve's neck. Deneuve hurries Sarandon away but mergence between them has begun. Sarandon imagines she hears the telephone ringing in a fantasy in which Deneuve is calling her, then she hallucinates an image of Deneuve in the mirror. This signifies the haunting of desire, the obsessive longing for the loved object.

Sarandon goes to visit Deneuve again, ostensibly to enquire about Bowie, but Deneuve's all-powerful look makes Sarandon admit, 'I don't know why I'm here.' Deneuve lets her in with a full recognition of her desire. The narrative can now explore the lesbian content prefigured in the look of desire between the two women.

Sarandon is in awe of all the beautiful antiques. Some are two thousand years old, and Deneuve says most of them belong to her family. She possesses both history and wealth. Sarandon looks at a bust of a woman, and says 'I love this piece.' She tells Deneuve it looks like her and, yes, there is a resemblance. This is a double visual joke as Deneuve says the bust is Florentine, five hundred years old. The audience knows that Deneuve is an ancient vampire and could well have been the model for the bust, but obviously Sarandon cannot know this. There is delight at both her acute observation and its apparent naïvety.

In the seduction scene that follows, we cannot know who is doing what first. There is again a disjuncture between the spoken and the visual. At first it appears that Deneuve is talking and Sarandon is listening, but really, neither of them is talking during the scene where they salute each other with their glasses while gazing into each other's eyes. The conversation that takes place during this scene is really from a future scene that we cut into. This disjuncture has a charming effect, playing with our desire, evading direct spectatorial address in the interest of anticipation.

While they look at each other, Deneuve says with an off-screen voice, 'I'm sure we could talk for hours, you and I, but I suppose you're very busy.' Sarandon's voice is also off-screen as she answers, 'Not too busy.' We see her sipping at her sherry on the right of the screen, and we hear her ask, 'What about you?' The moment shifts into the future present with Sarandon on the left of the screen, sipping sherry for continuity, when Deneuve says, 'Me?', as she sits at the piano playing a piece. She tells Sarandon, 'You would think me mostly idle, I'm afraid. My time is my own.'

We have here established two powerful women, one a professional, the other an aristocrat, both successful, beautiful, and desirous of each other. Together they have everything. They are phallic women in the sense of being and possessing what they desire. Later, when they have sex, they enact the completion of the fantasy for the phallic mother, that is, the child's desire for its mother whom it fantasizes as being omnipotent. To take this fantasy further, the child also desires the mother to be the subject of a desire for the child. The fetishization of their *beauty* signifies the quest for completion around which their desire revolves. In their mutual beauty, their reciprocal desire conveys a closure of sorts.

Again, who is doing what? Sarandon asks, 'How do you spend your time? Do you get lonely?' Deneuve replies 'No.' She continues to play the piano, self-contained in the sense of containing a self that is 'full', 'whole', with its promise of plenitude. Sarandon is obviously seduced by her beauty, her wealth, her power of completion. She says, 'I, rea . . ., I like your pendant.' The syntactic confusion conveys her nervousness. She obviously appreciates Deneuve's musical skills and asks her what she is playing. Deneuve tells her it is from Delibes' *Lakmé*, the story of an Indian Brahmin princess with a woman slave Malika. Sarandon asks, 'Is it a love song?' Deneuve says, 'I told you, it was sung by two women.' Sarandon says, 'It sounds like a love song.' Deneuve says, 'Then I suppose that's what it is.' Again, the lesbian possibility is made explicit. But it still needs further spelling out. Sarandon asks Deneuve if she is trying to make a pass at her. Deneuve says not that she's aware of, and Sarandon laughs. The music switches from Deneuve's solo playing to full orchestral score as Sarandon spills sherry on her T-shirt top. She says 'Oh no' in a deep guttural voice, as the red of the sherry stains the white top. Slow motion as she tries to wipe the stain off. Deneuve touches her shoulder and neck from behind, then sits down seductively. Sarandon uses this as a cue to take her top off. She is seen as if through a window frame as she reveals full breasts and a look of offer, of promise as well as possession. She gazes at Deneuve, who is also seen through a frame as she gets up and approaches Sarandon. Deneuve puts out her right arm to touch Sarandon's neck and breast. They look at each other, kiss, look, kiss again. With the same Delibes score now in full choral flow, switch to a bedroom scene with them partially dressed, kissing. The movements are clearly orchestrated. Deneuve is the initiator, Sarandon is responsive. This scene starts intercutting with another position of them in bed, with what we realize is Deneuve at Sarandon's right arm, though it takes a few glimpses of this to realize who is who, doing what. Deneuve bites into Sarandon's right arm, then we get a shot of Sarandon in a similar position biting into Deneuve's left arm. Again it is difficult to be sure who is doing what to whom, as we make the unknown intelligible.

There follows a superimposed cut to a massive piece of rare meat, a visual joke that combines sex with hunger for food into one funny image. Indeed, the next scene is very humorous. Sarandon is unable to eat, and is distracted as her lover Tom questions her about her appetite. The scene is set in a restaurant overlooking a swimming pool, but again we have to arrive at this knowledge in a way that renders our vision a conscious look of enquiry. For instance, while interrogating Sarandon on her afternoon with Deneuve, Tom expresses surprise that Deneuve should have given Sarandon the present of an ankh after only one meeting. Sarandon is looking at what turns out to be a diving space, as she says Deneuve is European by way of explanation, and we get an image of a diver to establish our vision. This is an 'othering' of Deneuve that the audience will laugh at, intercut as it is with lustful looks at scantily clad bodies beside the pool. Sarandon is hungry for flesh. The previous sex scene loads this scene with the physicality of love-making, as we know that Sarandon has had satisfying lesbian sex. But this lesbian sex is to be secretive, dishonest, in that Sarandon cannot tell Tom about sleeping with Deneuve, though it is left ambiguous whether she does not tell him because he is her lover. Sarandon and Tom fight, he tells her to see a doctor, she tells him 'I am a doctor.'

That night she is vomiting and the next scene starts with an image of blood under a microscope. It emerges that the medical team is examining Sarandon's blood. She is ravenous but cannot eat, and has an alien strain of blood in her veins, non-human and fighting for dominance. She is seen to have a bite on her left arm. When she is twice asked how this could have happened, Sarandon lies, but the sex scene with Deneuve biting into her arm is intercut to show she has knowledge of how it happened, though she does not know why.

Sarandon goes to visit Deneuve, saying her colleagues think she has gone to a blood specialist, and that she wants to know what is happening: 'What have you done to me?' Deneuve says it is natural she should be frightened because she doesn't know what is going on, but to give her time, to trust her. Sarandon says she did trust her, but Deneuve has done something to her. She undoes her sleeve and shows Deneuve a wound. Deneuve says it is a bruise, it will heal. She tells Sarandon that she has given her everlasting life, but Sarandon finds this derisory. She tells Sarandon that it is her, Deneuve's, blood in her veins, that they each made an incision. She shows Sarandon the mark on her own right arm. Deneuve tells Sarandon, 'You belong to me, we belong to each other.' Sarandon leaves the house but goes back as Deneuve predicts. She is imaged as having heroin withdrawal because of having to feed her hunger for flesh. Hallucination again figures to convey desire. Sarandon does what she can to resist eating human flesh, but her initiation is complete when she kills Tom for the purpose of feeding. But we know that her position of moral strength provides a genuine space for conflict, that she cannot collude with this arrangement with Deneuve, who tells her, 'You are a part of me now. I cannot let you go.' Deneuve wants to share eternity with her. 'You will begin to love me as I do you. Forever. Forever and ever.'

Our identifications may have been shifting, but the value system in operation in the film is generated by Sarandon, whose desire we share, whose seduction we enjoy, but whose ambivalence and resistance we also identify as morally right. The conflict is genuine, as Sarandon cannot become a vampire without validating destruction and the nihilism of murder. Despite desire, despite the apparent parity between the two women, power has to be asserted through resistance to a corrupt value system.

To conclude briefly, the apparently immortal Deneuve is destroyed. There is a kiss between a young girl and Sarandon in the penultimate scene. Is it a maternal kiss, a sexual kiss? Does it figure lesbian desire? We cannot be sure. Full knowledge is denied to us, leaving us in a state of closure without completion.

I conclude this account of the film summarily, because by the end it degenerates into the horror genre which holds no interest for me. I have concentrated on the use of avant-garde strategies to show how the film keeps us at a distance, makes us aware of our own activity of spectating. At the same time, there is the conventional use of filmic languages in the deployment of spectatorial identifications and narrative engagement, but this I find to be a strength, especially given that the explicit lesbian content is so fascinating. It is no coincidence that both avant-garde strategies and a lesbian sexuality are highly oppositional practices.

Let us look again at how the lesbian is figured in the film, powerful, phallic, holding the promise of completion. First there is their desire, which is initially articulated through their looking at each other. The agency and effectivity assigned to the look that the women bear gives them the power to enact lesbian desire. In phallocentric terms, when the two women acknowledge their desire for each other, and make love, they both 'are' and 'have' the phallus, the latter through the sexual 'possession' of each other's body. Then the notion of lesbianism as contamination is raised, as when Sarandon repeatedly asks Deneuve 'What have you done to me?', an implied accusation being that she has corrupted her sexuality by sleeping with her. The moment when Sarandon tells Deneuve, 'Don't you touch me', when she wipes a tear off the edge of her face, supports such a reading. Sarandon is frightened, in a rage because she is so vulnerable. I think this rage is the key and I think what we recognize in the women's desire is not a fear of contamination but of the rage that lesbian desire is prey to. It is this rage that I find the most 'convincing', in terms of representations, not only because it has a narrative place, but more because it conveys the loss of control, the sense of impotence at being so much in the (usually emotional) power of the other. As the lesbians are seen in mergence, so their loss of boundaries precipitates them into that shifting space of simultaneous intimacy and invasiveness. Rage can be the only response, re-emerging from the moments of impotent dependence on the m/other. 'You are a part of me', Deneuve tells Sarandon, drawing on the levels of both the maternal and the sexual relationship. This is the complexity of lesbian mergence. I see the capacity for mergence as the ability to access the state of the pre-Oedipal, that time of fusion with the maternal imaginary. During the pre-Oedipal stage, our sense of self would not have the boundaries of subjecthood, but would be blurred in identifications with the figure of the mother. In a similar blurring of boundaries, mergence in lesbian relationships can entail a mutual fusion, where separateness and individuation are in temporary abeyance.

I suggest that we can read the women's relationship through the subtext of a mother–daughter dyad. After the initial exchange of looks which establishes their mutual attraction, there is a deliberate depiction of mergence between them, which climaxes in a seduction and sex scene. This speaks to me of a parallel with the child's pre-Oedipal mergence with the mother. Because such a phase belongs to the realm of the imaginary, it cannot last, but must break through into the symbolic order of the phallus, a moment of fracture, lack, rupture, loss. Therefore the dyad must be interrupted through separation so that sociality can take place. The separation we see enacted in the film entails destruction to remove the relationship from the grip of its mergence. At the end, with the destruction of Deneuve and the survival of Sarandon, we have a scenario of the mother–daughter dyad as described by Luce Irigaray, where the mother is symbolically murdered, and where the daughter has no representations of her to help with mourning (Irigaray, 1992: 47; Whitford, 1990: 115). The film works for me on multiple layers of meaning, and it is particularly the place of the mother as other that I locate in the text. Although the constraints of a vampire narrative mean that lesbian desire is destroyed here in the form of Deneuve's destruction, there is both through her and through Sarandon a clear imaging of the mother as other, that is, a mother who holds meaning and desire, whose identity speaks of self-determinations.

Looking at the figure of the mother, Jessica Benjamin confirms 'she is not the subject of her own desire' (Benjamin, 1988: 88). This is because 'we have no female image or symbol to counterbalance the monopoly of the phallus in representing desire' (*ibid.*). Due to the definitional appropriation of desire as phallic, the mother can only be seen in relation to the phallus. This relation takes contradictory forms. She can be perceived as the phallic mother when she is pre-Oedipally merged with the infant/child, who sees her as containing the phallus. She can also become the castrated mother with the onset of or exit from Oedipus by the female and male child, where her lack of a penis confirms her social subordination under phallocentrism. We see that the mother can also activate the split processes of fetishism, whereby we disavow her lack, and/or our own lack as female subjects, in a play with oscillating positions. What these configurations confirm is that the mother is defined in relation to the phallus and her desires are constrained within phallic identifications. Teresa de Lauretis reminds us that feminine desire is either the 'desire to be desired', the feminine narcissistic position of the female object, or it is 'the desire to desire', which is seen as a subject position and therefore a form of usurpation of masculine privilege by the female who is attempting 'rivalry with male desire' (de Lauretis, 1994: 187). Because desire is seen as a subject position, and because desire itself is associated with a male subject endowed with a penis, the agency of the mother as a subject of desire is suppressed by the phallocentric appropriations of her desire.

Elizabeth Wright reminds us that the mother is only seen from the point of view of 'those who lay claim to her', that is, the father or the child (Wright, 1990: 145). The mother is not seen as a subject with her own needs, or with needs 'in relation to other women or to her work' (*ibid.*). The mother's subjectivity is suppressed and her agency is denied even though she is for many subjects the first source of enculturation into sociality, as well as primary caretaker. Kaplan finds that 'the mother is the one through whom we come to be subjects' (Kaplan, 1992: 44) and she is interested in the psychical as well as the social mother (*ibid.*: 32). The mother exists both as a figure-head implanted in our psyche through the social and economic organization of marriage and maternity and as a person, a being, a social subject operating in a symbolic order that derogates women and denies us the place of agency and autonomous desires. Because it is the same mother who enculturates the child into contact and communication, we can see that the denial of her desire signals her derogation to and by the child, so the transgenerational cycle of devaluing the mother and taking maternity for granted is perpetuated.

The subjectivity of the mother's desire is denied even while she is the object of sometimes impossible demands. Parveen Adams references the work of Donald Winnicott on the mother, who has to provide the infant with 'ego-support' by 'establishing predictabilities' for the infant so it can experience some sense of agency (Adams, 1983: 320–1). This can involve feeding fantasies of omnipotence that the infant experiences to secure an illusory sense of control. Benjamin records the infant's entrance into the phase of 'rapprochement' at about fourteen months onward, in which the infant has 'to reconcile his grandiose aspirations and euphoria with the perceived reality of his limitations and dependency' (Benjamin, 1988: 34). Because of the conflict involved, an accumulation of tension will become attached to the figure of the mother. Nancy Chodorow reports that children 'will maintain a fearsome unconscious maternal image as a result of projecting upon it the hostility derived from their own feelings of impotence', and this is maintained by 'children of both sexes, even with kind mothers' (Chodorow, 1978: 122).

I am drawn to some of Melanie Klein's work on infant and child behaviour, and especially to her work on the ambivalence of love and hate for the mother as she is experienced as a good and bad object (Sayers, 1986: 50). Janet Sayers reports how Klein finds that the child's fear of the mother can stem 'from the child's idealization of her as containing within herself the means of satisfying its every desire, and from its envious attacks on her for seemingly withholding this goodness from the child' (*ibid.*: 53–4). This intense vacillation between idealization and aggression connects with the impossible demand on the mother to anticipate and meet all the child's needs appropriately. It is obvious that the register of demand as unattainable desire makes this an impossible task to achieve. The mother is caught between the bind of 'maternal overprotection', where she maintains 'primary identification and total dependence too long', and the bind of 'maternal deprivation', where she makes 'premature demands on her infant's instrumentality' (Chodorow, 1978: 84). In other words, the mother has to magically know how much to shield the child without blocking its development of a sense of self, and she has to know how much to expose the child to reality, without challenging it too soon in a way which can damage its fragile sense of subjectivity. I reiterate that to find the correct balance is at best completely random, and more often impossible.

As Adams reminds us, the subject of the mother is constituted in lack and she cannot 'manage desire' any more than the child can, as this would be to control the unconscious, another impossibility (Adams, 1983: 323). Yet although impossible demands are made on the mother, and she cannot guarantee the psychic health of the child, the frequent response to the mother takes the form of 'mother-blaming' (Segal, 1992: 267).

I am especially drawn to Irigaray's work on the mother, which Margaret Whitford sees as recognizing 'women's ambivalence towards their mothers, without blaming mothers as individuals' (Whitford, 1992b: 263). Whitford refers to Irigaray's theorizations of the 'unsymbolized mother/daughter relationship', where we have practically no representation of this relationship, whether 'linguistic, social, cultural, iconic, theoretical, mythical, religious' or otherwise (Whitford, 1990: 108). Irigaray finds that with the exception of the Greek myth of Demeter and Persephone, which Marianne Hirsch and Adrienne Rich also reference (Hirsch, 1989: 35; A. Rich, 1976: 238), there is a near-complete absence of representations of the mother–daughter relationship (Whitford, 1990: 108). This absence in representations of the mother–daughter dyad is what Rich refers to as 'the great unwritten story' (A. Rich, 1976: 225). This erasure of the mother is brought about because women are not individuated and recognized as agents of desire; 'there is only *the place of the mother*, or the *maternal function*' (Whitford, 1990: 112; original emphases).

A solution that Judith Roof proposes is to 'detach maternity from heterosexuality', which involves a 'repositioning of maternity outside the nuclear, familial, patriarchal organization' (Roof, 1991: 105–6). Roof is in favour of seeing motherhood as an activity, where 'mothers can be (and are) lesbian, adoptive, unmarried, celibate, sterile, grandmothers, aunts, hired nannies, or males' (*ibid.*: 106). Such a repositioning of maternity has begun when we consider that marriage 'does not occur universally between two people, nor between two people of the opposite sex, nor is it always viewed as linked to reproduction' (Gittins, 1985: 63). The position of maternity as seen as natural in biologistic thinking is being challenged, and Diana Gittins reports that 'We cannot assume that wanting children is natural, nor that it is necessarily a result of, or a reason for, marriage, nor, indeed, a necessary result of sexual intercourse' (*ibid.*: 110). It is with such reworkings of ancient and outmoded paradigms that we may be able, as Roof terms it, to 'escape the Oedipal to new scenarios of desire' (Roof, 1991: 118). To move away and outside of such paradigms

> would involve conceptualizing the mother–daughter relationship outside the terms of the oedipus and the castration complexes, and it is not clear yet whether this is a regressive fantasy of return to the pre-oedipal . . . or a genuine glimpse of a post-patriarchal future. (Whitford, 1992b: 265)

Kaja Silverman takes the Lacanian view that it is a 'regressive fantasy' for the female subject to situate her desire in a position of mergence with the pre-Oedipal mother (Silverman, 1988: 124). In an attempt to move further from the pre-Oedipal, Silverman wants to locate the daughter's desire for the mother within Oedipus, 'to make it an effect of language and loss' (*ibid.*: 123). By situating desire and sexuality in the context of the symbolic, Silverman seeks to avoid speaking 'from the place of a mutely resistant biology, or sexual "essence"' (*ibid.*: 123–4). She argues that feminism is impossible without a 'homosexual-maternal fantasmatic' (*ibid.*: 125), and in this I read that we need paradigms of same-sex bonding through the model of the mother–daughter relationship. Although I agree that we need representations of such a relationship, Patricia White correctly identifies a danger in the current obsession with the figure of the mother in its 'writing out of lesbianism', where the 'homosexual' consists of same-sex relations without the 'otherness' of lesbian desire (White, 1995: 89).

De Lauretis also sees dangers in subscribing to a maternal imaginary, which reduces female sexuality to maternity, thereby threatening feminism once again, and which also erases the fact that lesbianism 'as a particular relation between women . . . is not only sexual but also sociosymbolic' (de Lauretis, 1994: 198). De Lauretis finds that the model of the 'homosexual-maternal metaphor' does not allow us to clarify distinctions between heterosexual and lesbian feminisms, and their respective sexualities and subjectivities. She concludes that some identifications, whether 'Oedipal or pre-Oedipal', do 'not alter the operation of the metaphor a great deal' (*ibid.*: 190), where all that is effectively being achieved is the transposing of the maternal metaphor and the paternal function (*ibid.*: 166). Although I think it is usually the mother who enculturates the child into sociality, this is suppressed in favour of seeing the father as the third term intervening in the mother–child dyad. I think it is the mother herself who initiates and institutes the separations necessary for the enculturation of sociality, and not the father who inevitably introduces desire. I would want the mother's autonomous subjectivity and her separate desires to be acknowledged, where we celebrate her agentic status rather than suppress it as has been done under phallocracy. However, I do not think the mother should carry the burden of supposedly holding the completion of the child's desires. To set up a maternal metaphor as a means of pursuing plenitude is a foolish project.

What is important is the constitution of an autonomous female desire. As Benjamin states, a solution to the 'dilemma of woman's desire must include a mother who is articulated as a sexual *subject*, one who expresses her own desire' (Benjamin, 1988: 114; original emphasis). I think such a desire must not be predicated on phallocentric formulations, but must move beyond them. This is possible if one resists automatic maternal identifications and deconstructs desire away from plenitude. Roof locates such a progress at work in lesbian narratives, which 'erase the preoedipal' by having 'an already differentiated and very independent protagonist daughter' (Roof, 1991: 116). Not only are identifications separate from maternal mergence here, but desire is also deconstructed, 'where the lack represented by the absent mother is displaced into the lack constituting desire itself' (*ibid.*). In a further deconstruction of desire, Roof reports that lesbian narratives 'frustrate the possibility of total knowledge', where mastery as knowledge is unattainable, where 'to desire is to desire . . . an unfulfilled desire' (*ibid.*: 111).

Such a strategy is not necessarily a plea for frustration, but the acceptance of lack and loss. This is an achievable project if we can come to terms with the impossibility of desire as it is currently defined. Rose points out that the child's desire for the mother is not simply enjoyment or possession of her, but the desire to be what she wants (Rose, 1982: 38). Therefore, if the mother's desire is taken to be for the phallus, the child will want to have or be the phallus for her. However, if the mother's desire is diverted from the phallocentric appropriations of it, and if desire itself is deconstructed away from the quest for completion, away from an economy where the phallus signifies plenitude, we will be that much closer to divesting desire from its investments in illusory gratifications. We know that desire 'exceeds the bounds of the imaginary satisfaction available to the demand' (Gallop, 1982: 13). This is in the context of theories where 'the subject is split and the object is lost' (Mitchell, 1982: 25). I would suggest that we accept that we are constituted in severance and lack. I can reject identifications with a maternal imaginary because I think we must not be duped into looking for origins and causes. It is a doomed project to recover what is lost. Just as prehistory is unknown to us, what is unrecorded cannot be subjected to the same scrutiny as what is documented. Rather than seek origins and causes, if we are accepting of gaps in our knowledge, we will also be more able to accept the unknowability and alterity of the unconscious, and the fragile and fluid status of desire.

Looking for 'solutions' to the absent significations of an autonomous female desire, I reiterate that it would be detrimental to replicate phallo-centric formulations of desire. However, I do not endorse separatism or an exclusion of men, but agree with commentators including Benjamin, Chodorow and Rich that equal parenting by mothers and fathers can reduce the tensions attached to the figure of the mother, and decrease the relegation of her social subjectivity to a maternal function. Benjamin is 'arguing here for simultaneity and equality, not exclusion or privileging of either male or female experiences and capacities' (Benjamin, 1988: 130). And Rich sees the project of fathers involved in primary caretaking as 'the most revolutionary priority that any male group could set itself' (A. Rich, 1976: 215). However, dangers and doubts attend this. First, the high incidence of child sexual abuse, incestuous or not, organized or familial, indicates that some men's interest in children can be perverted and damaging (Armstrong, 1994). Also, there is some doubt about how substantive the increase in the 'involved' father actually is, and Kathryn Backett's research studies find evidence that 'popular belief in the more "involved" father must therefore be seen as something of an illusion' (Backett, 1987: 88). Although the extent of men's participation may still make the mother primarily responsible as caretaker, I do think there is a movement towards the figure of the father as more present and engaged than the prototype of the absent and removed father. The active and caring involvement of the father can be useful, and indeed in addition to the more traditional familial unit of mother–father–child there are male-parent households as well as communal parent households with men where the child receives attention from several carers. A father who is seen to recognize the agency of the mother would greatly encourage the enculturation of the child to an alert awareness of the mother's subjectivity.

It is the conceptualization of the mother as an other with agency that can probably best encourage the child to recognize her subjectivity and to achieve its own individuation. Therefore I am in favour of Benjamin's proposing '*mutual* recognition' as a paradigm for such a relationship (Benjamin, 1988: 23; original emphasis). Kaplan refers to work done on the '*mutual* gazing' of mother and infant, and she asks whether a reluctance to engage in such mutuality might be a reflection of our being threatened by intersubjectivity (Kaplan, 1992: 49–50; original emphasis). It is precisely this intersubjectivity that we need to encourage, to move away from structures of domination around objectification and into a dialogue of mutuality and respect. Additionally, for this reason, the mother–daughter relation can provide a model for the stabilization, however tenuous, of the self who can then recognize the other. Irigaray makes the point that if we do not address the vertical relation contained in the mother–daughter relation, we might be unable to process the horizontal relations we have with other women (Whitford, 1990: 109). Therefore to theorize the mother–daughter dyad can help with the question Irigaray poses for feminism on 'how to construct a female sociality' (*ibid.*).

In order to rescue the mother from the phallocentric appropriations of her desire, we would need first to divest her of the phallus she contains in the pre-Oedipal fantasy of the phallic mother, just as we would need to see her post-Oedipal castration in the context of her social subordination. Jane Gallop is aware that to use the term 'phallic mother' is 'to subsume female experience into male categories' (Gallop, 1982: 117). If we are to use such oxymorons, it is, as Gallop suggests, to undo the connections 'between phallus, father, power and man' (*ibid.*). Gallop confirms that 'The Phallic Mother is undeniably a fraud' and she would like to see exposed 'the joint imposture of both Phallus and Mother' (*ibid.*). In exposing the phallic mother as a fraud we need not resort to seeing her as subjectively castrated, but as castrated symbolically as defined by the privileging of the phallus under patriarchy. We need to see her so-called castration in the context of the social reality of her subordination and derogation. This is to move away from the limitations of psychoanalysis which has yet to adequately theorize our subjectivity in relation to cultural, social, economic and political conditions, as well as in terms of our identities as constituted by race, sexuality, class, ability and other configurations. Sayers finds that Freud was unconcerned about the sociological constructions of sexual difference as they are affected by women's subordination, and that he did not attend to the historical, crosscultural and individual conditions which impact on subjectivity

(Sayers, 1986: 111). If psychoanalysis cannot wake up to the complex configurations of subjectivity outside of purely familial structures, it will continue to invite the frequent criticisms of its ahistoricism and its positing of false universalisms.

It is again the lesbian positioning that can destabilize some of the heterosexist and phallocentric formulations of female desire. De Lauretis confirms that the lesbian can be 'both – even at once – desiring subject and desiring object' (de Lauretis, 1994: 156). As a model for female desire, de Lauretis is referring not to the reality of lesbianism, whether psychic or social, but to *'its fantasmatic place* . . . from where female homosexuality figures, for women, the *possibility* of subject and desire' (*ibid.*; original emphases). Therefore, if lesbian desire is the obvious imaging of the woman as desiring and desirable, we have in this reworking a possibility for figurations of female desire to move away from the phallus. Rather than readopt its terms, we need to see lesbian desire as the model for a desire which is about questing and not completion. This does not invite frustration as much as it allows desire to defer its demands, so that the gratifications of desire we receive can accommodate its fragmentations in a reworking of desire away from an illusory plenitude and into achievable pleasures. In Roof's key strategy, 'Adopting a desire for desire' would deploy 'the lure of knowledge beyond certainty, identity, and mastery' (Roof, 1991: 254).

In *The Hunger* I am so pleased to see two women articulating the look of lesbian desire that I can tolerate its phallocentric framing. And there is much that pleases me about the film. It lends itself easily to simultaneous enjoyment and analysis, as we are both engaged and kept at a distance. For instance, our involvement in the narrative flow and our investment in spectatorial identifications are kept intact, while at the same time we have a space to be critical and inquiring as we construct our readings. Our knowledge unfolds intermittently in a process of making sense, so that we consciously produce meanings in the absence of given knowledge. This mirrors the process of intelligibility, whereby we attach meanings as social subjects, and our participation in such processes evokes a more conscious and critical state of spectating, a political project. In terms of agency, the spectator has the space to enjoy some practices and to resist others.

The film borrows from different traditions and genres to form an eclectic but coherent product, one which nevertheless takes away any ultimate knowledge of, or 'mastery' over, what happens. Although the narrative is full of satisfying detail that links the film together, it is also left open-ended. Consider, for instance, that Sarandon reveals the blood-bite on her left arm, when in fact in the bedroom scene she was bitten on her right arm. Consider also that Deneuve shows a bruise on her right arm, when she was bitten on her left arm. Are these just continuity errors? Or do they evoke a deliberate uncertainty in our spectating?[2] Either way, this use of the obverse serves to detract from a definitive reading. The closure without completion that the film enacts in its conclusion is also progressive. And the self-reflexive strategies, including watching television, having a video security system, taking and looking at photographs, setting up and monitoring video tapes, commenting on the resemblance of visual artefacts, are all devices which remind the spectator of the process of watching, where what is seen is constituted at a remove. Moreover, the use of both temporal synchronization and disjuncture conveys the 'uncanny', the known unknown, both familiar and frightening. In using the myth of the vampire, the film exercises a metaphor we deploy to convey our obsession with the buried, the hidden, the unacknowledged. Our cultural obsession with the vampire as signifying the undead connects with the psychic mechanisms of the repressed, that material that returns, re-emerges to haunt us in our adult lives.

If *The Hunger* conveys so well the complexity of lesbian desire, this is achieved partly through a conventional imaging of the woman as stunningly beautiful. I think spectators fetishize the woman's beauty, insofar as they see in that beauty a plenitude, a promise of completion that the search for the phallus signifies. There are implications in scopophilia of 'lookism', where the pleasure in seeing often consists of the pleasure of looking at beauty. It seems that we cannot yet avoid this fetishization of the woman's beauty. But perhaps we can begin by being conscious of how we constitute desire.

The look of lesbian desire is ultimately what engages me. I think the film does address the specificities of lesbian spectatorship, not just because it erotically evokes lesbian desire, but because that desire is figured as complex. It is about rage, resistance, refusal (just as much as it can be about passion and compassion). We can receive the lesbian content as both the fact of women's desire for each other, and as the fiction that this particular narrative takes. Made by a man and edited by a woman, the film feeds our hunger to see the look of lesbian desire given articulation on the screen.

I think we need to appropriate what gives us pleasure as women, and if this involves the adoption of mainstream practices around narrativity and spectatorship, we should go ahead with this appropriation, attempting to realign such mechanisms according to our own needs. But the notion of a 'unitary' subjecthood in the spectator is to be resisted, which is where the avant-garde questioning of form and languages comes in. By resisting the interpellation or evocation of the unitary subject (seen usually as white, middle-class, male, heterosexual and able-bodied), and by challenging filmic languages that attempt to disguise their own materiality, avant-garde strategies offer an obvious method for making certain mechanisms of pleasure fit into an alternative or 'oppositional' mode. Mulvey also outlined the common objectives between the avant-garde project and a feminist aesthetic attempting to bring about change in form and content (Mulvey, 1979).

A synthesis of the two traditions we have available to us can allow a way forward. Mainstream practices create pleasure, while avant-garde techniques are closely allied to a political project. Such a project is possible because avant-garde strategies bring in an altered perception of the filmic text. By making the spectator critical and self-conscious, narrative and identificatory processes can be *consumed consciously*, without apparent contradiction, so that we can simultaneously enjoy and analyse how certain responses in us are being evoked. This is to resist cinema as a mere manipulation of response, and to see it more as a way of examining how meaning is produced. This focus on intelligibility, on how we make sense, is, I think, the future for cinema as it reflects on itself self-referentially.

Parallels can be misleading if made automatically without due respect to the need for differentiations. Nevertheless, I persist in drawing some parallels between the paradigms of gender and race. Just as the 'male' has been seen as the norm for all subjects, so 'white' has occluded black subjectivity. A mythic anecdote demonstrates how the gendering of 'man' is false when seen as including women:

> 'When you say Man,' said Oedipus, 'you include women too. Everyone knows that.' [The Sphinx] said, 'That's what you think.' (Rukeyser, quoted by de Lauretis, 1984: 157)

In the same way, human is nominally taken to include the black subject, while in actuality our humanity has largely been excluded from history in racist discourses. Blackness must be seen as partly dependent on the naming properties of white supremacism and white cultural imperialism, but 'whiteness' must also be recognized as a racial category which has also been socially constructed in relation to the history of slavery and colonialism. We all share that history though our positionings differ. It really is inadequate at this point in history to continue not to acknowledge the impact of race and racism. 'Racism is a white issue as much as it is a black one' (hooks, 1990: 111). The deconstruction of whiteness as a racial and ethnic category has begun. Young makes the point that although this is necessary, it should not be used to refocus on the white subject yet again at the expense of representations of black subjectivity (Young, 1996: 33).

While there has been a much greater global politicization around race than gender, much of this work is marred by the operations of tokenism, as well as insidious and unconscious racisms. The poverty of images of black people means that 'however hungry' we are to receive these images, we know 'this iconically impotent cinema' has not offered us adequate representations of our lives (Alexander, 1991: 54). Rather than renounce the pleasures of the cinema, we have engaged in a strategy of selection, extracting what is beneficial and rejecting the offensive (Bobo, 1990: 96; Nataf, 1995: 58). Z. Isiling Nataf celebrates how 'pleasure in the place of erasure, invisibility, misrepresentation and othering is already progress' (Nataf, 1995: 57).

I am in favour of engaging with the pleasures of the mainstream while bringing to the text the politicized positions of the margins. As a woman who is black and lesbian, I favour oppositional or progressive practices from the vantage of being 'triply other', a status I celebrate. In terms of films, I have been a critical spectator because my identity as a black woman has meant I have often identified with screen personae at a racial remove. On the few occasions when I see images of black people in the white mainstream, they are often of servants and criminals. Denied easy identification, I have had to reconstruct my own mechanisms of making sense. In that reconstruction is a clarification, a demystification of mythic notions of a single and stable subjectivity. I know from my position of reconstruction and resistance that truly oppositional practices remain on the periphery, but it is precisely this distance, this dissociation, that gives the oppositional its cutting edge, its ability to analyse and re-envision.

When the production of meaning is achieved by making the unknown intelligible in ways that are self-conscious, a text can be 'progressive' in allowing social subjectivity a prominent place. Our ability to make the text intelligible will depend on how our identities have been constituted, not just along the lines of gender, but of race, sexuality, class, culture, language, age, ability, and of course our political positionings. By insisting on the presence of cultural diversity, sexual dissidence, racial difference, political divergences, and other sources of power differentials, the progressive text invites a plurality of positions in our identifications. If the text can accommodate the plural by allowing us to be conscious of ourselves as subjects with diverse subject positions, it will activate the pleasures in producing meaning. I feel sure that intelligibility, or the process of making sense, is crucial as a strategy for both producers and consumers of meaning.

Notes

1. Claire Johnston (1973: 217).
2. The transferring of the left and right arms in the film is a use of the obverse as a device, whether intended or not. This parallels a use I made of the device in an unproduced play I wrote, where the final scene has all the stage decor arranged in reverse, and where the word 'Horror' appeared spelt right to left. By reversing the representation of this scene through the use of the obverse, I wanted to denaturalize the mode of realism in the play, and to alert the spectator to a sense of altered readings brought about by defamiliarization.

An earlier version of this chapter appeared in Liz Gibbs (ed.), *Daring to Dissent: Lesbian Culture from Margin to Mainstream* (London: Cassell, 1994). Material from it is reprinted here with her kind permission.

2

The Castration of Lesbian Desire in Cinema

A Matter of Some Agency:
Sister George Not at Her *Personal Best*

Pourquoi Pa?

Jacqueline Nacal[1]

The signs point towards the end of the twentieth century being the turn of the dyke.

Rosa Ainley[2]

While deploying the metaphor of castration to signify severance and loss, we will see how *The Killing of Sister George* and *Personal Best* both show the castration of a lesbian who loses her partner, to a woman and a man respectively. The two films demonstrate how representations of the lesbian have moved from depictions of the pathological to the more favourable. For example, in *Sister George*, castration takes the form of an abandonment of agency, while in *Personal Best* the lesbian's agency is left intact. We will look at ideas around spectating positions available for women in order to gain what pleasure we can from such representations. In the first film, stereotypes of the dyke as self-destructive proliferate in the person of George, and what is unfortunate about this is that we may approve of her castration. The second film is less problematic, where the eventual erasure of lesbian desire is so contrived that we can see the castration as a transparent prelude to introduce heterosex.

Before pursuing how castration features in the two films, I wish to randomly explore over twenty-five years of feminist film theory, from the 1970s to the 1990s, to show how it has led to currently held ideas of active spectatorship. What I find at issue in both the films and in this film theory is that the concept of agency has achieved the prominent status it deserves, in some ways allowing for a reworking of gender paradigms. The concept of agency allows us to define passive and active spectating as a conforming or critical subject position irrespective of gender binarisms that locate the male as active and the female as passive. This is to reformulate agency away from the masculinist appropriation of it. Indeed, I would suggest that because the woman spectator can often be actively more critical of the film text than the man, the alignment of agency as masculine is disrupted. I take this view because the male spectator's investment in the malestream is likely to be confirmed by the film text, while the female spectator who is alert to certain processes may find more meaning in supplying an oppositional reading. The position of the active female spectator therefore reformulates the concept of agency to include the woman as agentic.

In order to structure this brief and selective overview of feminist film criticism, I will suggest that the readings of dominant, negotiated, and oppositional positions can chart the progress from a passive consumption of material to a critical and eventually politicized reception of it. I deploy these terms here as borrowed from Stuart Hall's work (Hall, 1980: 136–8), where dominant, negotiated, and oppositional positions correspond respectively to fixed, variable, and resistant readings. We will see a movement between these positions that suggests an agentic spectatorial response in our viewing practices.

First, the 1970s. Feminist film criticism started to emerge, drawing its impetus from the second wave of white Western feminism which had begun in the 1960s, and which really gathered momentum in the late 1960s. This coincided with the Hollywood discovery of 'the modern women', and the 1970s saw a series of films aimed at this audience, including *Klute* (1971), *Alice Doesn't Live Here Anymore* (1974), *Julia* (1977), *Three Women* (1977), *Coma* (1977) and *Nine to Five* (1980) (Brunsdon, 1987: 119). These films could be said to involve the 'recuperation' of women's concerns, 'whereby radical and oppositional ideas' are co-opted and contained so that they become incorporated into 'the culture of domination' (*ibid.*: 119–20). Charlotte Brunsdon argues against the fixing of a text as either progressive or reactionary, as this reifies the meanings of the text as if they were permanently the same (*ibid.*: 122). However, the debate in the 1970s was very much focused on whether a film was progressive or retrograde. And the feminist consensus for a time was to reject Hollywood and the cinematic codes it typified. Laura Mulvey, for instance, had used psychoanalytic theory to demonstrate 'the way the unconscious of patriarchal society has structured film form' (Mulvey, 1975: 57). Clearly this means that the consumption of images can be suspect if such representations are received uncritically. The initial response was to turn away, to eject what we had previously enjoyed.

So by the late 1970s, many feminist film-makers and theorists had decided to reject the aesthetic and technical practices that characterized the classical Hollywood film, as they were 'saturated with ideology' (Mayne, 1993: 78). In America, film-makers turned in large numbers to the making of documentaries on women's issues, as there was a feeling that this medium was more authentic in conveying our concerns (Erens, 1990: xviii; Kaplan, 1983: 125).[3] The American work drew on socio-cultural and journalistic traditions (Kuhn, 1982: 76). In Britain more than America, feminist film-makers and theorists favoured a radical break from all traditional regimes of representation (Doane *et al.*, 1984: 8; Kaplan, 1983: 125). The British work was more dependent on theory, initially semiotic and structuralist as well as psychoanalytic, and then later poststructuralist (Kuhn, 1982: 76–80). The shift in attention was away from the semiotic/structuralist position of seeing the 'film text as autonomous and discrete' to the poststructuralist position of attending to 'the text–reader relationship' (Creed, 1992: 15).

Pam Cook refers to 'the 70s tendency to "fix" spectators in abstract, closed positions' (Cook, 1993: xii). This 'fixing' of the female spectator coincides with the notion of the text as producing 'dominant' readings. Effectively, this implies that the way technical and aesthetic codes are employed in the text serve to elicit a pre-programmed response, where spectatorial readings are predictable and uniform. This is patently not possible, no matter how manipulative the film medium can be. But rather than consider the degree of dissident readings attendant on a text, the notion of dominant readings presupposes uniformity, as decodings correspond to the intentions and techniques of encoding. Therefore both textual readings that ignore social histories, and psychoanalytic readings that do not account for how the spectator subjectively constructs the text according to social specificities, fall into misguided notions of a passive spectator, whose response is to concur with dominant ideologies. Jackie Stacey points out that the term 'spectator', used in the singular, posits a passive model of consumption with fixed readings, by implying 'a unified viewing experience' (1991: 149).

If dominant readings were the only ones available, we might indeed be in danger of facing a monolithic social order. Deidre Pribram makes a necessary distinction between the dominant and the monolithic. For while dominant ideologies allow a coexistence with alternative practices competing for ascendance, a monolithic structure is not amenable to transformation (Pribram, 1990: 3). However, we know that readings are variable and resistant, and this suggests a space for contestation and change, so that the 'monolithic' can be seen as the mask of its own rationalization to cover its false pretensions as inevitable, natural, unchangeable.

The 1970s dismissal of Hollywood was effectively to break from cinematic systems that seemed to focus on an endless recycling of images of women as defined by male fantasies. Claire Johnston's work was a 'notable exception' to the large-scale rejection of Hollywood in the 1970s (Penley, 1988: 5). I believe Johnston's work is characterized by an emphasis on 'negotiated' readings as well as an attention to 'oppositional' practices in her call for a 'counter-cinema'. Johnston did not want to foreclose on the pleasures and engagement offered by Hollywood and 'the entertainment film', but she was clear that pleasure without politicization is an empty project (Johnston, 1973: 217). Together with Cook, Johnston developed the 'symptomatic' readings of texts in a strategy similar to the *Cahiers du Cinéma* editorial group, who sought to locate the '*structuring absences*' of a text so as to expose its contradictions (*Cahiers*, 1970: 496; original emphasis). Johnston's early adoption of the practices of reading against the grain spells for me the position of the alert spectator. I see in this position the possibility of reconciling pleasure with political consciousness, where we engage critically with a text rather than passively accept its dominant encodings. This is to offer negotiated readings.

In her essay, 'Pleasurable Negotiations', Christine Gledhill favours negotiated readings and sees them as a way to bridge 'the gap between textual and social subject' (Gledhill, 1990: 67). That is, in negotiated positions, the text does not merely produce meanings because the spectator supplies them as well, which I see as an assertion of agency. Gledhill refers to Gramsci on how hegemony cannot be secured, because ideologies are not simply imposed but renegotiated through contestation (*ibid.*: 68). Gledhill's essay confirms the greater emphasis now given to the variable subjectivities of spectatorship, where response cannot be uniform. Meaning must be negotiated in relation to the differentials of race, gender and sexuality, class and culture, age and ability, social status, employment category, religious persuasion, geopolitical positionings, and so on. Gledhill is clear that negotiation 'stops short at the dissolution of identity suggested by avant-garde aesthetics', and she does not want identity to be abandoned, but 'its dominant construction as total, non-contradictory and unchanging' (*ibid.*: 72).

We see that the greater emphasis on the socio-historical differentials of spectator positions allows negotiated readings to be a strategy of response that is both conformist and critical, where both the text and the spectator are in active and mutual process. I believe we are now seeing a further emphasis on the socio-historical specificities of spectatorship, where the 'resistant' and 'radical' readings of the text redefine pleasure, not as a passive absorption of dominant meanings, not even a negotiated response of critical engagement, but as an actively split spectator, who can be simultaneously seduced by the film's codes, be aware of its contradictions, and be in complete opposition to its ideological operations.

Z. Isiling Nataf argues that 'the black lesbian spectator has a schizophrenic response to mainstream, popular film' (Nataf, 1995: 57). She suggests a fourth term of response to those of dominant, negotiated and oppositional positions, that of 'deviant', which as she says is aligned to oppositional readings (*ibid.*: 58). I prefer the term of a 'split' rather than 'deviant' reading. For me, the oppositional and resistant reading is different from the split reading. Let me explain. If I were merely to accept the text without questioning its terms, I would not be split but conformist. Similarly, if I were to refuse the processes of the text, I would not be oppositional but alienated in my response. As Judith Mayne suggests, '"pure" instances of dominant or oppositional readings' are 'highly unlikely', and it is possibly 'more useful to designate all readings as negotiated ones' (Mayne, 1993: 93). I am redefining the negotiated and the oppositional as a new configuration of split spectating. It is precisely the meeting on common ground within an oppositional framework that allows for engagement as well as resistance. For me, the split spectator is not one who evidences contradiction as confusion, but one who is alert to the demands of conflicting discourses. This allows me to consume consciously, to be engaged and seduced, as well as critical and resistant. I prefer the term 'split' to 'multiple', because the former allows for contradiction while the latter conveys to me a tendency to confusion.

I am therefore making a distinction between oppositional and split readings. It is also worth clarifying a possible confusion on how to distinguish between negotiated and split readings if both involve split processes of engagement with critique. I would say the negotiated position allows for more pleasure in reading the text within its own terms, but consciously, while the split position allows for alternative pleasure in reconstructing and rewriting. Intelligibility in negotiated readings permits us to feel we are responding in complex ways which favour an active response, say, through exposing the competing discourses in the film. But in the split spectating position, intelligibility has to be reconstructed consciously, and this is not only active, it is agentic, because we have to supply readings that exceed the textual confines of the product, sometimes to the point of rewriting or 'righting' what we receive.

Because I am now more aware of my own political and subjective identity, I am able to respond critically while remaining captivated by the use of narrative and other codes. This allows me to critique the material I consume. I would want to develop further identity in an aesthetic that foregrounds intelligibility through self-consciousness. This is to favour the active reading as agentic.

Let us turn to the films and see how they invite dominant, negotiated, oppositional and split responses. I suggest that *Sister George* relies on dominant readings, even though there is space to supply negotiated readings. And *Personal Best* offers more possibility for an oppositional response, from which we can extract additional pleasure by supplying split readings. These positions can mix and merge, and the availability of split spectating allows for their reconciliation, so we can absorb, assess, and oppose meanings simultaneously.

Both the films play with spectacle, one through the use of screens which serve as self-reflexive, and the other through the use of cinematic devices such as slow motion and unusual camera work. Such usage forefronts spectacle as received through structuring devices, rather than pretending it is received without mediation. Both products can be celebrated as fine pieces of film, *Sister George* for its technical expertise, *Personal Best* for its stylistic inventiveness. But for me both films are more flawed than substantial. Male direction and heterosexual vision dominate, and a lesbian aesthetic of sorts is created only to be dismantled by stereotypes of destructiveness on the one hand, and commonplace assumptions about the centrality of heterosex, on the other.

The Killing of Sister George could be subtitled as the castration of a lesbian. I am taking castration as signifying loss, here the loss of a partner to a third party. George is the fictional character in a TV soap played by Beryl Reid, who lives with her lesbian partner Childie, played by Susannah York. The film records how George is killed off on-screen, and how she is rejected by Childie, who leaves her for another woman. Both the killing off and the rejection of her embody the castration that George undergoes. As spectators we respond with a fascinated ambivalence towards George. While we receive her sympathetically, we also endorse her castration. This suggests that dominant encodings are in place, which we are inclined to decode with more conformity than contestation. However, our ambivalence points to a space for negotiated readings where we can supply additional meanings.

Effectively, the castration of George in the film is a denial of her agency. She faces adversity she cannot triumph over; she has desires that become demands that cannot be met. She is humiliated, eliminated, rejected. By the end her castration is complete, and confirms that any claims she might have had to agency are now foreclosed.

This denial of her agentic being takes the form of a systematic disempowerment, while those around her achieve status, recognition, success, all in contrast to the way she herself is losing control. While we see her fall from grace from her point of view, we also see her relating to others with frequently alienating behaviour, which serves to justify our response that her castration is invited and even inevitable. This is not to blame the victim, this is to see that agency involves responsibility, and that George loses her agentic status because she does not take responsibility for the alienating effects of her actions.

I will retail the narrative with an emphasis on the two threads of this castration, the killing off of her in her professional life, and the rejection of her by Childie in her personal life. Both serve to divest her of her agentic capacities.

Alcohol is immediately established as an explanatory framework for George's sometimes over-the-top behaviour. The film begins with her drinking in a pub, where she is obviously a regular. She returns home in an explosive state and tells Childie that they are going to kill her. If this were American cinema we might take this literally and believe her life is in danger. Another response is to see this as a paranoid delusion, with George thinking she is the victim of a murder plot, one which exists more in psychosis than reality. However, it is quickly established that George is not literally in danger, nor is she having delusions, but that she is an actor and she suspects her character is going to be killed off. At the studio where they are filming the soap, she is so aggravated by hints of this happening that she unprofessionally storms off the set in a fury and gets raving drunk at another pub where she is also obviously a regular.

To what extent does she herself invite her elimination? This is crucial to considerations of agency. On one hand she is aware of the effects of her actions, on the other she courts adversity and actively seeks confrontations in ways which invalidate her right to agency. For instance, she sexually harasses two young nuns in a taxi. Although this is funny, it also indicates a lack of maturity and decorum. George is reprimanded by Mrs Croft from the BBC, in a scene reminiscent of the best of Oscar Wilde, with a wit that goes to the heart of social convention and establishes its tyrannical hold over the respectable and the reprehensible.

Mrs Croft tells George that the BBC has received a letter from the Mother Superior of a convent responsible for the two novitiate nuns involved in the incident in the taxi. George asks how was she to know they were novitiates, an in-joke about the incidence of lesbian activity among some nuns.[4] Mrs Croft's reply is crushing: 'Their status in the hierarchy of the church is totally irrelevant.' Mrs Croft is clear that George must write to the Mother Superior and apologize. George says, 'You mean, humble myself.' This is the first cutting off of her dignity. The route to her castration has begun, as from humility she has to move to her humiliation.

At work this humiliation takes the form of her being supplanted by a male actor, who plays Ginger the barman in the soap and has overtaken George in the popularity ratings. Ginger is a pompous and conceited being who obviously revels in the way he is on the rise while George is declining. The production assistant and the script-writers are particularly sycophantic to him, flattering him, lighting his cigar, giving him central screen time at the expense of George. At a script rehearsal meeting, George realizes she has been written out for two weeks with flu, and she is particularly vulnerable because this might be the killing off she fears. She again storms out, which is not tactically wise given that future work depends on one's previous record. In acquiring a reputation as difficult and disruptive, she is shown as actively courting disaster. This is an example of her agency being at odds with itself, where her ability to protest against her treatment has taken a trajectory of self-defeating or even self-destructive behaviour.

When the next script arrives at their home, George and Childie are both delighted that George has been written in again. They call Mrs Croft at Childie's suggestion, and George leaves a message inviting her to join them at Gateways for a drink. Mrs Croft arrives at the club and tells them that 'It's the end of Sister George.' The character is to be knocked off her moped in an accident with a ten-ton truck, and her death will be instantaneous. When George protests that this is a ridiculous ending, with no dignity, and that she will challenge the decision, Mrs Croft cuts her off by saying it is a policy decision made at the highest level. She offers some hope about the possibility of a part in another serial, but George is unable to contemplate the future at that moment.

On the day of the last shoot with George, where she is killed off, she is apparently drunk and sabotages several takes with her silly behaviour. Although most of those present genuinely find her more funny than offensive, there is an element of self-defeating behaviour in this attempt at resistance. Similarly, at a sending-off party where George is apparently very drunk, she alienates BBC heads as well as a possible employer. Again, this is spirited resistance, found funny by most present, and certainly we also laugh with her as she expresses outrage at the job offer of playing the voice of an animated cow. However, the extent of her antisocial behaviour shows that she is developing a reputation as disruptive and is therefore unemployable. At the end of the film, she returns to the studio where she is so enraged by the fake coffin they are going to bury her in that she smashes glass, lights, equipment, all of which confirm her destructiveness and aggression.

The disempowerment of her agentic capacities is most evident in her relationship with Childie, her glamorous younger lover. George's jealousy over real and imagined male rivals is a recurring conflict between them. Childie is presented as a toy-girl, sexually initiated but emotionally immature, and her large collection of dolls is the dominant visual motif to convey her infantilization, also evident in her name.

The scene that takes place between them early one morning encapsulates the action of the film, showing George at first in possession of agency, then dispossessed of it, and finally left abandoned in her despair. It begins with her writing fake fan letters to the BBC, which for us as spectators is funny, but which portrays George as becoming increasingly pathetic. She awakens Childie as arranged so she can go to queue for ballet tickets, and at first Childie wants George to join her and the gang. This shows that George invites inclusion, she is wanted, she has the agency to affect others favourably. She is in possession. However, when she asks Childie to stay home instead of getting the tickets, so they can have a cosy breakfast together, and Childie declines, George's claims to agency are challenged. Agency includes the ability of the self to evoke a favourable and desired response from the other. The request for them to have breakfast is simple enough, but because this exchange holds such an immense symbolic value, signifying George's losing of agency and the eventual rejection of her, the moment is dramatically charged. George immediately suspects that Childie is being unfaithful, and when Childie admits her attraction for a man, George is physically violent and grabs and shakes Childie. Childie tells her she's got no right, and George lets her go when Childie says 'I'm not married to you, George.' This serves as castration. George is not a man, she is not Childie's husband, as if these would constitute possession of agency. George admits to Childie that she is afraid, and if there were more agentic emphasis attached to her needs, Childie would have possibly stayed to comfort her. But because George's behaviour is so alienating at times, with its jealousy and aggression, Childie is probably glad to escape, as she does in the end. George is left to weep on her own. This scene prefigures the conclusion.

George and Childie do have fun together. We see George has agency as the ability to elicit spontaneous laughter. But by now their humour has become aggressive and silly, as when they are dressed as Laurel and Hardy indulging in slapstick horseplay. When George invites Mrs Croft to join them at Gateways, she quells Childie's hesitation by saying someone has to broaden Mrs Croft's horizons. She is referring to the lesbian membership of the club, a public place where women could be openly out. In the 1990s we can take that for granted in London. But the scarcity of such a venue for late 1960s London makes the scene filmed at Gateways quite significant for the purposes of historical documentation. Mrs Croft is in for a revelation. She looks around at the women couples dancing close together, she takes in the possibilities and calls it 'most entertaining' in her prevaricating style of speech. She has come to the club to give George the news about her being killed off. But we realize she also has an interest in Childie, who sent her some of her poems. Mrs Croft says some of them are very mature. She questions Childie about George's treatment of her, and encourages her to leave George. She tells her to call her at the BBC, and when Childie says she is frightened, Mrs Croft says they won't let anything happen to her. This is in stark contrast to Hollywood, where in the film there is no play of suspense around danger for Childie. In American cinema such a line would have suggested or confirmed the jeopardy of the female's safety.

George's castration through losing Childie to Mrs Croft has begun. When George asks Childie to join her for lunch on the last day of the studio shoot for her, Childie does not understand how much George needs her support, and she declines the invitation. It emerges she had a prior arrangement to meet Mrs Croft, and when George forces the truth out of her about her whereabouts, Childie admits they met to discuss her poems. George knows at once that Mrs Croft's interest is a sexual one, and has little to do with the aesthetics of poetry.

Sure enough, after George causes several scenes at a sending-off party, Mrs Croft seizes on her behaviour as a reason to get Childie out of George's flat and into her own '*pied-à-terre*'. We first see the visual imaging of Mrs Croft's sexual desire for Childie in the way she fondles and caresses Childie's favourite doll. There follows a sex scene between them at George's flat. What is so castrating for George is that she witnesses the latter part of this encounter, and it is unclear just how much she has seen of their love-making. She is enraged at this betrayal.

George wants Childie to stay with her, and calls on the long shared history of their years together in an attempt to assert her needs. But her demands cannot be met any longer, and she has lost the agentic status of evoking a favourable response. She compounds her abandonment by inviting further alienation. She lashes out by revealing to Mrs Croft that Childie is thirty-two years old and had an illegitimate child at the age of fifteen. This detail dates the film, because we no longer see thirty-two as beyond the pale, and because illegitimacy carries less stigma. Childie and Mrs Croft leave, and George tells them, 'You two are going to be very happy together.' She says it ominously, but after their exit she repeats 'very happy' lamentingly, as the realization of her rejection and loss starts to sink in.

By the end she is in a state of breakdown. We have witnessed her decline from agency to abandonment, from possession of a job and a partner to a dispossession of both. What is stereotypical about such a disempowerment is that it takes the form of a systematic castration. Although we see George in sympathetic ways, with other characters admiring and respecting her, our own admiration and respect are marred by the spectacle of her antisocial behaviour, where she often uses alcohol to mask her aggression, and she ends up paying for her alienating actions by a gradual loss of her agentic capacity. Ultimately she exhibits more self-destructiveness than agency.

Now let us look briefly at the concept, rather than the 'fact', of castration. In a wider sense it is a 'decisive metaphor' for all loss (Metz, 1982: 69), with death as the ultimate severance. As a concept, it explains how the series of severances we undergo structure us in lack. The concept has been deployed to account for how we perceive and internalize sexual difference, and some feminist commentators have taken it on board to rework how we receive gender.

According to Freud, castration solves the enigma of sexual difference for the puzzled child. The boy child sees he has a penis which the girl child lacks, and by privileging the visible over the invisible, by emphasizing a supposed presence over an apparent absence, this penis becomes the signifier of difference. Stephen Heath says of castration that it is 'the articulation of the symbolic to a vision', where 'difference is brought down to a matter of sight' (Heath, 1978: 49). Anatomically but only coincidentally linked to the penis, the phallus becomes the symbolic marker of a social order that disempowers women and privileges men. Therefore, when the girl child sees she 'lacks' a penis, this is an anatomical confirmation of her castration, her lack of power under patriarchy. The girl child, again according to Freud, can negotiate castration in three ways. She can despise her femininity and its social position, often becoming neurotic, frigid, inhibited. She can stay 'arrested' in pre-Oedipal identifications with a female figure, retain her active clitoral position, and remain within a 'masculinity complex' that characterizes the lesbian position (Mitchell, 1974: 96). Or she can take the 'normal' road to femininity, which Juliet Mitchell refers to as 'the tortuous path to womanhood itself' (*ibid.*: 119). This is done by supplanting the mother with the father as love object, by substituting her active clitoris for the passive vagina as a site of sexual activity, and by accepting her castration and remaining fixed within Oedipus, where she tries to make good her lack through the libidinal acquisition of the penis through a male partner, or possibly through an eventual child, ideally male (Mitchell, 1974: 96–7; cf. Bronfen, 1992: 42–3, and Showalter, 1985: 199).

Let us look at how castration is seen to be the means of transmitting culture. What in fact is taking place is the transmission of a patriarchal social order, which we see in the way the boy child negotiates the complex. While the 'normal' girl child's acceptance of castration binds her to Oedipus for life, the boy child's acceptance of the possibility of castration allows him to resolve Oedipus by leaving it. In other words, the boy child has the promise of becoming a subject of desire. For the patriarchal culture to be transmitted, he must accept the prohibition of the mother's body by accepting that she desires not him but his father, not his deficient organ but his father's more powerful member. What comforts him in this prohibition is his ability to defer his desire on the promised gratification of it being met at a future date. The boy child therefore contains the rivalry he feels with his father, and starts to identify with him. By accepting the law of the father, the boy child is acceding to cultural prohibitions against exclusive access to the mother, thereby being heir to the eventual investiture of phallic privilege that will give him access to women's bodies as a subject of desire.

Castration takes place as the primary separations from the mother's body, with secondary separations when the father is said to intervene in the mother–child dyad. Jacqueline Rose summarizes Lacan's account of castration, where 'the phallus stands for that moment of rupture' when the father intervenes and introduces desire through lack (Rose, 1982: 38). For Lacan, the phallus signifies desire through the figure of the father as position of law and prohibition, functioning as a *'paternal metaphor'* (Lacan, quoted by Rose, 1982: 39; original emphasis) where the presence or absence of a real father is not at issue. Rose says of this account that

Castration means first of all this – that the child's desire for the mother does not refer *to* her but *beyond* her, to an object, the phallus, whose status is first imaginary (the object presumed to

satisfy her desire) and then symbolic (recognition that desire cannot
be satisfied). (Rose, 1982: 38; original emphases)

Rose recognizes that this status attached to the phallus is 'false' (*ibid.*) so
that a major issue revolves around the dismantling of the phallus as
signifying desire.

Ellie Ragland-Sullivan suggests a way of countering the effects of
secondary castration. She recounts how the mother communicates to the
child her unconscious desire for the phallus as contained in the father,
confirming the child's own castration through the preference for the father.
She suggests, 'To short-circuit this system', that either the primary
caretakers must become the fathers, or the mothers must alter their
unconscious desires, because these mothers, 'by accepting their femininity
at all, support a system of phallic values' (Ragland-Sullivan, 1986: 298–9).
This of course presupposes that the mother is a heterosexual woman who
is desirous of the phallus. As I argue here and elsewhere, it is precisely a
lesbian desire that could communicate a non-phallocentric frame of desire
to a child, with the mother as a subject of desire, desirous of another
subject of desire who desires her. This is to counter castration at its
secondary stage.

Rose also references Moustafa Safouan's work which confirms that
the intervention of the third term need not be figured by the father (Rose,
1982: 39–40). To go further, as Kaja Silverman does, we can challenge
the notion that it is the father's intervention as the third term in the
mother–child dyad that signifies the separation that precipitates the child
into symbolization and language. The severances or splittings from the
mother's body can begin with the trauma of birth, of being weaned from
breast-feeding, of experiencing the mother as absent, and so on.
Therefore, Silverman finds that the infant's exposure to lack and loss
predates any inkling of sexual difference or language (de Lauretis, 1994:
218). These severances predate the father's intervention. Moreover, the
beginnings of language also predate the secondary castration of the father
as the third term. Silverman wants to dismantle the phallus as signifier
of desire, and she finds that entry into the symbolic order is not affected
by the phallus, but by the prior entry into language. 'The only immutable
law of desire is . . . the Law . . . of Language' (Silverman, quoted by de
Lauretis, 1994: 220).

This is not to deny or repudiate castration. The position of repudiating
castration for the woman can identify an endorsement of the phallus.
More crucially, the position can topple over into the delusional. Elizabeth
Grosz says of the female lesbians who believe themselves to be male,

'These girls border on psychotic because they repudiate rather than disavow the psychic reality of castration' (Grosz, 1993: 109–10). Previously, I have been drawn to the position of 'accepting' castration as a way of staying in sync with the symbolic order. Now I have come to the position where I agree with Teresa de Lauretis that we need a disavowal of castration. The position of disavowal allows us to oscillate between symbolic acceptance and subjective resistance, while the position of repudiation can only persist in being at odds with the symbolic while in fact underwriting its permeance. De Lauretis argues 'that the lesbian subject neither refuses nor accepts castration, but rather disavows it' (de Lauretis, 1994: 204).

Personal Best charts two white American women's lives as they train to take part in the Moscow Olympics. The film could be subtitled the bisexual at her best and worst. This presupposes that the central character is Mariel Hemingway, playing Chris the young bisexual woman, and that the secondary character is Patrice Donnelly playing Tory, a lesbian. This preference in hierarchy of the bisexual over the lesbian is echoed in the opening credits, Mariel Hemingway followed by a male actor (the coach), and then Patrice Donnelly followed by a male actor (the boyfriend). The deliberate insertion of male presence dilutes the lesbian content, gradually supplanting this content with a movement towards heterosexuality. This movement takes the form of castration again, but what is encouraging is that agency is still permitted some place. Tory the lesbian loses Chris the bisexual to a man, but her own agency and their friendship are maintained. She is not left embittered and abandoned, but survives with her subjectivity left intact. Tory may be castrated, in that her desire is cut off, but she retains agency. Indeed, lesbian audiences see her as the film's main protagonist, reversing the attempted peripheralization of her by rereading her as making an endorsement of the centrality of lesbian desire (Ellsworth, 1986: 193–5; Weiss, 1992: 77).

For the purposes of this analysis, I will recount the film's narrative in two parts, from the two women's viewpoint. Lesbian desire features prominently in the beginning half, and I will retell it from Tory's point of view, just as the second half moves into heterosex, told from Chris's viewpoint.

The beginning of the film focuses on Tory as powerful. She is an initiator of action who takes control, is knowledgeable, and evokes favourable responses in those around her. The opening shots establish her as a subject watching Chris as object. The spectacle is relayed from her viewpoint as we observe Chris running a race in which she does badly. Tory's victory in her own race event contrasts with Chris's poor performance. That evening in a bar, the two women meet, introduced by Chris's father. When Chris breaks a glass by accident because she is overwrought, Tory takes control and looks after her. In Tory's car, Chris is tearful and Tory holds her, comforting her in a maternal way. Not only is Tory more powerful, she is obviously more the mother to Chris's child at this point in the narrative, the phallic mother who can complete the child. We cut into a scene with them laughing, smoking grass. Tory is knowledgeable. She knew from watching the race that Chris panicked. This serves to establish her as the acute observer, whose spectating is accurate. Chris thinks this casts an aspersion on her competitiveness and wants to arm-wrestle with Tory to prove she can beat her. Of course, as subtext we know that this is an excuse for physical contact, and in this case a prelude to physical engagement.

Their arm-wrestling is a confrontation that shows their power shifting, then arriving at deadlock, as Chris's determination and will to win put severe pressure on Tory's greater strength. However, Tory does win, and again it is she who holds the greater power between the two. Tory's astute faculty of observation has allowed her to recognize Chris's sporting potential. Rather than be competitive, she actively encourages Chris's ability. There then follows a sex scene, with Tory kissing Chris on the lips, then a cut to them in bed.

Tory the seducer is also the initiator of support for Chris, and she persuades the coach to allow Chris to train and then to run with them. At first the coach sees none of the potential that Tory has seen in Chris, but he eventually allows her to join the team. We see in Tory's character-ization that she represents vision, victory, control, action, support. As a seducer she is also an initiator, who acts agentically by evoking a return of lesbian desire. The two main themes of sex and sport meet and merge in their partnership, as they sleep and train together in the same team. Tory is fiercely protective over the needy Chris, as when the latter falls ill from food poisoning. Tory comforts the vulnerable Chris through the night at the expense of her own performance on the field, which suffers while Chris does well. Clearly a mother–daughter dyad dynamic is at work. Linda Williams finds that 'the failure to define the lesbian nature of their relationship as anything other than a regression to mother–daughter narcissism is one of the major disappointments of the film' (Williams, 1982: 151).

From this point, Tory's decline is charted, but with such clumsy contrivances and careless editing that a lesbian spectator will be alert to the forcing of heterosex into the narrative. Lesbian desire is cut off and left out, a gaping omission that locates heterosex as constructed possibly on false consciousness in this instance.

To demonstrate what I mean by the imposition of heterosex, I will deconstruct the next few scenes to show how their poor editing exposes the narrative's illogicality. When Tory does badly and Chris does well, Chris tells the coach her performance is because of Tory's support, not his coaching or her ability. Her loyalty is clear, and there has been no sign of swerving. This, however, is immediately followed by a party scene where Chris allows herself to be chatted up by a man. Tory is understandably upset and makes a drunken fool of herself. What might seem realistic is exposed as contrived, and an alert spectator would want more explanation as to why their lesbian desire is being challenged. If Chris is becoming less desirous of Tory, we need more visual proof for this to register as convincing. Instead of this, Chris expresses her continued desire by seducing Tory when the latter is upset that they will be competing. What could follow – a sex scene between them – is instead a slow-motion filming of them running up a hill, their heavy breathing reminiscent of making love. Again, sex and sport meet and merge as themes, the one being supplanted by the other. There is some suggestion that running up and down hills is an absurd activity, or at least that is how I read it. I wonder if all this expenditure of energy and risking of serious injury is socially all that productive. Certainly it is justified in the name of 'sport', but the culture of sport is itself highly suspect with its emphasis on competition and victory.

I myself am critical of competitiveness in the name of national aggrandizement, so from the start I have reservations in the way I receive the sporting content of the film. However, I am able to quell my objections because of the unusual way the women's rivalry is treated, where it is not the women who are in competition, but the coach who wants to bring out their competitive killer instinct. Tory wants them to split up because of the pressure in their training together, but it is Chris who insists they stay together, because she is still needy.

Tory's roles as actor, agent and initiator have all been reconfirmed by the narrative. Chris meets her desire with a return of desire. Suddenly, however, Tory is to be disposed of and her desire erased, and this is done with a contrivance that leads to their splitting up. It comes about through an accident, when Tory advises Chris to approach her high jump by running from further away. The marker that indicates the starting-point of the run is accidentally moved and Chris hurts herself as a result. The coach implies that Tory deliberately did this to stop

Chris competing, and Chris is confused, not really believing the coach. What has been a three-year relationship is now called off on the assumption of a guilt that Chris does not really believe. This contrivance is compounded by another, when Chris meets a young Olympic gold-winning water-polo player and immediately falls for him, becoming his mentor and partner, much as Tory had been for her. Chris and the new man go to a bar where Tory happens to be seated upstairs, another clumsy contrivance. On being questioned by the young man about Tory, Chris says they used to be roommates, and when he asks why they separated, she laughingly replies, 'I don't know precisely what happened', again alerting us to the illogicality and confusion in the way lesbian desire has been erased.

Later, Chris's new boyfriend again questions her about Tory. It seems he knew about them, since he refers to them as the two greatest looking girls there and that their relationship was no secret. Chris says there is nothing to tell about the relationship, and they don't see each other anymore. And that is the end of that. Three years are discounted with nothing to tell, either of their love or of Tory's support for her. Lesbian desire is completely erased in this non-account.

However, Chris is loyal to Tory as a friend, and this saves her from descending into villain status. But her loyalty is only in relation to Tory as a sportswoman, not to Tory as a sexually desiring subject. There is no question of their lesbian desire surfacing again. While I approve of the sporting solidarity that Chris demonstrates towards Tory, replacing competitiveness with shared loyalty and changing what could be confrontation into cooperation, I am disappointed that there is no acknowledgement of lesbian desire in their contact. They do not even refer to the fact that they used to sleep together intimately.

Tory is reluctant to take part in the last event that will decide who goes to Moscow. She has hurt her knee and aggravated an old injury. This injury of her knee could stand in visually for her castration at losing Chris to a man. Chris tries to persuade her to take part, telling her she's not that hurt, she can run. Tory says, 'Oh yeah, you know how hurt I am?' She is of course referring to her emotional pain at the rejection of her lesbian desire. Chris answers, 'I know exactly how hurt you are.' Close-up of Tory crying. We are obviously waiting for some recognition of the content her pain, instead of which Chris says, 'You can do it, you can run the race.' Sport has again supplanted sex. Sport is about winning, while lesbian sex is to be erased in favour of heterosex.

Tory does run. What is more, she wins the race with Chris's support and secures her place on the American team, as does Chris. But as the commentators say, with the American boycott of the 1980 Moscow Olympics, 'They're all dressed up with nowhere to go.' When Tory and Chris accept their laurels and stand at their winning positions, Chris asks Tory what she thinks about her boyfriend. Tory's answer concedes the heterosexual attraction for Chris, while remaining resistant herself: 'Well, he's awful cute . . . for a guy.' The film ends on this joke, which both endorses Chris's newly found state of heterosex, and confirms Tory's agentic status as a lesbian. Indeed, we could subtitle the film as the lesbian at her best through the worst, with Tory emerging triumphant despite her castration, a determined lesbian who concedes the attraction of heterosex for Chris, but who knows better for herself. There is room for more than one winner.

Let us briefly consider questions of agency in relation to social structures. One way I have used the term agency is as the ability to affect other subjects and bring about a return of desire. bell hooks defines agency as 'the ability to act in one's best interest' (hooks, 1990: 206). Agency of course operates on wider structures of sociality, as that which allows us to remain functioning subjects in the symbolic order while we are in the process of rewriting that order. This is possible because 'structures are only constituted through the practices of social agents, who produce these structures anew in the process of reproducing them' (Felski, 1989: 56). As Rita Felski argues, this allows us to move away from the model of a pre-given subject constrained by structures we cannot modify (*ibid.*). As she states,

> Human subjects are not simply constructed through social and linguistic structures, but themselves act upon and modify those structures through the reflexive monitoring of their actions. (Felski, 1989: 57)

This suggests to me a model of agency which permits an interactive process between the social order and the subject receiving and responding to that order. Rather than follow a Freudian paradigm where masculinity is associated with agency and femininity with passivity, we need to destabilize the genderings of the social subject. We can attempt this by reformulating how we receive gender. Some of Julia Kristeva's work, for instance, challenges the alignment of masculinity with the third term that intervenes in the mother–child dyad (Meyers, 1992: 145–6). This confirms for me that lesbian desire for a desirous lesbian would significantly alter the apparently universal adoption of Lacan's father figure as signifying the entrance of desire, through the mother's assumed desire for his so-called phallus.

Allison Weir references Kristeva when she seems to follow 'the original Freudian-Lacanian position', that the mother desires the phallus, and therefore the child identifies with the phallus in wanting to be or have what the mother desires (Weir, 1996: 181). However, Weir also cites Kristeva where she 'argues explicitly that the "imaginary father" is simply a metaphor for the "third term"' (*ibid*.). Kristeva suggests that the third term, that which introduces the social into the mother–child dyad, need not be the father/husband/lover, although it can be. Rather, it is 'meaning' in the mother's life that can initiate the separation and the entrance into sociality. Kristeva is clear that the mother 'has to have another meaning in her life' besides the child (Kristeva, quoted by Weir, 1996: 182). It is this other 'meaning' that Kristeva thinks could be what Freud formulated as 'the father of prehistory' (*ibid*.). Similarly, Lacan's 'paternal metaphor' is just that, a metaphor that privileges the masculine.

Elsewhere, Kristeva seems to find, like Lacan, that the only alternative to the acceptance of the law of the father is psychosis (Leland, 1989: 130). I prefer the view that alternative positionings are possible. Dorothy Leland argues:

> For even if we accept the (arguable) view that we enter society *via* the Oedipus complex and submission to the Law of the Father, it does not follow that we cannot *subsequently* reject, at least in part, our paternal heritage. (Leland, 1989: 130; original emphases)

While I do not endorse a return to the mother in terms of a regressed state of early identifications, I do favour a reworking of the mother as an autonomous subject worthy of respect, whose desires are not phallo-centrically defined, but separate and active affirmations of her equal subjectivity.

To return to the question of agency in relation to the postmodern formulation of the subject as shifting and unstable as a category. How can we present a fractured and fragmented subject as a model for agentic practices if that subject is irremediably split? I suggest that we do aspire to coherence but that we rethink how our identities are arrived at. On this I agree with Diana Meyers, 'that people need to consolidate a tolerably unified subjectivity is indisputable' (Meyers, 1992: 157). I think we can attain social coherence without phallocentric formulations. I do not deny that a fractured subjectivity can be a liability if incoherent. But I do think that this same position of fracturation allows the subject to reconcile contradictions and juggle differences, and that this fractured subject can maintain coherence and consistency. Feminists have pointed to how the postmodern dissolution of the subject has coincided with the historical moment when women are finding their voice. As Felski says, 'The assertion that the self needs to be decentered is of little value to women who have never *had* a self' (Felski, 1989: 78; original emphasis). Rose makes a similar point:

> Feminists could legitimately object that the notion of psychic fragmentation was of little immediate political advantage to women struggling for the first time to find a voice, and trying to bring together the dissociated components of their life into a political programme. (Rose, 1986: 94)

I would argue that the split positionings of the fractured subject enable us to be more alert to how we are constituted in lack. This can alleviate the threat of loss that castration signifies for us, although it cannot remove that threat. To persist in notions of wholeness, in an order where plenitude is signified by the phallus, is to reproduce the same structures that have enchained us socially. In the famous words of Audre Lorde, 'the master's tools will never dismantle the master's house' (Lorde, 1984: 112; original emphasis removed). Therefore to transform certain structures we have to reformulate how we receive them, deploying different methodologies and alternative epistemologies.

One reformulation I repeatedly argue for is a refiguration of the mother. Sandra Gilbert and Susan Gubar also argue against the father figure as representing the third term that introduces the child to language, referring to the father as a 'supreme fiction'. The *'nom du père'*, the name of the father, is 'secondary', they argue, because 'it symbolises no more than the autonomy of the mother – the *"aplomb de la mère"'* (Gilbert and Gubar, 1989: 96). They venture to ask if it is 'possible that verbal signification arises not from a confrontation with the Law of the Father but from a consciousness of the lure and the lore of the mother?' (*ibid.*: 98). Similar to Silverman's theory, they quote Anika Lemaire and C. Stein on how 'linguistic communication has already been established' by the time of the Oedipus complex, which therefore cannot be what brings about 'the primal repression which establishes language' (Lemaire and Stein quoted by Gilbert and Gubar, 1989: 96).

I see castration in the films as taking the form of removing access to a previous partner through the prohibition by a new partner. This new partner need not be male. And the prohibition spells loss as severance, a cutting off of desire. Although George and Tory lose Childie and Chris, there is a vast difference between the two castrations. In the first, agency as productive instrumentality is eliminated, while in the second it is endorsed. In this difference lies a key strategy which we can extrapolate for our own ends. I think that these male fantasies show that the castration of lesbian desire can only be realized if that desire takes its reference point from phallocentrism. If that lesbian desire is able to reinvent itself outside the phallic frame, it can negotiate castration through disavowal rather than as defeat.

Let me explain. George's behaviour attempts to replicate the phallus, insofar as she tries to pass as male, and is therefore positioned outside the phallocentric order because she fails. Because she has not questioned this order, her failure takes the form of allowing herself to be acted upon without agentic signification. Tory on the other hand accepts the phallus as signifying the symbolic order, but she could be said to take her frame of reference from outside of it, from a still functioning but radically other subject position, and as a result, she remains agentic, not passing as a male, but acting as a female who can coexist with the symbolic order because of having negotiated it differently. It is precisely her lesbian desire as a non-phallic desire that enables her to disavow her castration and accept the loss of Chris so gracefully.

Consider an early joke Tory has with a black male friend, who complains that winning in sport is like coming in sex, sometimes it's just not enough. Tory laughs and says, 'Speak for yourself, buddy.' There is an ambiguity here. Is she speaking of sport or sex? Could it be that winning is enough for her? The more likely reading is that lesbian desire and lesbian sex are enough for her, that they deliver the pleasure they promise because they are positioned outside a phallocentric order. Her castration at losing Chris will not destroy Tory because her desire is fluid, and not fixated on one object, as is George on Childie.

Let us now consider some critics on the films, whose findings connect with my argument that spectatorial positions are agentic when allowing for a mix of responses. I have suggested that it is the split spectatorial position that allows for engagement simultaneously with resistance.

Sister George largely evokes dominant readings, but there is also spectatorial space to supply negotiated readings. Caroline Sheldon finds that the three women represent the 'major stereotypes' of lesbian films, with George as 'the essence of revolting butch', Childie as 'the neurotic (regressed) lesbian', and Mercy Croft as 'the successful and sophisticated career woman', who functions as 'the castrating bitch' by enabling Childie to leave George (Sheldon, 1977: 12–13). As Sheldon says, what we are presented with is 'quite emotionally repellent' (*ibid.*: 13), but there is room to receive these images differently. I would suggest that Vito Russo's reading of George offers a more negotiated response, in which he evinces sympathy for her, contrasting her 'honesty and openness' with 'the cartoon treachery' of Mercy Croft and 'the loveless opportunism' of Childie (Russo, 1987: 172). These readings of George as repellent and sympathetic of course attest to the the diversity of response available in spectating positions.

Elizabeth Ellsworth's analysis of spectatorial responses to *Personal Best* also attests to this diversity. She finds that liberal and socialist feminist reviewers 'assessed the ending within its "own terms"' (Ellsworth, 1986: 192). This for me suggests a negotiated rather than a dominant reading. Probably, as heterosexual feminists, these women were able to enjoy the content of lesbian desire but accepted its demise in the film without protest. Ellsworth finds that lesbian feminist viewers took a more active line. They reimagined the ending and reemphasized the lesbian content, by redefining Tory as the centre of narrative interest (*ibid.*: 194). This is without doubt an oppositional and resistant reading.

As far as the split reading goes, I am also able to engage with the text and enjoy its representations of lesbian desire, no matter how brief and inaccurate they may be. While there is material I dislike, such as the recycling of racist jokes, and while I find Chris at fault for rejecting Tory, I can enjoy some of the text even while I critique the rest of it. My split reading allows me to see Tory's castration as engineered, whereby her relegation to off-screen space to make room for a male partner is an obvious contrivance carried out in the name of the phallus. Williams finds the erasure of Tory quite in accord with Hollywood's treatment of lesbians. 'Instead of death or suicide, the punishment has simply been reduced to narrative banishment' (Williams, 1982: 152). And her reading of the film confirms the tradition of heterosexual pornography, where the content of lesbian desire is 'so much titillation before the penis makes its grand entrance' (*ibid.*: 154).

Silverman cites Serge Leclaire on how, having the penis, the male is on the right side of the symbolic order but on the wrong side of knowledge. Conversely, the female, lacking the penis and therefore castrated, is on the right side of knowledge but the wrong side of the symbolic order (Silverman, 1990: 111). As Silverman argues, the phallus is not part of some 'sacred time', but can be divested of privilege and dismantled from its status as that which signifies desire (*ibid.*: 113).

As we have been examining castration and agency in relation to the lesbian I would like to discuss how the black subject is also exposed to attempts to castrate our agency. Our castration under white supremacy has taken the form of dehumanization, and our ability to act agentically has been marred by the operations of stereotyping. First, castration as the denial of our humanity. The Combahee River Collective attest that for the black subject, 'to be recognized as human, levelly human, is enough' (Combahee River Collective, 1978: 16). It is clear that the attempted hijacking of our humanity through white ascriptions of black animality and bestiality have served to castrate black people. This castration has historically included taking the form of lynching black men and raping black women, and justifying such atrocities by projecting fantasies and wish fulfilment onto us through the use of stereotypes. Black men are portrayed as rampant rapists and black women as promiscuous at least, if not prostitutes.

In stereotyping, black men are violent and dangerous criminals, and black women are 'primarily mothers, domestics and prostitutes' (Lindsey, 1970: 88). The paradigm of projection through fantasy and wish-fulfilment remains intact. White readings need to be rewritten. It is white men, whose sexual fantasies of rape get projected onto black men, who have historically raped black and white women. These men's fantasies that their white women are in particular danger from black men are belied by the fact that rape is far more often intraracial than interracial (Davis, 1984: 43; hooks, 1990: 60). It is also these men's wish-fulfilment for black women's bodies as sexually available that enables the projection of sexual promiscuity onto us.

It is precisely through the operations of stereotyping that racist ideas achieve ideological currency. Sander Gilman traces the evolution of the term 'stereotype' from the use of a mould to make papier mâché copies, where as a mould, the stereotype was originally seen as an 'immutable structure' (Gilman, 1985: 15–16). Gilman's interest in the stereotype concerns its manifestation as a text, and hence, like a text, the stereotype is not immutable but 'inherently protean' (*ibid.*: 16–18). In an attempt to understand but contain the multiplicity of the factual, the stereotype attempts to delimit its object by setting up crude definitions of what it is. This is a form of controlling behaviour, and as Homi Bhabha points out, stereotyping reveals its anxiety as it attempts to fix its false assertions (Bhabha, 1994: 70), so that the '*same old* stories' are 'differently gratifying and terrifying each time' (*ibid.*: 77; original emphasis).

To return to the question of our castration through the attempted elimination of our agency, black subjects can adopt a double conscious-ness which involves the disavowal of our castration and the affirmation of our agency. There is evidence to suggest that we have always done this. Patricia Hill Collins documents how black women, confined to being seen as 'mules and mammies', in fact 'resist by creating their own self-definitions and self-valuations' (Collins, 1990: 142).

I conclude with the opening quotation. From '*Pourquoi Pa?*' ('why father?'), we spell out the implied *Pourquoi pas* ('why not?') and move to *Pourquoi pas Pa* ('why *not* father?'). While the father can indeed be primarily instrumental in the child's social and psychic structuration as a subject, I think it is much more likely that the mother carries this weight.

Lesbian desire can offer paradigms to counter desire as inevitably masculine and phallic. Not only have representations of us moved from the abnormalization of our desires to the granting of agency to them, but these desires can reformulate female desire away from the phallus as a 'privileged signifier' (Lacan, quoted by Butler, 1993: 77). Whether we reproduce and replicate phallocentric desire or can resist and refuse its terms remains to be seen.

Notes

1. Jacqueline Nacal, quoted by Sandra Gilbert and Susan Gubar (1989: 81). Barbara Laplace has pointed out to me that the name Jacqueline Nacal has an uncanny (and uncoincidental?) resemblance to Jacques Lacan.
2. Rosa Ainley (1995: 12).
3. Eileen McGarry was alert to the problematic nature of seeing documentary film as a privileged purveyor of 'truth' (Erens, 1990: xviii; Kaplan, 1983: 126–7).
4. See Rosemary Curb and Nancy Manahan (eds), *Lesbian Nuns: Breaking Silence* (1985).

3

European Lesbians in Film

Reformulating the Fetishization of Beauty:
November Moon Falls *At First Sight*

The film star is an institutionally sanctioned fetish.

Anne Friedberg[1]

In this discussion of *November Moon* and *At First Sight*, I will suggest that the mechanisms of fetishism are not the exclusive province of the male, because they describe certain processes which women also negotiate. I deploy both film and psychoanalytic theory to explore how we can reformulate some of these processes. I suggest we interrogate the mechanisms of psychic processes as they have been defined by masculinist thinking, and extract what is useful for us. This involves a critical act of reappropriation, whereby we choose to claim what is socially productive, and refuse that which adheres to patriarchy's nihilistic and death-dealing order. First, I will venture into an exploration of oppositional positions of spectatorship, expanding on the concept of the split spectator, whose fragmentations reflect the processes of fetishism. I will also look briefly at second-wave feminisms. In addition to discussing the films in detail, I will also cover some material on the phenomenon of fetishism in relation to lesbian desire.

I begin with the premise that film does not merely reflect certain social positionings, it can actively produce our social subjectivities. As Annette Kuhn states, 'Cinema is a discursive process in its own right', where films can be 'actively instrumental in discursive constructions of the socio-sexual' (Kuhn, 1988: 108). This confirms for me the power of film in the project of reconstituting identities. What cinema can in theory deliver is the imaging of women, black women, lesbians, and especially black lesbians, in contexts that reformulate how we have been received under orthodox regimes of representation. This I will argue can involve redefining pleasure away from plenitude and more through fragmentation. A cinema for women, with women as subjects of desire *as* women, is certainly a starting point in the re-enculturation of social subjectivities. We have made some inroads on the journey to reformulation and reappropriation. Let us now look at some of the progress in terms of active spectating.

We start with the contested argument that the film gaze belongs to the male, whereby cinema represses the female on screen as well as the female viewer engaged in watching. This lack of space for the woman has been re-theorized, and work on spectatorship provides evidence that women have a great capacity for critical receptivity. B. Ruby Rich, for one, has questioned the notion of the woman as passive spectator by countering 'with a conspicuous absence of passivity' in her reception of the film text (1978: 278).

Active spectatorship may not have been theorized as such until comparatively recently, but the concept explains recurrent viewing positions that women have brought to film. Black spectators have traditionally been selective in what we accept gladly and what we tolerate with difficulty. We enjoy what little pleasure we can extract from mainstream images of us, few as they are, and we tend to remove ourselves from the rest, so as to resist negative imagings of us. As Jacqueline Bobo says, black subjects 'understand that mainstream media has never rendered our segment of the population faithfully', and so 'we have learned to ferret out the beneficial and put up blinders against the rest' (Bobo, 1990: 96).

bell hooks states that 'as critical spectators, black women participate in a broad range of looking relations', and that we 'contest, resist, revision, interrogate, and invent on multiple levels' (hooks, 1992: 128). Oppositional strategies are also supplied by bringing to bear the lesbian gaze, which 'determines the subject's position of the lesbian viewer' (Testaferri, 1995: xvi). Jane Gaines, for instance, suggests that lesbian studies of films 'show that the female "look" cancels the male point of view and that active reading resists the flow of classical narrative' (Gaines, 1984: 84–5). Z. Isiling Nataf finds that 'the black lesbian spectator, as a resisting spectator, has a schizophrenic relationship with the cinema interdiscourse' (Nataf, 1995: 61).

Molly Haskell also points out the phenomenon of active spectating, whereby in the memory of the films certain women watched, what they remember are women's 'intermediate victories', and images of their 'intelligence and personal style', not their humiliation and punishment in the narrative on-screen (Haskell, 1974: 31).

In this selection of memory we resist the dominant meanings of film by supplying our own readings and achieving our alternative pleasures. We add to these positions of active spectating the notion of the woman as the 'ultimate dialectician', with Rich referencing Brecht on the exile who 'lives the tension of two different cultures'. Rich suggests that 'the woman spectator is an equally inevitable dialectician' (B. R. Rich, quoted by Williams, 1984: 155). Rich ventures that women respond to film much more dialectically than men, and I would agree that as female subjects we are more likely to be contesting and critical than male spectators who benefit from staying with the same because of the confirmation of their privilege under the current social order. As Laura Mulvey has found, 'mainstream film coded the erotic into the language of the dominant patriarchal order' (Mulvey, 1975: 59), and so obviously most men will have less reason to contest certain imagings. Women have more at stake, for instance our equality has still to be recognized and respected. We are much more likely to engage with texts in 'a deconstructionist spirit' (Fischer, 1989: 3). Linda Williams suggests that women spectators are not merely adopting the positions of masculine mastery or feminine over-identifications, but are 'juggling all positions at once' (Williams, 1984: 155). By bringing politicized pleasures to the text, we can challenge the mainstream orthodoxies while selectively engaging with the pleasures of narrative, identifications and desire. What this confirms for me is the concept of a split spectator, who is adept at making unusual and contesting connections, and who supplies meaning in a perpetual process of intelligibility.

What we can assume from the above is that the black lesbian feminist position offers a multiple vantage point of active spectatorship. But how can we transform our oppositional responses into a social force that would actively court the transformations we desire, in film and elsewhere? Bobo offers a theory of 'articulation' as precisely the means to achieve change. Referencing Stuart Hall and Ernesto Laclau's work, Bobo defines an articulation 'as the form of a connection, a linkage, that can establish a unity among different elements within a culture, under certain conditions' (Bobo, 1990: 104–5). Bobo refers to Hall's distinct preference for articulation as 'joining up' rather than as 'giving expression to', because the latter implies a unity in the social group which is clearly not a possibility. An articulation is formed through a 'social alliance', it is cohesive for a time in focusing on political change, and when 'an articulation arises, old ideologies are disrupted and a cultural transformation is accomplished' (ibid.: 105).

Both black and white feminists have successfully begun an articulation on our subjectivities as equal, and not as subordinate as we have been historically defined under phallocentrism. The notion of articulation as 'joining up' has allowed us to form coalitions, but the absence of a uniform 'expression' in our struggles testifies to the innumerable differences between women. The solution would not be to attempt to dispel difference, an impossible and undesirable task, but to explore equality and celebrate difference, a fetishistic position.

Let us look at feminisms in relation to fetishism, that is, to the split positions of equality and difference as the project that feminist theorizing must resolve. Before proceeding, I think it best that I state my endorsement of the usage of 'patriarchy' and 'women' as workable terms. In this I agree with Sylvia Walby, who references the critique of the concept of patriarchy as involving 'essentialist' and 'ahistoric' analyses that do not account for the experiences of women of different cultures, classes and ethnicities, racial and otherwise (Walby, 1990: 2). This is apparently due to the dominance of white middle-class women in the women's movements, whose appropriations of feminism have sometimes served the purposes of exclusion. Walby argues that the concept of patriarchy can adequately describe the phenomenon of women's experiences as subordinated, and that it can be developed to be more inclusive, 'over time, class and ethnic group' (*ibid.*). Some also object to the use of the category 'woman'. Black feminists, for instance, refute the notion of a unity in this category. While I obviously agree with this, at this point I do not go into black feminisms, I merely follow Walby in her argument that the categories of 'men' and 'women' have a discernible 'historical and cross-cultural continuity' to justify the usage of these terms (*ibid.*: 16).

We begin with Simone de Beauvoir's famous formulation of the man, and of the woman in relation to the man: 'He is the Subject, he is the Absolute – she is the Other' (de Beauvoir, 1949: 16). There has been much theoretical work on why and how this has come about. Mostly, as I will demonstrate, biology is confused with the social in explanatory accounts. Carole Vance quotes Gayle Rubin on the 'sex–gender system' as 'the set of arrangements by which a society transforms biological sexuality into products of human activity' (Rubin, quoted by Vance, 1980: 381). That is to say, we are born within fixed biological positions determined by our sexed bodies, but the 'gendering' of these bodies as 'masculine' and 'feminine' is a social process, and hence not fixed but subject to alteration. However, as Vance points out, sex–gender systems see 'gender categories as unalterable', because 'natural' and 'given' (Vance, 1980: 382). While sexed bodies remain fixed for the main part, in that genitalia are likely to remain the same, gender need not be, and it is this confusion of the two, this fixing of the changeable, that shows the attempted suppression of social construction in favour of biological reductionism.

Countless authorities have attempted to put into place theories of 'origins' and causes, but these explanations usually founder on the conflation of sex with gender and are always determined by pre-suppositions. For instance, Lacan cannot account for why the symbolic order is patriarchal. Similarly, Rosalind Coward finds that Engels's account of the division of labour between the sexes cannot escape the lure of the 'natural' as an explanation, and that his account of the division 'is presupposed, excluding consideration of this division itself as a construct' (Coward, 1983: 152). Elizabeth Cowie also finds that Lévi-Strauss's attempt to explain society as a set of kinship structures involving the exchange of women is one where this exchange 'is itself predicated on a pre-given *sexual division*, which must already be social' (Cowie, 1978: 126; original emphasis). Again, there is a conflation of the biological with the social, and this is a danger in attempting to provide explanatory accounts of origins. We find that 'in ascribing "origins" the trap is set for the inscription of a fundamental sexual difference into the social' (*ibid.*).

I would agree with Jean-François Lyotard's proposition that, rather than seek 'grand narratives of legitimation', we should be glad that postmodernism has discredited them (Lyotard, quoted by Fraser and Nicholson, 1990: 22). Nancy Fraser and Linda Nicholson report how since the beginning of the 1980s, feminists have abandoned the 'project of grand social theory', no longer 'looking for *the* causes of sexism' (Fraser and Nicholson, 1990: 31–2; original emphasis). As Nicholson suggests, radical feminism may be correct in identifying the pervasiveness of women's subordination, but 'wrong in searching for a singular cause' (Nicholson, 1986: 9).

Looking at the re-emergence of white Western feminism, the 'second wave' of the 1960s onwards, Walby both summarizes and critiques the main strands of the women's movements. In Britain, radical feminists and Marxist feminists dominated the movement, while in America, liberal feminists and radical feminists followed distinctly different directions (Walby, 1990: 2). Walby reports that the critique of radical feminism is that it offers essentialisms, biological reductionisms and false universalisms by locating patriarchy as a definable system of domination in an account that does not address the many differences between women (*ibid.*: 3). Walby also exposes the analysis of liberal feminism as inadequate for not addressing the overarching structures of women's subordination, seeing it rather as the result of isolated instances of inequality (*ibid.*: 4). Marxist feminists are also critiqued for their exclusive focus on capitalism as determining women's oppression, which fails to recognize the impact of gender as an independent dynamic of inequality (*ibid.*).

Nicholson also charts some of the developments in feminisms in America. Liberal feminists were known as the movement for 'women's rights' whereas the radical feminists were dubbed 'women's lib', in a pejorative diminution of the word 'liberation' (Nicholson, 1986: 19). This latter title acquired media exposure at the 1968 Atlantic City Miss America Contest, where radical feminists protested by throwing bras, wigs, false eyelashes and other items into a 'Freedom Trash Can'. Although there was no instance of any bras being burnt, the media took hold of the image, and members of 'Women's Lib' became known as 'bra-burners', seen as sacrilege (*ibid.*: 29; cf. Bordo, 1994: 187).

Nicholson characterizes the different movements as involving the liberal feminists engaging with social reform at the level of state legislation, while radical feminists sought 'root causes' for subordination as stemming from the family as an oppressive site for women (Nicholson, 1986: 39, 26). There were also Marxist feminists who concentrated their analysis on capitalism, and saw changes to the organization of the economy as the means of effecting social transformation. Some women identified as socialist feminists who sought to integrate the findings of radical feminism with a Marxist analysis (*ibid.*: 39–40). We must add to this the presence of some 'cultural feminists', who saw women as essentially 'superior' to men (J. Evans, 1995: 18).

Judith Evans refers to the 'tension' (*ibid.*: 2) between liberal feminism and radical feminism in the fight for equal rights in the name of sameness, and the struggle for change in the social order in the name of difference. Julia Kristeva in 'Women's Time' refers to the beginnings of the movement with the suffragists fighting for equal rights, and the post-May 1968 feminists, who insist on change. Kristeva suggests that both 'attitudes' prevail in Europe (Kristeva, 1981: 197–8). Toril Moi summarizes Kristeva on these positions. First, there is liberal feminism with the demand for equality and 'equal access to the symbolic order'. Then there is radical feminism which celebrates difference and a rejection of the male symbolic order (Moi, 1989: 128). There is also a third position that Kristeva takes, a rejection of 'the dichotomy between masculine and feminine as metaphysical', where we see such a dichotomy as an abstract theorizing, and move beyond its constraints. Rather than define 'femininity', Kristeva sees it as a '*position*' and not an essence (Moi, 1989: 128, 127; original emphasis).

Kristeva finds that all these positions, or 'attitudes', are possible in a '*parallel* existence of all three in the same historical time' (Kristeva, 1981:

214; original emphasis). That is, we aspire to equality, fight for transformation, and attempt to transcend gender. In keeping with the fetishistic position that enables a confluence of contradictions, I obviously support the synthesis of these 'attitudes', or 'generations', or at least the first two positions, which Kristeva characterizes as wanting an *'insertion into history'* as opposed to a 'radical *refusal* . . . in the name of the irreducible difference' (*ibid.*: 198; original emphases). We must subscribe to both positions, encapsulated in what Evans refers to as 'the hope of attaining *radical equality*' (J. Evans, 1995: 25; my emphasis).

To polarize equality and difference as mutually exclusive opposites is to set up a divisiveness in feminisms that reminds me of what Adrienne Rich has called a 'false historical necessity' (1979: 286). She is referring to the divisiveness with which suffrage was sought and granted in America, 'playing off sex against race', where black men got the vote first and not black women or white women (*ibid.*). In parallel ways, I think it is unnecessary to set up equality and difference as opposed terms. We must seek equality and celebrate difference. As Moi finds, 'feminists have to be pluralists' (Moi, 1989: 118). Therefore we must work within the same order while effecting its transformation into a different social order.

It is clear that while we must challenge the symbolic order, we must select what to dismantle and what to retain for the system of sociality to remain functional. We do not wish to destroy language and communication, identity and expression, but what we do wish is to reformulate the framework of their inscription. As Kristeva points out, a threat to the symbolic order also threatens 'the very principle of sociality' (Kristeva, quoted by Weir, 1996: 147). As Allison Weir states, we need to distinguish 'between the necessary conditions of a social community, and of language, and the pathological conditions of domination' (Weir, 1996: 147). Weir quotes Kristeva on a possible solution through an 'interiorization of the founding separation of the sociosymbolic contract' (Kristeva quoted by Weir, 1996: 148, emphasis removed). Weir explains how Kristeva wishes to differentiate between 'the violence of separation, which is unavoidable, and the violence of domination, which can perhaps be overcome' (Weir, 1996: 150). This entails the adoption of an identity based not on 'a defensive opposition to the other, but on an acceptance of internal differentiation – an acceptance of the otherness within the self' (*ibid.*). Locating in ourselves the presence of the other would more easily facilitate a positing of our self in the position of the other, for the purposes of tolerance if not conversion. We could understand each other's mindsets more easily, so as to enable a dialogue characterized by its openness to other positions. This would be less about suppression and more about the celebration of the subject, specifically the woman, 'to bring out the singularity of each woman, and beyond this, her multiplicities, her plural languages' (Kristeva, quoted by Weir, 1996: 152).

Let us turn now to the first film. *November Moon* (*Novembermond*) is the story of two lesbians who meet in France during the Second World War. November is Jewish and stateless, recently orphaned and unemployed, a refugee seeking French citizenship. Férial is French, has a job and lives with her mother and brother. They are all white. November and Férial fall in love just before the German occupation of France. November is caught by the Nazis but escapes to Paris where Férial shelters her in her flat. They are both in danger of losing their lives. To avoid suspicion from the Gestapo, Férial gets a job with a Jew-baiting newspaper where she has to consort with German officers. This enables her to be alerted beforehand when the Germans plan to raid her flat, and November is saved from capture. After the Allies liberate France from Nazi occupation, November and Férial are in theory free to enjoy their life together. The film ends on a closure of sorts, with the restoration of order through the removal of the Nazi threat. But as we will see, this is a closure without completion, where we are left in a state of suspension.

While retailing the narrative in more detail, I hope to demonstrate the visual motif of fetishism in the film and to suggest ways of renegotiating how we receive the fetish. I find that there is a deliberate fetishization of the woman's beauty as signifying her desirability. This is common to much of cinema, where many films depend on this beauty to carry the narrative. What is crucial here, however, is that this fetishization of beauty seems to be exposed as a conscious motif, working visually and verbally through the filmic text. From that early moment when we first see November's face, a close-up on her beauty, we immediately perceive her as attractive, aesthetically pleasing, desirable. This response is mirrored throughout by other characters in the film. When November goes to the officials in charge of her application for French citizenship, one suggests she marry a Frenchman to avoid nationality problems. When he tells her she is certainly attractive enough, she looks away, she looks down. She does not wish to address this idea. It is clear that her beauty can be an obstacle.

November goes to see Chantal, who runs a bistro. Chantal allows November to work there illegally, eating free meals and keeping tips. Chantal had met November's father in Paris years ago. He too had fetishized her beauty by staring at her across a café room, then approaching her with a straightforward declaration of interest. Chantal had liked his directness, and when she tells November about this meeting, we see how visible beauty itself is being fetishized as representing the woman's desirability.

This is also evident when November meets the young man Laurent for the first time, introduced by Chantal. There is no demonstrated passage of time from their introduction to their having a meal in a restaurant. Although they have only recently met, he tells her he is in love with her. She tells him she is not in love with him, indicating she is not his partner, but that she does like him. His expression of love so soon after meeting confirms that he too fetishizes her beauty, seeing it as signifying the reason for his desire, and reading that desire as love.

Beauty has its penalties, as does vulnerability of course, as when November is sexually harassed in a bakery. She is rescued from the verbal abuses of two men by a young woman. They exit to a café where they talk, and it emerges that the woman is Férial, Laurent's sister.

November meets Férial at her home with her mother and Laurent. They become close, with Férial protective about the danger November is in from the Nazi threat. Later, we see them at a restaurant, where they publicly hold hands and gaze wordlessly into each other's eyes. Without saying anything they get up and start dancing. They have an equivalent height and body-frame and look physically well-matched. We are surprised at their daring, as all present are scandalized at seeing two women dancing quite intimately in a restaurant. They are urged to leave and exit laughing – it turns out this was a ruse to avoid paying the bill. However, because we see the spectacle of their dancing without knowing it was planned, we read desire in the two women's behaviour, a desire brought about by the mutual fetishization of their beauty.

They return to November's room, and the desire we had read in the earlier scene is spelled out as they kiss for the first time, passionately. Cut to the next morning, pan to them asleep together. The landlady bursts in to say they are at war. This is a funny moment when she sees them in bed, but deadly serious as well.

After a passage of time, when the Germans invade France, the two women are forced to leave their homes. There is a sequence of refugees walking for days, geographically displaced and in danger. November shelters with Férial's uncle at his farm in the south, while Férial and her mother go to Paris. When the Germans occupy the south, November is caught by the Nazis. She is raped by an SS officer, her arm is branded, and she is set to work in a brothel. She hits a German officer with a statue to avoid sex and escapes with the help of another officer, who is shot dead for his intervention. Her treatment by the SS officers also confirms the fetishization of her beauty. The officer who rapes her is acting on the sick wish to humiliate the object of desire. And the officer who saves her is motivated by compassion, because she reminds him of his mother. She manages to escape to Paris where Férial shelters her.

Here the film shifts in focus to include more of Férial. We had seen her earlier rejecting the invitations of Marcel, a friend who is also fixated on her beauty. After the occupation, she decides to benefit from Marcel's attraction to her as a way of securing a job with him at a newspaper run by the Nazis. This is to divert suspicion from the dangerous secret of her hiding November. Marcel tips off Férial that her flat is to be raided one night, and this information saves November. What is effectively a secret collaboration between Férial and Marcel has a long tradition in cinema, based on involvement through sexual desire, but here it is done refreshingly differently. From corrupt insurance man to incorruptible private eye, from implicated to involved detectives (*Double Indemnity*, *Klute*, *Eyes of Laura Mars*, *Basic Instinct*), this tradition of sexual engagement and mutual seduction has located the woman as the object of male desire. In *November Moon* what is refreshing is that the secret collaboration has a sexual tension for Marcel which is left taut by Férial's clear refusal of his desire. Moreover, this refusal occurs in the context of an unambiguously clear lesbian desire. The rejection of Marcel, which actively favours the affirmation of lesbian desire, is treated generously within the film narrative, an example of the overriding goodness that the text expresses, and Marcel does not try to punish Férial for choosing November over him. An aggressive logic and a homophobic jealousy might lead some heterosexual subjects to seek vindictive pleasure through punishment, but Marcel helps save November. Because order is restored, this act of mercy is his own saving grace when the Nazis fall.

Lesbian desire is set against a backdrop of war, a predominantly masculine activity of aggression and destructiveness. Because this desire is about equality, and not about power positioning, the two women share their jeopardy and face their oppressors with a common front. While it would be possible to set them up as respectively more or less oppressed, I do not read them this way. It is too easy to say that November suffers more, because she is Jewish, because she is raped and beaten, and branded by a hot iron, because she literally has to run for her life with bleeding bare feet. It is also easy to say that Férial suffers less because as a French subject she can work legally, she is not raped and she is successful in fending off male advances. However, there is something psychically so scarring about the experience of war that it is silly to attempt to quantify her oppression against that of November.

I think the ending of the film is one of suspension and not completion. After the liberation of Paris, Férial is seized by neighbours who think she was a Nazi collaborator. Her hair is chopped off, a punishment that was meted out to subjects who slept with Nazi officers. The film ends with a frozen image of her in shock, staring at November. It is worth asking what is achieved by leaving the spectator in a state of suspension. Although the Nazis have been removed and order has been restored, there is no neat tying up of narrative links, no filling in of gaps to make us feel whole in our knowledge, and this has the effect of altering our pleasure. One central narrative question in the film is whether the two women will survive. First November and then Férial are in increasing danger of losing their liberty and their lives. There is much tension around the question of whether they will survive, and that is why I think Férial goes through the hair-cutting scene, as a way of activating our fears for her danger. She does not die – cutting hair is not itself painful – and we know the truth of her resistance to the Nazis will vindicate her apparent treachery. So this ending might seem anti-climactic and disappointing. However, because her treatment has shown that psychic and emotional violence are just as traumatizing as physical abuse, we end with a closure of sorts, with a ready-made ending. But it is a closure without completion, where we are not able to exit feeling full with the plenitude of cinematic satisfaction. We are presented with their survival as a closure to the central narrative question, we are allowed to infer that their relationship will also survive, if that is what we also want, but we are not given some cosy completion to their trauma. Instead we can read that their trauma will be carried beyond the concluding frame of the film, and hence our pleasure in completion will have been diverted from plenitude to fragmentation. More on that later.

So what the ending confirms for me is that trauma is not just about physical violence being more oppressive, because emotional and psychic violence are also very damaging. And so if one sets up a counting game of competing oppressions, one is in danger of missing the point that all oppressive practices are interconnected, and equally detrimental to the interest of all subjects, including the oppressors. I do not wish to belittle the specificity in the experience of being at the receiving end of oppressive practices. But it is important not to just quantify and measure oppressions, but to qualitatively assess their impact.

To expand further, if I claim that as a black lesbian I am at a particular juncture of interlocking oppressive social systems, my 'triple jeopardy' under racism, gender and sexuality is not to think I am more oppressed than the white lesbian, the black heterosexual woman or even the infamous white middle-class heterosexual man. It would be strategic to remember that we all face multiple jeopardies, including those around age, illness and disability. Some of us will have to confront poverty, and all of us are under threat from environmental catastrophe. Our lives are fragile, and the planet itself is in danger, from warfare and weaponry, an unfolding population explosion and ongoing pollution. Our history of violence and our capacity for destruction make the future frightening. In this global context of jeopardy as a multiple condition, it would be foolish to measure danger and oppression in quantifiable terms. So when I claim that there is a unique position of the black woman who is lesbian, I am not attempting to be more oppressed than thou. I am merely being mindful that I have access to an alternative analysis, where my position as a black lesbian has enabled me to rethink practices from the outside, where I can connect the oppressions, see through the deceptions, and create alternative practices to the ones received in the malestream.

Oppression fosters the necessary resistance that follows if one is to affirm the values of survival, of autonomous subjectivity, and emotional strength. That is why the logic of the phallus, with its inherent structures of inequality, has to be challenged, why phallocentrism itself needs to be dismantled, so that its destructive properties can stop damaging all subjects, oppressor and oppressed.

What is interesting about this film is the way it apparently reworks the lesbian look, starting with the fetish and rewriting lesbian desire according to a non-phallocentric logic, where we can read the fetish as detached from genitalia. By fetishizing the woman's beauty, we subscribe to the dominant cultural and psychic mechanisms around how we constitute and perceive beauty, but we can divest our desire for beauty from its linkage of the fetish with the phallus.

The term *fetishisme* was coined in 1760 'as the term for "primitive religion"' (McClintock, 1995: 181). Anne McClintock reviews the history of the term, moving from Marx and commodity fetishism to Freud's use of fetishism in relation to sexual perversions (*ibid.*). Robert Nye reports that the term fetishism in relation to sexual activity was first documented by doctors and psychiatric specialists in the 1880s and 1890s, coinciding with the 'golden age' of sexology (Nye, 1993: 13). The phenomenon of fetishism had a 'prehistory' in terms of practice, but it was the turn-of-the-century naming of it that made it 'a culturally evocative concept' (*ibid.*: 13–14).

Freud and later Lacan were unconvinced that there were versions of female fetishism, seeing it as an exclusively male perversion. Feminist theorists are now rereading fetishism, seeing that its mechanisms of disavowal and processes of splitting are not exclusive to men (Grosz, 1993: 112; Schor, 1992: 115). McClintock agrees that 'recognizing female fetishism radically challenges the magisterial centrality of the phallus and the castration scene' (McClintock, 1995: 183).

Let us look at initial definitions of fetishism and the fetish:

> The fetish is a substitute for the mother's missing penis; it commemorates the scene where the little boy sees the mother's genitals and simultaneously denies his perception of her castration, lest the same fate befall him. (Schor, 1992: 114)

The male fetishist puts in place contradictory assumptions. He sees the mother has no penis and is horrified at her lack, because he has fantasized her as the phallic mother in possession of a maternal phallus, and because her lack frightens him by giving him a bodily but phantasmatic figuration of what might happen to him. The fetishist is an expert at negotiating contradictions, which exist in flux rather than resolving in fixity, to allow for oscillation between belief and disbelief, avowal and disavowal. Rather than accept that the mother is castrated, the fetishist incorporates another mindset which enables the figuration of a maternal phallus to coexist with the lack of such a phallus. The fetishist therefore believes the mother is both castrated and not castrated. He sees her as not castrated by supplying the concept of a maternal phallus, a penis elsewhere. The fetish itself is that which signifies the maternal phallus, which could be an object, attribute, body part, appearance, etc. Using the fetish to signify the missing maternal member, the fetishist both accepts and denies the mother's castration. The fetish is 'a compromise formation between the horrified recognition of female castration and its vehement denial, or disavowal' (Schor, 1992: 114).

Naomi Schor refers to the fetish as 'a testimony to the ultimate undecidability of female castration' (*ibid.*), and Emily Apter reminds us that this 'undecidability' is its 'defining feature' in psychoanalysis (Apter, 1991: 80). Moreover, like the phallus which is 'fundamentally transferable' (Butler, 1993: 83), the fetish object or attribute is not confined to penile representations. McClintock confirms that 'far from being universally phallic substitutes, fetishes can be any object under the sun' (McClintock, 1995: 185). What all this suggests to me is that women can benefit from the processes of splitting and the mechanisms of disavowal that the fetishist deploys. Disavowal allows for multiple and plural possibilities.

Like Teresa de Lauretis, I think the lesbian subject disavows her castration (de Lauretis, 1994: 204), and I think this is possible by playing with symbolic registers and subjective realities in new alignments which allow both to coexist. As a female subject living in a patriarchy, I do 'accept' my symbolic castration as it has been defined for me by pre-existing orders of language and sociality that will post-date me. On another subjective level, I also resist this symbolic reading of castration as it does not coincide with my own perceptions of empowerment and pride in being a woman. There is in this acceptance and this resistance a median point, that of disavowal, so that contradictorily, I neither fully accept nor fully reject my castration, but disavow it, in an oscillating play of working within the symbolic order while rewriting its terms as far as I am able.

The reappropriation of fetishism as a lesbian possibility has begun. Schor claims that 'the female homosexual is a successful female fetishist' (Schor, 1992: 115). But we must resist setting up the fetish as a counter-penis, and work rather with the possibility for alternative pleasures to be opened up. It is precisely the detachable status of the fetish away from the penis, or from the body, that gives it the possibility of transcending phallocentrism.

Elizabeth Grosz also finds that, contrary to Freud and Lacan, female fetishism does exist, and that 'lesbianism provides its most manifest and tangible expression' (Grosz, 1993: 101). She argues that the girl child is likely to disavow her own castration, not her mother's (*ibid.*: 113). Grosz outlines three possibilities for the girl child who disavows her own castration, those of heterosexual (secondary) narcissism, hysteria, and the masculinity complex (*ibid.*: 110). Those girls who choose a masculinity complex are commonly identified as lesbian (*ibid.*: 112). Rather than phallicize or hystericize their bodies as do the narcissist and the hysteric respectively, the 'masculine' woman takes on an external love object in the form of another woman (*ibid.*: 113). Grosz then suggests, countering the usual associations of fetishism with misogyny and hatred of female genitalia, that the lesbian fetish 'is the result of not a fear of femininity but a love of it' (*ibid.*: 114). It is exactly this act of appropriation for our own productive ends that we need to keep activated, and what enables this particularly in the concept of the fetish is its fluidity, its potential of freedom from the penile.

De Lauretis references a model of desire that no longer affixes itself to the phallus as privileged signifier of desire (de Lauretis, 1994: 223). She argues that 'the lesbian fetish is any object, any sign whatsoever, that marks the difference and the desire between the lovers' (*ibid.*: 228). She suggests that 'in lesbian perverse desire . . . the fantasmatic object is the female body itself' (*ibid.*: 231). In what is a crucial overturning of phallic privilege in favour of more authentic figurations of lesbian desire, de Lauretis suggests:

> What the lesbian desires in a woman . . . is indeed not a penis but a part or perhaps the whole of the female body, or something metonymically related to it, such as physical, intellectual, or emotional attributes, stance, attitude, appearance, self-presentation . . . (*ibid.*: 228)

What this confirms for me is that we can fetishize attributes linked not only with character but with appearance, more specifically with beauty. I do not wish to subscribe to the objectification involved in 'lookism', but I do think that often what we find pleasurable is the beauty that activates our desires. Not beauty as cardboard cut-out or chocolate box clichés of the desirable woman (frequently figured as white, young and able-bodied), but a subjective working of what we find attractive. The plurality of this subjectivity escapes rigid taxonomies of what does or does not constitute beauty. Each subject can have different imagings of the beautiful, based on our own previous attractions and affairs as well as those images that get circulated in mainstream media representations of women. If I think it is the woman's beauty we fetishize, it is often because this beauty is what is satisfying our scopophilia, our pleasure in looking. Commercial cinema is heavily dependent on the beauty of women to carry the weight of desire and narrative. Claire Johnston writes, 'The star system as a whole depended on the fetishization of woman' (Johnston, 1973: 211), and I believe it is the woman's beauty that signifies her obvious visual desirability.

In *The Interpretation of Dreams*, Freud notes how sexual repression frequently draws on transpositions of body parts, and one example he gives of such a transposition is 'the replacement of the genitals by the face in the symbolism of unconscious thinking' (Freud, 1900: 509). Although he is talking about repression rather than the processes of splitting here, this supports my hunch that we especially fetishize the woman's beauty, by apparently seeking the maternal phallus in the woman's face, the shape of her mouth, the structure of her cheek-bones, or the 'glint on the nose', and so on. What could be a permanently patriarchal set of responses to beauty can probably be divested of their phallocentrism if we rethink the fetish. It might be productive to engage in making certain psychic mechanisms conscious, by reworking how we enact psychic structures in our lives.

At First Sight (Coup de Foudre aka *Entre Nous)* is another story of two white women who meet and fall in love in France. The film begins in 1942, is set during the German occupation, and intercuts their experiences. Léna's marriage is one of convenience, Madeleine's of love and friendship. Léna is Jewish and is able to escape an internment camp by marrying Michel. They have a perilous time escaping, and their displacement parallels that of refugees forced to leave homes and motherlands. Madeleine is widowed at the age of nineteen when her husband is shot dead in her arms. Both women are aware of danger and loss. The recent death of Léna's mother and Madeleine's loss of the man she loves put them both in a state of mourning, even trauma. The Nazi occupation directly impacts on their lives but the film's focus is later, when they meet in Lyons in 1952. Léna is still married to Michel, Madeleine has remarried, and they both have become mothers. Their immediate attraction leads to a firm friendship and, later, to an implied sexual relationship. They leave their husbands, take their children and plan to set up a home in Paris, where they will support themselves running a clothes boutique. The film ends with the film-maker's dedication to her mother (Léna), her other mother (Madeleine), and her father. The ending presents a closure of sorts, but again this is a closure without completion, leaving us with a sense of fragmentation.

In this particular film I concentrate on key scenes that convey the women's desire for each other. As the opening sequences so clearly intercut the two women's lives, we justifiably anticipate their meeting, and it is with their *coup de foudre*, their immediate attraction 'at first sight', that I wish to begin. They meet at a school, where Léna's two young daughters are performing in a school show. Léna is looking after Madeleine's little son. When Madeleine arrives to collect her son, they meet for the first time. Madeleine is late. She says she was with a clairvoyant, and asks Léna if she believes in such people. Léna answers she does not know, she has never been to one. Madeleine looks at Léna's profile, and takes in her beauty – the shot suggests a falling at first sight. The two women are both beautiful (of course). This first exchange typifies the way they begin their friendship. Madeleine is direct, inquiring, interested, she wants to know. Léna is unknowledgeable, she has little experience, but she is open to finding knowledge. Their mutual beauty, their parallel height and weight, their complementary style of feminine French costume, all point to a common physicality. We read desire in the look that Madeleine gives to Léna. I am reminded of a line from the Doors, 'Hello, I love you, won't you tell me your name?', for its evocation of an immediate attraction based on the fetishization of the woman's beauty. But what is refreshing is that there are possibilities for a recontextualization of the fetish.

At the same first meeting, within minutes, a second exchange takes place that again typifies for me how their relationship will evolve. Léna notices she has a ladder in her stocking, and immediately looks at Madeleine's legs and notices she is not wearing anything. Madeleine says she wears suntan lotion. She puts her hand on her bare leg and then offers it to Léna to smell. Léna's response is delightful. She at first expresses surprise at this intimate gesture, then meets it fully by holding Madeleine's hand in her own. She smells the scent and says it's good. We could read in this that Léna already looks to Madeleine as a mirror, and that Madeleine already mirrors back a desire for intimacy which Léna finds good to meet.

Cut to them walking, talking about their names. Léna is about to say something but stops herself, despite prompting from Madeleine. They arrive where Léna lives, and Madeleine asks her if she would like them to meet again. Léna admits it was precisely this that she had wanted to say, conveying the mutuality between them. Madeleine gives Léna her number, and they arrange to speak the following day. Next cut to them at Madeleine's home. It is as if nothing that has elapsed in the interim has any significance: all that matters is that they meet again, and soon, again conveying the immediacy in the fetishization of a woman's beauty.

As the two women get to know each other, they relate their previous history and conduct their present lives in the context of male attentions that also fetishize the woman's beauty. At the beginning of the film, Michel fetishizes Léna's beauty to the extent of proposing marriage before speaking to her. Madeleine too is fetishized for her beauty, and her first husband's last work of art is an unfinished attempt to capture it in a sketch. Male attention is everywhere. Léna is harassed by young men, and she has an encounter (albeit apparently voluntarily) with a soldier on a train journey. She admits to Madeleine that she came for the first time. Madeleine meanwhile is sexually active. She is having an extra-marital affair, and is also subject to male sexual harassment, from Michel specifically. The male attention serves to divert and distract from lesbian desire, so that the two women constantly skirt around their desire for each other, often wondering about the extent of their feelings for each other. There is no imaging of their desire in direct representations of sexual activity, but nevertheless it can be inferred that their growing intimacy will incorporate physical closeness. I think a reason for omitting any direct representation is because the film is partly biographical, written by the film-maker Diane Kurys as a testimony to her love for her parents, biological and social, real and fictive. It is as if the daughter cannot quite bring herself to image the lesbian parent and lesbian lover together sexually, possibly because it is too traumatizing to take on.

A heterocentric sensibility would possibly find the castration of the men in the film to be uncomfortable or even alienating. However, my reading as a lesbian allows me to celebrate lesbian desire, especially when it can dismantle phallocentric film languages. The men are castrated but the women are not phallicized as a consequence. Although we also fetishize the actors' beauty (and Miou Miou and Isabelle Huppert playing Madeleine and Léna are beautiful), the lesbian look can reformulate the fetish by removing its phallic association. This is to rewrite the phallus, not as a sign of completion or plenitude, but as being fraudulent and empty. If we could expose the over-inflated importance attached to the phallus, all subjects, male and female, would benefit.

Let us look again at how the women's desire is suggested despite an omission of specific representations. The reading to be inferred is that their desire is sexual, and that they mirror and meet the other's need for intimacy. It is clear that they find each other attractive, from the first meeting. In one scene, after they have been swimming and are dressing in front of a mirror, they reassure each other about the size of their breasts. They exchange looks of obvious admiration and apparent attraction, and their gaze is mediated through the mirror. Madeleine asks, 'Why do I feel so good with you?' The question is not answered in images of desire, but its suggestion is clear. Later, when Léna goes to fetch Madeleine from her parents, where she has been resting after a breakdown, we can assume their relationship is already an issue. Léna takes Madeleine to her shop, appropriately called 'Magdalena', a phonetic merging of the two names. They drink champagne, exchanging mutual support. Léna says she is deliriously happy. These are the last words they exchange on screen. Michel attempts to intervene and the film's resolution follows shortly, with the two women deciding to live together with their children. Although there is more footage, it does not include them speaking together, which serves to omit any spoken representation of their desire. We can assume that they will strive for an autonomy separately from the men, where together they can meet each other's needs without recourse to financial dependence or emotional involvement with men. They will do this by remaining loyal to each other to the extent of setting up home together in a feminine economy. From the mutuality of their desire to the equality of their subjectivities, we can assume their partnership is one of parity, not of power politics around sexual domination or emotional manipulation.

The film ends on closure without completion. The narrative question around whether they will commit themselves to each other is answered in the affirmative, providing a resolution, but this closure does not have the completion we might have visually experienced, say, through a sex scene. The omission of any direct representation of their desire serves to open up enigmas, gaps in our wish to know. I have suggested elsewhere that this is a way forward, because such a strategy allows us to reconstitute what gives us pleasure. Closure without completion allows pleasure to be diverted from plenitude to fragmentation. On this latter point, I would like to reference Barthes on *plaisir*/pleasure and *jouissance*. Jane Gallop summarizes Barthes' distinction 'between *plaisir*, which is comfortable, ego-assuring, recognized, and legitimated as culture, and *jouissance*, which is shocking, ego-disruptive, and in conflict with the canons of culture' (Gallop, 1988: 121).

Oppositional readings can destabilize structures through their contestation of 'comfortable' practices. By resisting notions of completion and plenitude, and by affirming lack, severance and splitting, we can reformulate pleasure as that which allows for fragmentation. Also referencing Barthes, Constance Penley finds that fragmentation punctuates an utterance, it emphasizes 'its uncertainty rather than its authority' (Penley, 1989: 104). It is this space in between that provides a locus for the spectator to supply meanings. I think the split spectator is particularly able to access the processes of intelligibility that enable her to make sense. And I need to reiterate that the split spectator is not the incoherent social subject. I agree with Christine Gledhill that 'we are in a very weak political position if rupturing the place of the subject in representation is our chief point of entry' (Gledhill, 1978a: 35).

However, I do stay with my speculation that it is the fractured subject who can best negotiate lack and loss and the fragmentations of contradictory discursive constructions. It is this same split subject who can work around language as shifting, identity as precarious, and subjectivity as defined by an unknowable unconscious. I am drawn to Julia Kristeva's formulation of the subject in process, '*le sujet en procès*'. In this positioning, the '"speaking subject" is the split subject of psycho-analytic theory' (Leland, 1989: 124–5). This subject in process is 'an agent who acknowledges that fixed identity is illusory and yet sustains a tenable subjectivity by alternating between destabilisation and "provisional unity"' (Meyers, 1992: 146). As I argue, I am in favour of fragmentation being recognized as a quality to celebrate rather than as something to deny or compensate for. Kristeva's formulation of the 'subject-in-process' signifies for me a position of alertness to our being constituted on shifting terrains of discourse and desire.

By conceptualizing a fragmented or split spectator, I am not subscribing to the idea that this entails incoherence. On the contrary, I think the concept of a fragmented subjectivity is one that accommodates contradictions and can juggle the potential conflicts between different positions by reconciling them without inconsistency. This split subjectivity, in this instance, enables me to enjoy the closure of sorts that takes place in the two films, without feeling that I must also experience completion to achieve pleasure. Although there is something unsettling about both films, the pleasures they afford have been redirected onto fragmentation. Here, fragmentation creates spaces of meaning and we then have to fill the gap by supplying meanings and connecting some of the splits. I think it is the split spectator who paradoxically has a developed ability to 'only connect', to borrow from E. M. Forster, who furthermore is best equipped to fill the spaces and bridge the gaps with unusual and alert connections.

For example, in *November Moon* we are informed that November was named after the month of her birth, and we might assume her zodiac sign is Scorpio. During the winter when she is hiding at the farm, Férial visits her from Paris, bringing her clothes and books. That night November tells the allegorical tale of the scorpion desperate to dance and live in freedom. It is clear that November identifies with this creature. In her story it emerges that it is a November evening. Our capacity to supply meaning, to make intelligible, is immediately activated, so that we connect fragmented moments in a bid to make sense, from knowing that November is a Scorpio to thinking this is her birthday. We are given the information that informs this reading not in significant cinematic moments, but in the spaces where we receive meanings by supplying them. This device of understatement works to encourage the processes of intelligibility, whereby we make sense according to our subjective capacities to supply meaning. This example from the film confirms for me that pleasure is not only about completion through closure, but about the fragmentations of subjectivity that empower split spectatorship. Because I have acquired meanings from the text in the absence of their explicit imaging or expression, this has activated certain processes of intelligibility that are pleasurable.

A similar process takes place with *At First Sight*. Andrea Weiss says of the film's ambiguity about the nature of the women's relationship that it 'leaves space for the lesbian imagination' (Weiss, 1992: 125). What my lesbian imagination supplies is a relocation of desire, which is evidenced not in the text but in what is left out of it. As Judith Roof says of this film, 'We are finally left with a dislocated desire represented by the absence of any consummation' (Roof, 1991: 81), and this for me involves a redirection away from plenitude and into intelligibility and the making of meaning as a source of pleasure. Consider the final moments of the film, with the women on the beach with their children. The decision to leave their husbands and set up home together has been taken. Might they acknowledge their commitment to each other now with a more familiar address of a 'tu' instead of the formal 'vous' they have so far used with each other? Yes, they might. Because they no longer address each other on screen at all, there is in this silence a suggestion of familiarity, though unspoken. Silence can sometimes bespeak intimacy. Instead of speech, we get a title, what Judith Mayne calls 'a very literal authorial signature' (Mayne, 1990: 126), where Kurys as author-daughter situates the work as autobiography, by coming out as one of Léna's daughters now watching her father leave her mother for the last time.

It is worth noting here that although the Jewish women in the two films are not practising or devout, their identity as Jews makes them take up certain positionings, so that it is less a matter of religious persuasion and more a cultural formulation that frames their identity. Although this is a digression, and not historically or geographically connected to the film heroines, I think it is now appropriate to explore some material on the Jewish subject, first in relation to black women.

African-American lesbian activist Barbara Smith outlines some of the many issues. She points to the tension between black and Jewish communities, where black women are seen not to address their anti-Semitism and where Jewish women do not acknowledge their racism (1984: 67–8). Smith recounts the thinking of black subjects who remain as a social underclass while Jewish people arrive as exiles and manage to 'make it' (ibid.: 69). While Smith clearly recognizes the commonalities of oppression and persecution, from segregation to genocide (ibid.: 72), she asserts the fact that 'white skin and class privilege make assimilation possible' for the Jewish subject in a way barred to the black subject (ibid.: 80).

Elly Bulkin, speaking as a white Jewish woman among other positionings, recognizes that there are commonalities as well as differences in the experiences of Jewish and black subjects, and she parallels the infamous Middle Passage, where kidnapped black subjects were transported under horrific conditions to the 'New World', with the transportation of Jewish subjects in cattle cars to the Nazi extermination camps (Bulkin, 1984: 105).

Bulkin makes other connections, with Native American women, Chicana women, Asian-Black, Arab-American and Jamaican-Jewish women, among other subject positionings. She knows 'the frustration' of seeing non-Jewish women of colour 'reflect society's prevalent anti-Semitism' by not acknowledging or confronting it (ibid.: 103). Of course non-Jewish white subjects can also be anti-Semitic, and it is not the sole responsibility of the black subject to address the issue. Bulkin correctly deduces that 'the problem is societal, not individual' (*ibid.*). I would certainly agree that anti-Semitism is another face of the same phenomenon of setting up targets to receive hatred and persecution, to hold the projections of violence and the justifications of oppression.

We can see the connections made historically between black and Jewish subjects, both peoples being subjected to systemic violence and persecution. Sander Gilman has traced historical links made between black and Jewish subjects and reports that in the nineteenth century, blacks and Jews were interchangeable categories (Gilman, 1985: 34–5). In Europe and elsewhere, 'being Jewish meant being marked as different' (Gilman, 1993: 12). Similar in process to the othering of the black subject and of the woman, 'The Jew defined what the Aryan was *not*' (*ibid.*: 9; original emphasis). This confirms that the processes at work in oppression and persecution have similar foundations, and can only be addressed through large-scale action and long-term transformation.

Melanie Kaye/Kantrowitz concurs that 'solutions must also be global' (Kaye/Kantrowitz, 1992: 90). She identifies the stereotypes of 'the Jewish Landlord and the Black Rapist', where 'Jews are rich and Blacks are violent' (*ibid.*: 123). She wishes to address the facts that not all Jews are rich professionals and not all blacks are poor and homeless (*ibid.*: 141). She wants there to be a mutual recognition by both black and Jewish subjects of the horrors of the Holocaust and of black enslavement (*ibid.*: 128). Kaye/Kantrowitz finds domination both wrong and unnecessary, and she proposes respect and not confrontation (*ibid.*: 136, 126). This accords with Smith's proposal of 'ethics and respect' as a necessary basis for political and personal interaction (Barbara Smith, 1984: 83). In what is now a familiar motif in my argument, that of the benefits of a fetishistic maintenance of multiple belief systems, I agree with Smith that we need to develop the 'usually politically motivated desire to work out differences, at the same time acknowledging commonalities' (*ibid.*: 73).

Not only have we reformulated the concept of the fetish, we have also seen that the splittings of disavowal can be appropriated to serve more crucial ends than the fascination with the penis/phallus that the fetish has traditionally represented. Let us now extract from the splitting mechanisms of the psyche a more productive use of fetishism, insofar as it allows us to disavow the symbolic castration of the black subject. Fanon, for one, refuses 'to accept that amputation' (Fanon, 1952: 239) and in this refusal lies the basis of our resistance. Black subjects can be aware of racist readings of us while disavowing their claims to truth, literally disbelieving the dominant order because it does not correspond to our own readings. This involves for some of us a tenuous balancing of the social realities of racism and the subjective realities of our own self-affirmations.

I of course argue that it is the decentring of the subject which enables us to negotiate our contradictions. Rather than attempting to make whole, or make good the gaps in the self, if we can accept our fragmentations we will be empowered to receive the fractured and the fluid in ways that can benefit us. I am aware of some of the implicit difficulties and coincidental dangers in this position. Robert Stam quotes Elizabeth Fox-Genovese on how it is surely no coincidence

> that the Western white male elite proclaimed the death of the subject at precisely the moment at which it might have had to share that status with the women and peoples of other races and classes who were beginning to challenge its supremacy. (Fox-Genovese, quoted by Stam, 1991: 235)

I suggest that rather than allow what could be a dominant strategy of co-option to deflect us, we could extract and retain what is beneficial for all social subjectivities. I think it is precisely the fetishistic position of multiple beliefs and plural possibilities that allows the decentred subject to negotiate different positionalities. The black subject's decentred and double consciousness allows us clearly to see the 'construction of culture and the invention of tradition' (Bhabha, 1994: 172). It is this knowledge that enables black subjects to initially occupy positions 'on the shifting margins of cultural displacement' (*ibid*.: 21). I agree with Homi Bhabha that it is 'the "inter" – the cutting edge of translation and negotiation, the *in-between* space – that carries the burden of the meaning of culture' (*ibid*.: 38; original emphasis).

Stuart Hall also argues that 'new ethnicities', separate from race and nations, could be 'predicated on difference and diversity', in a celebration of the 'ethnicity of the margins, of the periphery' (Hall, 1993: 258). It is certainly a fact that it is at the edge and not in the malestream culture that we find ways of rereading and rewriting the dominant order. On this, hooks quotes Gayatri Spivak's favouring of 'texts where so-called marginal groups, instead of claiming centrality, re-define the big word human in terms of the marginal' (Spivak, quoted by hooks, 1990: 22).

The split position of multiple beliefs and decentred fracturations can become a source of strength if used as a strategy for disavowing the dominant and affirming the alternative. As black subjects under white supremacism, we can disavow our symbolic castration while we affirm not some illusory wholeness, but our fractured positions of a decentred subjectivity. I think this is a key strategy for negotiating the plural, which can be helpful given the facts of multiple subjectivities and plural positionings. To be obvious, as fractured subjects who are often aware of contradictions, black identities involve more negotiations than being black. We are also women and daughters, some of us are lesbians, mothers, sisters, wives, workers, writers, activists, and so on.

Schor refers to the political appropriation of fetishism by feminists as a 'paradigm for a typically deconstructive strategy of pressing claims for equal rights while asserting sexual difference' (Schor, 1992: 115). Not only do I endorse this view, I see it as the only negotiation possible if we are to progress beyond foolish debates and false dilemmas.

Note
1. Anne Friedberg (1990: 43).

4

Lesbian Desire for Bedding
Lesbians in Cinema

Plural Positionalities: *Claire of the Moon*
Wants to *Go Fish* . . . *When Night Is Falling*

Desire functions much as the zero unit in the numerical chain – its place is both constitutive and empty.

Jacqueline Rose[1]; original emphasis

It is evident from *Claire of the Moon*, *Go Fish* and *When Night Is Falling* that the pleasures of narrative are often attached to a trajectory of desire and identification. Looking at narrative in relation to desire, we will see how narrative positions us as subjects of desire. We will also look at the historical masculinization or phallicization of desire, with some speculation as to how to resist it. Material on the representations of black subjects will show the paucity of images available to us, much in the same way as an autonomous female desire has yet to be figured.

First we look at some of the issues concerning narrative, and how feminist film-makers and theorists have critiqued its Oedipal obsessions with linearity and closure, as well as how we have responded to its lure with pleasure. I find that the close linkage of narrative with desire, or stories with sex, explains its continued hold over audiences, readers, spectators. The twentieth century has cemented the previous century's fascination with sex, so that desire becomes focused not so much on the spiritual, material, intellectual, political or even social, as on the sexual, project. This obsession with sex seems likely to increase as we enter into the new millennium. My analysis of the three films will centre on how desire for visual representations of desire, that is, for sex scenes, propels the narrative.

Narrative has been seen as the central support of classical cinematic languages, and some feminists have attempted to disrupt it by banishing structures of linearity and closure. Lesbian film-maker Barbara Hammer finds that 'conventional narrative' is a 'patriarchal and heterosexist mode' and to break free, one has to disrupt such modes, where 'radical content deserves radical form' (Hammer, 1993: 72, 70). This is of course a crucial issue, centring on how dominant ideologies saturate the mainstream text, and on how psychoanalytic constructions of the subject then subject the woman to silence and invisibility as the underside, the other, the minus-male. Calls to abandon narrative are a concrete strategizing of how to break away from concepts of pleasure that have been defined and deployed without reference to our equal subjectivities as women.

But do we really want to reject narrative? Can we not rework it? Many of us, myself included, feel that to abandon narrative is to reduce engagement and remove pleasure, even to the point of alienation. I am reminded of the acute discomfort I have sometimes felt while watching some avant-garde films, convinced that they are more an exercise in pretentiousness than art, and that their lack of substance and structure are evidence of an impulse towards alienation. What this probably testifies to more than anything else is my own endorsement of narrative as a cultural form. For one thing, I write short stories with a strong commitment to narrative. And I am also aware of its potential in music, where concept albums could be structured around the unfolding of relationships.[2]

Certainly, narrative is here to stay for the immediate future. It is of course a main characteristic of the commercial feature film. Television soaps depend on the cliffhanger techniques of narrative to maintain continuity of audience interest, where spectators tune in to resolve the what-next question. Even commercial advertising has woken up to the properties of narrative to engage curiosity and sustain interest. In fiction, although some attempts have been made towards disrupting narrative through experimental writing, narrative still dominates, taking the form of linearity as disruption and reinstatement of order, where the conclusion can involve closure, that is, a cutting off of open readings in favour of preferred readings.

Narrative can evidence less interest in 'what' happens, which is the suspense factor, and more in 'how' it happens, in the process, which can be repeated. And spectating as an activity of process is central to spectatorial positionings. I would suggest that we reappropriate the pleasures of narrative, and this in fact has been underway for some time. Jane Gaines refers to how black women film-makers are largely staying with standard filmic languages. 'It is more important to make comprehensible and accessible films than it is to experiment with subverting classical Hollywood narrative' (Gaines, 1984: 83). African-

American film-maker Julie Dash, formerly a maker of documentaries, has been inspired by black women writers like Toni Cade Bambara, Alice Walker and Toni Morrison to turn to 'dramatic narratives' because she 'wanted to tell those kinds of stories' (Dash, quoted by Alexander, 1993: 227). Other feminist film-makers, including Michelle Citron who was initially an advocate of the feminist avant-garde, have decided on 'going mainstream', which Deidre Pribram describes as 'an effort to recuperate a more generally shared filmic language' (Pribram, 1990: 7). This involves the reappropriation of 'cinematic forms (narrative, genres, aesthetic codes) previously defined as belonging to the patriarchy' (ibid.).

I think this reappropriation is a productive step, and reclaims for female pleasure the 'properties' not of patriarchy but of the human impulse to make sense of our lives through the telling of stories. Barthes asserts that 'narrative is international, transhistorical, transcultural: it is simply there, like life itself' (Barthes, 1977: 79).

Looking further at some theories of narrative in relation to desire, Teresa de Lauretis examines the development of semiotics as the study of 'a production of meaning which involves a subject in a social field'. She concurs that the object of enquiry here is not 'narrative but narrativity; not so much the structure of narrative . . . as its work and effects' (de Lauretis, 1984: 105). What is of course consequential to this theory is the address to the social subject as site and source of meaning. De Lauretis goes on to argue, and I agree completely, that narrativity entails 'the engagement of the subject in certain positionalities of meaning and desire' (ibid.: 106). That is, narrative enables us to take up positions as subjects of desire according to our social subjectivities.

De Lauretis quotes Barthes on 'The pleasure of the text' as 'an Oedipal pleasure (to denude, to know, to learn the origin and the end)' (Barthes, quoted by de Lauretis, 1984: 107). The question of Oedipus as framed by Sophocles' Oedipus Rex 'generates a narrative, turns into a quest', again linking narrative with desire (de Lauretis, 1984: 112). De Lauretis is clear that this 'desire is Oedipus's,' it is a masculine desire because 'its term of reference and address is man' (ibid.). Therefore, in addressing the social subject, narrative and Oedipus persist in a masculinization of desire. I reiterate that the lesbian positioning of subjectivity is placed to allow for a reworking of desire, where a politicized reception in our consumption can alter how we receive narrative.

Stephen Neale also writes on the link of narrative with desire. 'The representation of desire itself engages "directly", so to speak, the twin pleasures of narrative by giving them representation in terms of (a specific version) of desire itself' (Neale, 1980: 29–30). While desire is closely affiliated with narrative, narrative seems indissolubly linked with cinema. Neale argues that 'the cinematic institution exists predominantly to produce narrative', but that equally, 'it exists to produce narrative as cinema' (ibid.: 30). I would want to argue that a central narrative interest is obviously focused on desire, where the main narrative question in a text will revolve around whether and/or how sexual activity will be imaged. Representations of lesbian desire therefore become the staging of desire which meets the codes of narrative, the operations of desire, and the spectatorial pleasure of seeing such a staging. De Lauretis suggests that 'the spectator becomes the desiring subject of the film's fantasy; that is, the film becomes the mise-en-scène of the spectator's desire' (de Lauretis, 1994: 127).

Constance Penley has posed the question, 'What, for example, would feminine voyeurism or fetishism be?' (Penley, 1988: 22). I have suggested elsewhere that female fetishism would draw an advantage from the splitting processes that could enable a dislodging of the link between desire as signified by the phallus. To the question of voyeurism, I do of course accept its inevitability in the cinematic medium, but I think it can be reworked through alternative positionings of desire. To be obvious, desire here would not involve 'mastery', 'knowledge' as control or power politics, but would redefine the woman as autonomous, self-defined and self-determining in her desires and equal in her difference. To enable us to enjoy the voyeurism entailed in our spectating, without letting it be a means of reflecting merely illicit pleasures, we would need to move away from trajectories of desire as controlling, to a celebration of the woman as a subject of desire. For this we need a synthesis of politicized pleasures. This is a key to future cinematic representations, that they be respectful to their referents.

Annette Kuhn poses the question that had framed some film theory as to whether commercial cinema was for 'entertainment or enlightenment?' (Kuhn, 1988: 112). In television, the consensus is that the medium should be enjoyable as well as educational, and this precept of entertainment as instructive has been in circulation for several centuries. As far back as 1595, in the Elizabethan court, when Philip Sidney first published A Defence of Poetry, he defined the object of poetry as 'to teach and delight' (Sidney, 1595: 25).

Early feminist film theory also examined the issues of desire and pleasure. Claire Johnston was in favour of both enjoyment and education, and she suggested that the entertainment cinema be politically informed, and the political film draw on ideas from the entertainment film (Johnston, 1973: 217). Certainly, it would be foolish to attempt to forgo entertainment. As Charlotte Brunsdon says, 'The argument that entertainment is never politically or ideologically neutral' should not obscure how 'it is also, at the same time, by the same textual strategies, entertaining' (Brunsdon, 1987: 123). As we have already seen, the pleasure of narrative in cinema often revolves around desire and its enactment, and I think this voyeurism is acceptable provided we are alert to what we are consuming. As I have suggested elsewhere, we can defuse the implications of 'mastery' involved in voyeurism by supplanting the gaze with the look, thereby aligning ourselves more with the pleasures of fetishism than voyeurism in our spectating.

Claire of the Moon is an example where lesbian desire for explicit imaging of lesbian sex provides the primary narrative interest. We go along with what sometimes sounds like contrived dialogue because the representation of this desire has moments of recognizable lesbian behaviours. I wish to concentrate on the idea of attraction as antagonism, where the two women skirt around their desire for each other as something that threatens their self-imaging as autonomous. This antagonism is there from the start between them, but it is not because Claire is heterosexual and Noel is lesbian.

The two are both published authors and meet at a women writers retreat. All the women present are white. They share the same cabin and their differing lifestyles put pressure on their social relations. Claire smokes black Sobranie cigarettes incessantly, she writes when she is inspired rather than out of discipline, she lives for the pleasure of the moment, and has sex with men she meets in bars. Noel is a non-smoker, she is very serious about her research as a practising therapist, she is fixated on a tragic self-image, and she avoids sexual intimacy even though she identifies as lesbian. Their differing sexual identities could make their desire for each other take the form of lesbianism converting heterosex, where Noel seduces Claire. But Claire is no innocent. She is sexually knowledgeable, an initiator who controls men, and what is more it is she who seduces Noel. This is a welcome turnaround of the dynamic of initiation as a site of power, because effectively neither and both are being initiated.

The dynamic of antagonism between them connects with the rage in lesbian desire, where we can sacrifice autonomy to achieve intimacy. Significantly, Noel is researching the subject of communication and is aware that intimacy spells exposure and vulnerability. As a therapist she knows that all subjects have 'missing pieces', and she herself is obsessed with the impossible object of desire, where it is not mutuality she seeks, but the confirmation of her status as tragic. Claire's attraction for her is a threat to proceed beyond initial communication to intimacy, where desire suggests a desire for mergence. Noel's image of herself as tragic is a defensive protection of her sense of autonomy, because obviously if the object of desire cannot reciprocate, the desire remains safe, remains intact without the risk of its return. Reciprocation would involve an outing of desire into the realm of reality, where it would not be as easily controlled as in fantasy. So for Noel, it is much safer to stay with a self-image as tragic.

When Claire actively desires Noel, who is not on a par with a stranger date she can discard, but an attractive woman who arouses her, this desire involves confronting the loss of autonomy. Claire's sense of autonomy is based on the power she has as a woman who has seen through the construction of masculinities. She perceives men as lost and lonely behind the exterior of their masculine behaviours, and this gives her the confidence not to be controlled by them. When she starts fantasizing about her desire for Noel, she tries to resist, and she is afraid because this is not something she can control. Lesbian desire promises pleasure but it also threatens a loss of autonomy.

I have deliberately not retold the film in terms of its narrative progression, as I find that it is desire for lesbian desire that propels the narrative and the spectator's investment is in seeing the enactment of this desire. Let us now consider how the antagonism in the women's desire is figured filmically, as a way of setting up expectations and then meeting them through the resolution of a sex scene.

The expectation of desire is understood from the start of the two women meeting, and indeed their antagonism is based on an unconscious awareness of their attraction for each other. This becomes conscious desire, as they interrogate each other in an urgent need to make sense, know more, get close. As they reveal and learn more about each other, an erotic tension charges their contact, and we experience a void we need to fill with some representation of their lesbian desire.

This is teasingly done through a series of fantasies. First Claire has a dream sequence, where they start kissing. When we realize it is a dream, we are disappointed there is not more, delighted there has been some, and desirous that there be a fuller imaging of their attraction. Next, in a fantasy related by Noel, we see her cruising a woman in red. They start having sex in a public toilet, the woman becomes Claire, they are kissing but it is again a fantasy. This is very funny, playing consciously with our desire, presenting something that is quite satisfying, but still not enough. I think this is key, that we want to see a fuller imaging of lesbian desire within the realist frame of the film. It is not enough to have representations of lesbian desire. These representations and this desire must be embodied through imagings of a recognizable 'reality'. Our position as spectators has made us engage with the narrative logic of the film, so that it delivers representations of lesbian desire to meet our demands for its cinematic enactment. When we are given a bedroom love-making scene between the women at the end of the film, this serves as a narrative resolution to the expectations that have been set up for and by the spectator. I have suggested that the main narrative movement is to evoke and then represent lesbian desire, and it is precisely through our investment in seeing this explicit imaging of lesbian desire that the spectator is engaged.

It is now appropriate to turn to the subject of desire itself, and I return to Jacqueline Rose's opening words, where desire 'is both constitutive *and* empty'. By that I understand that desire can make us take up certain positionings, as process, but that the quest for completion as permanent plenitude is of course illusory. Rose finds it is 'the ultimate fantasy' to seek in the other a way to 'make good' the lack and loss in the subject (Rose, 1982: 32), something I concur with completely.

Rose outlines Lacan's account that 'the mother is taken to desire the phallus not because she contains it (Klein), but precisely because she does not' (*ibid.*: 38). Rose cites Lacan on the child's desire, 'which is the desire to be the exclusive desire of the mother' (Lacan, quoted by Rose, 1982: 38). According to Lacan, because the mother desires the phallus, and the child wishes to have or be what the mother desires, there is an intrinsic impossibility in desire as achievable, because no one, least of all the child, can have or be the phallus. Rose goes on to outline how 'the subject has to recognise' that there is 'lack in the place of the Other', and 'that the status of the phallus is a fraud' (Rose, 1982: 40). I certainly endorse this.

Possibly contradictorily, I am drawn to the view taken by de Lauretis, who finds that 'in lesbian perverse desire . . . the fantasmatic object is the female body itself' (de Lauretis, 1994: 231). Rather than seeking some fake phallus that does not exist, the lesbian finding of the female body enables lesbian desire to achieve a plenitude of sorts, not based on phallocentric formulations of desire, but on a type of completion which is less tendentious. De Lauretis references Adrienne Rich on how lesbian desire is 'limitless' (*ibid.*: 250), and that 'provided their fantasy scenarios are compatible, both subjects can find together, always for the first time, that fantasmatic body for themselves and in each other' (*ibid.*: 251). I know that lesbian love in lesbian love-making can engender passion 'always for the first time' and in this pleasure there is a brief but renewable capacity for completion without straying into the phallic frame. If we rethink desire, not in linear terms as a desire for an object(ive) that can be obtained and possessed, but in spiralling terms, where desire is a seeking out of the unknowable, the ineffable, we are close to Judith Roof's finding that desire perpetuates desire, that it is not about completion in a phallic sense, but the desire for desire (Roof, 1991: 111). We know that pleasure can be a problematic category in our unconscious. As Penley says, 'pleasure is not always a priority in the unconscious' (Penley, 1988: 20). Freud had also supposed that the sexual instinct was not regulated by an economy of pleasure, with linear arousal and release. Indeed, the sexual drive may contain a possibility of its non-gratification, so that there is always something that 'escapes', the something else or something more which could be the desire for desire.

Looking at desire as process, there is the desire for a recognition of the self through the desire of the other for the self. I think this is not so much a need for recognition as it is a need to solicit a response in the other, confirming one's sense of agency. But even if the other were to recognize and respond to the desire of the self, any 'completion' of desire would be pleasurable but illusory, because the demands of desire as process cannot be met. It is a false route to expect the other to compensate for the inadequacies of the self through the validation by the other. Rose quotes Lacan, there is 'no Other of the Other' (Lacan, quoted by Rose, 1982: 33). It is deceptive, sometimes psychotic, to assume such a positioning can be possible.

The desire for desire can be seen in terms of an insatiable hunger, a hunger that remains renewable because satisfaction is short term. Roof uses the trope of knowledge as an unending quest, a searching out of the unknowable, to create an equivalence in how we conceptualize desire. 'Not fulfilling the desire to know sustains desire' (Roof, 1991: 111). If we can accept that desire is like knowledge as an unending quest, then we can come to terms with a lack of permanent completion, and an indefinite deferral of our desire. It is a desire as 'a practice of penultimateness', that is, 'of deferring knowledge and mastery in recognition of the virtue of continuing to desire to know' (*ibid.*: 253). This is to deconstruct desire away from its masculinist appropriations. Therefore an obvious project to pursue if we want to effect transformation is to dismantle the phallocentrism of the symbolic order, whereby we discard those practices which falsely promise plenitude through the values of mastery and control.

I am in favour of de Lauretis's view when she references Martha Gever in 'reclaiming the cinematic function of voyeurism and rearticulating it in lesbian terms' (de Lauretis, 1994: 122). John Ellis distinguishes between the look of voyeurism as 'curious, inquiring, demanding to know', and that of fetishism, where the 'gaze is captivated by what it sees, does not wish to inquire further, to see more, to find out' (Ellis, 1982: 47). I think fetishism can allow us to enjoy the spectacle without loading it down with the weight of our demands. The lesbian look can enable the spectator to engage with narrative, identifications and desire without wanting to see the woman subjugated. I see this as a move away from subjecting the woman to a gaze of mastery and control. Looking with rather than watching the woman can suggest a pleasure uncontaminated by controlling behaviours. This is to engage with the image rather than treat it as an object of omnipotent surveillance.

I find that viewing *Go Fish* is an exercise in conscious voyeurism, where we are both aware of our subject positionalities, and engaged in narrative consumption. The largely linear narrative is given temporal twists, which again allow for its conscious consumption. Several effective devices – voice-over, hands clasping, a spool spinning, pages turning, papers falling, writing on canvas – serve to punctuate the narrative, and give it a temporal progression. These devices both naturalize the narrative, making it assume an illusion of real time and space, while drawing attention to its constructedness, for instance, through the voice-over and hand-held camera, which confirm its experimental mode of film-making. The effect is that we are held by the film's seductive qualities even while we maintain some distance.

The narrative trajectory of the film offers a reworking of the classic romance, where the quest is to find the ultimate partner. Certain obstacles have to be negotiated, leading to closure of sorts in a sex scene, and the conclusion that lesbian coupledom will triumph. What makes this compelling for lesbian spectators is that we are offered a window to view lesbian communities, where the desires, issues and agendas often reverberate beyond the immediate moment of consumption. What is so charming about *Go Fish* is that it communicates the lived experience of lesbian lifestyles as perfectly productive, where our wish to set new agendas is given affirmation.

The film follows the lives of members of two lesbian households. Max has been celibate for ten months and is desperate to find a partner. When Kia suggests Ely as a potential candidate, Max finds the hippie-looking lesbian with long hair to be ugly. First obstacle. But Max introduces herself to Ely, then goes along with a date that Kia has set up. Max and Ely see a film, argue about it in the best tradition of film spectating, and end up exchanging a kiss on the sofa, as one does. It then turns out that

Ely has a partner. Second obstacle. But not really – this too is negotiated without complication, as the relationship is long-distance, suffering from lesbian bed-death and about to end. With the help of their flatmates Kia and Daria, the two women are brought together, and again, the central narrative movement reflects our desire for lesbian desire to be articulated on screen. Here, this desire is given a charming temporal twist, and because we are aware of our voyeurism, we effectively negotiate it on lesbian terms.

Voyeurism is also forefronted by being enacted within the film, so that it becomes clear that participants like Kia and Daria and Evy are analysing not just what Max and Ely have told them, but what they have seen. We have the distinct impression that they too are 'watching' the narrative, and this highlights our own voyeuristic pleasures by making us aware of our positions as spectators.

Let us consider the sex scene finale, where the temporal playing with it makes us consume the images at a slight remove. Ely and Max meet for a serious date which begins with Max cutting Ely's nails. This is both intimacy and practicality. Rather than evolve directly into the sex scene we have been waiting for, we are made to wait with a teasing delay, as a cut to the next morning shows Ely leaving Max's home and skipping home, delighted. That night they were not divided. But as lesbian spectators we need more, and hence there is pleasure in the resolution, as the sex scene is replayed when Max and Ely recount it to their flatmates. Because we have had to wait, because this account is at a remove, our consumption of it is both self-aware and merged, both conscious and engaged.

A voice-over ends the film: 'The girl is out there', the partner of your dreams, the romantic ideal we seek. The film has followed a narrative trajectory of romance, ending in coupledom, with an affirmation of lesbian desire as celebratory, lesbian sex as raw pleasure.

Go Fish offers plural positionalities. From the first image of a black man, to the representation of Kia as a black woman whose authority invites respect, to the way her Latina girlfriend Evy is welcomed into the family of lesbian community, all these are contextual moments that place the central narrative in a recognizable frame. During the course of the film there is the obligatory haircut, a ritual for many lesbians. There is a reference to the obliteration of lesbians from history which contextualizes our current project to be visibly out. And there is a discussion of different terms for oral sex, for which Kia favours 'the honey pot'. These are all credible moments from a lesbian lifestyle. There is also a confrontation when Daria sleeps with a man, although she identifies as lesbian. Her action reflects the stance of plural positionalities that many lesbians are adopting, including in relation to their choice of male sexual partners, often gay men.

Let us now re-examine the question of desire in relation to the castration and Oedipus complexes. According to Freud, these complexes are an account of the psychic structurations whereby the child receives and internalizes gender difference. The castration complex allows the boy child to acquire an identity as an agent of desire, in which he identifies with the father in possession of the phallus, and in which he defers his desire for the mother by negotiating the threat of castration through the acceptance of the father's prohibition. The girl child's acceptance of castration means that she has to come to terms with her anatomical lack and her social subordination. If she does not disavow castration, she remains fixed in phallic identifications and desires, in which she seeks the phallus for life in an effort to make good her lack. 'While for the boy accepting castration means leaving the oedipus complex, for the girl it means securing her in this position for life' (Bronfen, 1992: 43). Elisabeth Bronfen favours a view of castration as signifying 'human mortality', where the difference of gender based on the phallus would 'be secondary to a more global and non-individuated disempowerment before death' (*ibid*.: 45). I agree that this acceptance of castration as signifying the threat of inevitable death would mean that the severances and losses we undergo could be theorized separately from the genderings of the subject. However, in the current social order, the inequities of gender do need to be challenged as long as there is a patriarchy in operation. To borrow from the slogan on a T-shirt, we can be postfeminists when we have a postpatriarchy. Until such time, the feminist project of deconstructing gender must pursue the aim of dismantling the phallocentrism that keeps patriarchy in place.

Lacan augments Freud's theorizations of the Oedipus complex with a symbolic formulation, 'that the complex structures the infant's confrontation between desire and the law' (Stanton, 1992: 293). In this formulation, desire is for the phallus and the law is that of the father's prohibition. As Martin Stanton confirms, traditional formulations of the Oedipus complex evidence 'the total ignorance and suppression of the mother' (*ibid*.: 291). Although Lacan can be said to have progressed the usefulness of Freud's theories by locating them within linguistic and symbolic registers, the valorization of the father at the cost of the mother's devaluation has a patriarchal bias that must be resisted.

Although 'no imperative dictates that lack be exclusively identified with one sex' (Silverman, 1990: 112), it is the woman who represents this lack in her absence of a penis/phallus. If the masculine subject is so threatened by the reminder of lack, this is because 'the lack which the male subject must somehow disavow is finally his own' (*ibid.*). This is the Lacanian view, 'that male subjectivity is founded on castration' (*ibid*). Kaja Silverman records how Lacanian psychoanalysis attests to the symbolic castration of the subject as a universal event rather than as a variable process (*ibid.*: 112–13). She argues that we are therefore diverted from attending to how the phallus comes to be 'the privileged signifier within our cultural order', and we also do not address why it should be 'the signifier of privilege' (*ibid.*: 113). Because the phallus is founded on fraudulent notions of plenitude and potency, when it is really about the absence and lack equivalent to that projected onto the woman, it is constantly under threat of exposure as a sign of forced privilege. Silverman clarifies that 'phallic male subjectivity might also be said to be predicated upon a massive cultural disavowal of the lack upon which it rests' (*ibid.*).

Lacanians stress that no one, male or female, can have the phallus. But of course, if the privileged signifier is the phallus, and that is based on a linkage with the penis, it becomes obvious that there will also be a privileged relation between what the phallus stands for, a patriarchal order, and the male subject in possession of a penis, that is, a subject who is heir to that order. As Teresa Brennan states, 'no one has the phallus. Yet the tie between phallus and penis exists, and persists' (Brennan, 1990: 4). Jane Gallop also finds that although Lacan distinguishes between phallus and penis, 'the distinction seems, however, to resist clarification' (Gallop, 1988: 125). Although 'the signifier *phallus* functions in distinction from the signifier *penis*', it '*also* always refers to *penis*' (*ibid.*: 126; original emphases). I do not think I am taking this linkage too literally, as this would be to collapse the symbolic and representational with biology and physicality. There is, however, an undeniable conflation between phallus and penis that explains the symbolic order's investment in the patriarchy.

But why should that be the case? As Deborah Cameron finds, Lacan's account 'offers no explanation *why* the symbolic order is patriarchal' (Cameron, 1985: 124; original emphasis). Elizabeth Grosz suggests that Lacan's interpretation 'can only be descriptively accurate if it takes into account the historical, changeable nature of patriarchy and its key signifier, the phallus' (Grosz, 1990: 145). The obvious project becomes one of attempting to dismantle phallocentrism.

Ellie Ragland-Sullivan refers to 'the phallic signifier' as 'a function (Latin, *functio*: "performance")' (Ragland-Sullivan, 1989: 45). An element of performance, of imitating what we contest, is present in Judith Butler's work, where she recognizes the fragility of the phallus in its status as privileged signifier:

> The 'structure' by which the phallus signifies the penis as its privileged occasion exists only through being instituted and reiterated, and, by virtue of that temporalization, is unstable and open to subversive repetition. (Butler, 1993: 90)

Butler suggests that 'the lesbian phallus' can allow the phallus 'to signify differently', including by exposing 'its own masculinist and heterosexist privilege' (*ibid.*: 90).

I have argued elsewhere that performance can play into the co-opting strategies of the dominant order, where mimicry replicates what it wishes to replace. I think a dismantlement of the phallus is to be preferred to its resignification as lesbian, and therefore I am in favour of Silverman's project to 'dislodge the phallus' (de Lauretis, 1994: 220). Silverman wants to remove the phallus 'from its privileged position' (Silverman, quoted by de Lauretis, *ibid.*) so that it is no longer seen as a 'signifier of desire'. De Lauretis finds this consistent with Silverman's argument that symbolic castration takes place through the entry into language prior to the phallus introducing the name of the father (de Lauretis, 1994: 220).

Brennan asks, 'what would a non-patriarchal symbolic entail?' (Brennan, 1990: 5). This is a crucial question. Parveen Adams suggests that we do not take up 'the counter-celebration of other candidate organs as the model of female completeness', that this would be an irony because it is 'itself an act of phallic identification' (Adams, 1996: 50). I agree that to start valorizing female body parts and setting them up as penile equivalents would be to play dangerously into the practices we wish to resist. We need to be able to represent the woman as an autonomous subject of a non-phallic desire, and for that, 'another term would be needed – women as symbolic' (Whitford, 1990: 119).

This still does not resolve the question of how the term 'women' could be inscribed to bring about a change in the symbolic order, nor indeed how this term would operate. As Rose states,

> If the status of the phallus is to be challenged, it cannot, therefore, be directly from the feminine body but must be by means of a different symbolic term (in which case the relation to the body is immediately thrown into crisis), or else by an entirely different logic altogether (in which case one is no longer in the order of symbolisation at all). (Rose, 1982: 56)

I am drawn to Luce Irigaray's work here, which Margaret Whitford finds is about 'above all, a question of change' (Whitford, 1990: 120). Whitford realizes that the question of how to change the terms of the symbolic 'can *only* be addressed collectively' (*ibid.*: 119; original emphasis). Irigaray has been criticized for some of her leanings towards essentialism, but I agree it is best not to dismiss her work 'in the interests of an overwary anti-essentialism' (Doane, 1991: 174). I concur with Irigaray's vision that we need 'the creation of a powerful female symbolic to represent the *other*' (Whitford, 1990: 121; original emphasis). But this 'other' *must* be formulated differently from the phallocentric. It must be founded on the relational and celebratory, not on aggression and suppression. It must centre on a concept associated with Hélène Cixous, a 'feminine economy' of gift and exchange, of giving and sharing (Still, 1992: 90–2). This is to subvert the masculine economy of exploitation, use and surplus value. Nancy Hartsock suggests, 'To paraphrase Marx, the point is to change the world, not simply to redescribe ourselves or reinterpret the world yet again' (Hartsock, 1990: 172). Although some of us are only now starting our redefinitions and rewritings, I endorse the view taken by Audre Lorde that 'change is the immediate responsibility of each of us' (Lorde, 1984: 141).

When Night Is Falling records the lesbian awakening of Camille, a teacher of mythology at a theological college. She is in a partnership with a fellow teacher, Martin, and they are offered the possibility of a joint chaplaincy at the college, on condition that they marry. Camille's dog Bob mysteriously loses all signs of life and she is devastated. She goes into shock and stores the dog's body in the refrigerator at the apartment where she lives. She meets a black woman called Petra in a laundromat, who is comforting and understands Camille's grief at losing Bob. They say goodbye but meet again when Camille discovers they have switched their laundry.

Camille goes looking for Petra at the circus where she works, and Petra invites her into her caravan. Camille comes out about wearing one of Petra's tops. Petra assumes Camille's man would have liked it, but Camille says 'What man?', indicating that there is no male competition. Petra comes on to her with a compliment about Camille's exquisite mouth, and gives out a guttural breath indicating desire. It is erotic, charming, funny.

Petra confesses she switched the laundry on purpose. She wanted to see Camille again, she was moved by her. In one of the finest lines from the film, Petra declares, 'Camille, I'd love to see you in the moonlight with your head thrown back and your body on fire.' Camille is shocked. She says 'OK', not as acknowledgement of Petra's desire, but as a way to make her stop. She says that was uncalled for. When Petra tries to defend her behaviour, Camille feels out of her element. She insists on taking her laundry and leaving.

Petra pursues her to where she lives. Camille responds by initiating a long kiss, then rushes off in her car in some consternation. Later, at Camille's apartment, Petra attempts to seduce her but is interrupted by a visit from the priest from Camille's college. There is another male interruption in the form of a sex scene between Camille and Martin. Camille is active and receptive, and says 'I love you' to Martin while making love, mixed with images of Petra on a swing. 'I like the new you,' Martin tells her the next morning.

Camille has a fantasy that Petra kisses her on the neck. She goes to the circus looking for Petra and the two make love – there is mergence as body parts meet and melt into each other.

After the first love-making scene, the obstacles start. While Camille is with Petra, she is too fired with lesbian desire to question it. However, there is still the problem of Martin, who finds out about them and is distraught. Camille is guilt-stricken. She takes the body of Bob and buries it in the snow. She then attempts to commit suicide by lying down in the snow where she is nearly buried under snowfall with night falling. She is discovered by accident, and survives. The film ends with the two of them leaving town together in Petra's caravan, on their way to a circus in San Francisco. The credits intercut with the body of Bob reviving and running across the snow landscape in a bid for freedom.

The first prominent motifs I noticed in the film were images of ice, cold and snow. This signifies for me a subtextual layer of meaning, namely the movement from frigidity to passion, from a living death to a joyous life. Camille's first spoken words, 'Aren't you cold?', are, I think, a projection of her frigidity, which changes to a position of active enjoyment of sex during the course of the film. Hence the symbolic freezing of her dog, kept in a state of artificial life, which is similar to Camille's lonely existence. We learn that she and Martin have been together for three years, and we can suspect that she is only just starting to resist frigidity, with such clues as 'I like the new you' after a night of active love-making.

From those first images of water and ice, with its fluidity and coldness, we get a sense that there is more to the text than meets the eye. When Petra comes on to Camille, expressing a desire to see her body 'on fire', Camille says she is out of her 'element', fire is too threatening, it can melt the protectiveness of ice. Camille's attempt to commit suicide by lying in the snow, risking hypothermia, is metaphorically consistent with the visual motif of her as the ice maiden, frozen, in need of warming and sexual awakening.

Although it is Petra who first spells out her desire, it is Camille who actually initiates its enactment. It is Camille who first kisses Petra, it is she who goes to Petra when they make love for the first time, and finally it is she who suggests she join Petra and the circus. When the two leave town together, mapping their future and joining their fortunes, there is a definable moment of closure with the triumph of their partnership, cemented by the dog Bob's awakening in the snow.

I am so enamoured of the film, so seduced by its gentle beauty and tender vision, that I do not want to be critical about its deliberate evocation of closure as a 'feel-good' technique. Similarly, rather than criticize the depiction of Petra as another black character who is not seen to be articulating her blackness, I am convinced that in this case this does not matter. Petra is not attempting to pass psychically as white, because her blackness is a given. She seems integrated with the white culture without having become white-minded as a result of this contact. I am glad to see the imagings of her as strong though vulnerable, as capable and confident, desirous and desirable. It is so pleasing to see representations of black subjects as humanized without being pathologized. I take this view because, as a black subject who has been hungry for healthy imagings of us, and knowing many other black subjects share this desire, I am pleased to be able to receive positive models and progressive positionings of black actors. I will quickly outline the scarcity of such an occasion, putting it into the context of the pathologization of the black subject.

Sander Gilman's work states that 'the idea of black sexuality as pathological was well implanted in European consciousness' (Gilman, 1985: 113). He finds that the black servant was 'ubiquitous' in European art, and served to sexualize representations by being a signifier of eroticism (Gilman, 1987: 174). Gilman also reports the connection in the public mind between the 'concupiscence of the black' and lesbian sexuality (*ibid*.: 181). We can see racist ideologies around the morbidification of the black lesbian, whose sexual pathology is seen to hold a multiple location.

Turning to representations of black subjects, Tania Modleski asks whether the tendency in early cinema 'to cast white people in black face' might 'suggest that blackness may be so monstrous it can only be signified but not directly represented?' (Modleski, 1991: 118). When we have been represented in our own person, it is often as a backdrop. Mary Ann Doane finds that black subjects provide '"local color," a background for the unfolding of white dramas' (Doane, 1991: 230–1). Doane confirms that black women 'inhabit the textual sidelines, primarily as servants' (ibid.: 233). As Gladys (a pseudonym), a black lesbian interviewed in *Jump Cut*, says of how many black female actors she can name, 'We just can't remember all the names of the maids, that's the problem' (quoted by Whitaker, 1981: 117).

When I see the imaging of a black lesbian who is not a servant or a criminal, not infantile or predatory, not pathological or victimized, I can truly embrace and celebrate the principle this embodies for me, that a black subject is seen to have an equal subjectivity. I am accordingly delighted to be able to receive the character of Petra in *Night* as someone I can both identify with and desire, without embarrassment, punishment or alienation. She also evokes the issue of mixed-race relationships. As a black lesbian the majority of whose partners have been white, and as someone who moves largely in white circles, the emphasis on uniracial couplings and intraracial social associations does not apply to me. B. Ruby Rich says that desire for her 'has been inextricably linked to differences', that it was not sameness but 'difference that held the magnetic charge' (1993: 320). Similarly, my outlaw status as a black lesbian who 'dares' to actively desire white women is given an additionally erotic charge.

Looking at some of the issues concerning a black lesbian sexuality, Valerie Mason-John and Adowa Okorrowa report that although the white writing of history has suppressed much information on relationships between women, the historical evidence that does exist testifies that these relationships have always existed. 'Homosexuality was expressed more freely before colonizers came and suppressed it' (Mason-John and Okorrowa, 1995: 73). Mason-John and Okorrowa offer examples of woman-to-woman marriages in Africa and harems in Asia as part of a diverse history and tradition for black lesbians (ibid.: 73–4).

Savitri Hensman reports how 'some colonial powers had made gay sex a criminal offence' (Hensman, 1995: 36). She offers a reading of the sexual stereotyping of black gays and lesbians, 'for instance as "passive Orientals" or "sensual Africans"', where although the stereotypes differ, 'the principle was the same', where black subjects 'became a backdrop for other people's fears and fantasies' (ibid.: 45). As she points out, this can 'spill over into intimate relationships' (ibid.).

Black lesbians have differed about the acceptability of our having relationships with white women. Some have 'felt forced to make personal and political compromises' in such relationships although they do not necessarily insist on intraracial partnerships (Pratibha, 1984: 60–1). Shaila objects to the notion that relationships with white women mean 'sleeping with the enemy', because she can still see '*lots of other enemies around*' (Shaila, 1984: 60; original emphasis).

It also needs to be recognized that two black women in a relationship together are just as vulnerable to power differentials between them as are lesbians in an interracial relationship. Mason-John and Ann Khambatta make the important point 'that relationships can be healthy or unhealthy whether they are with Black or White women' (Mason-John and Khambatta, 1993: 29).

Rich points out that 'Race occupies the place vacated by gender' in some lesbian relationships, where race serves as a 'marker of difference' in the lack of gender differences (B. R. Rich, 1993: 321). Rich cites the work of art historian Linda Nochlin, who states that 'the conjunction of black and white, or dark and light female bodies, whether naked or in the guise of mistress and maidservant, traditionally signified lesbianism' (Nochlin, quoted by B. R. Rich, *ibid*.). Although this suggests that interracial contact must have a sexual basis, which is patently false, this also attests to how the tradition of lesbianism is closely connected with transgression, of which interracial relationships are one obvious instance. Rich names Lorraine Hansberry, Langston Hughes, James Baldwin and Pat Parker, 'all black queers who had white lovers' (B. R. Rich, 1993: 333).

Here in Britain, black lesbians have been written out of history until relatively recently. It is only in the last couple of decades that we have started documenting our activities in significant numbers. Mason-John details some of the organizing that black women have done in Britain, of which the Brixton Black Women's Group (BBWG) was a pioneering example. The group began meeting in 1973 and opened a centre to serve black women in 1979, which continued until 1986 when it was closed owing to the massive cuts made that year to funding grants (Mason-John, 1995: 9). Founder members of the BBWG were also affiliated with OWAAD, formed in 1978 and then known as the Organization of Women of Africa and African Descent. It was argued that the organization should incorporate more black women, including Asian women, for reasons of solidarity in campaigning, so in 1979 OWAAD changed its name and became known as the Organization of Women of African and Asian Descent (*ibid*.: 7). A newsletter called FOWAAD was issued. Mason-John reports that a major rift occurred over the issue of sexuality, where black lesbians were rendered invisible and their sexual identity was seen as an apparently trivial issue when set against the backdrop of the 1981 riots in Britain (*ibid*.: 7–8; cf. Hensman, 1995: 32–3). OWAAD disbanded in

1982. Mason-John refers to it as 'an important chapter in Black women's herstory' (1995: 8).

Since then, black lesbian groups have set up, with the 'We Are Here' conference in 1984, Zami I, the first national black lesbian conference in Britain in 1985, and Zami II in 1989. In 1988, Shakti was set up in London for South Asians, with women-only groups now meeting and groups forming outside of London. And in 1990, the sixth International Lesbian and Gay People of Colour conference was held in London, where black lesbians and gays met and which resulted in the setting up of Zamimass in the same year, a black lesbian-only organization (Mason-John, 1995: 10–13, 19–20).

Mason-John and Khambatta record how there existed in the 1980s a 'potential to create a community of, and for, Black lesbians', but that the feeling from the early 1990s was that 'the fragmented networks that exist do not constitute such a community' (Mason-John and Khambatta, 1993: 18). While some of us may not have much time to devote to organizing for reasons of avoiding burn-out, it is regrettable that spaces do not exist in significant configurations which could lead to political action and social transformation, with black lesbians at the vanguard, where we have always been.

The narratives of the films I have discussed here have had closure with a completion of sorts, but this completion is of a lesbian desire that in my reading is not phallocentric but fluid. These women are not obsessed with their partners but enamoured, not fixated but in love. Their desire seems not to entail permanent possession, control, domination or subordinaton, but respect and reciprocity. They support lesbian desire through the plurality of positionalities. I do not think it is a pure coincidence that all three films, explicitly lesbian and made by women, feature heterosexual sex scenes, because this imaging of heterosex is a reminder precisely of the plural in lesbian activities. Although this could be seen as a falling into phallic figurations, it also spells the possibility of multiple pleasures. Who is to say which is which? The imaging of these heterosexual sex scenes is also a playful turning round of lesbian sex as central. Whereas in pornography, lesbian scenes are 'preludes to the hetero-fuck' (Smyth, 1995: 132), here there is a reversal with the 'hetero-fuck' a prelude to lesbian sex.

It is precisely around the question of the phallicization of desire that the issue of lesbian sexuality revolves. Esther Newton reports how the late nineteenth- and early twentieth-century woman who expressed active desire had to do so in phallicized terms, because desire was seen as exclusively masculine (Newton, 1984: 287). Jeffrey Weeks reminds us that Havelock Ellis had pointed to the contradictions of the nineteenth-century woman, whose conceptualization as asexual was historically and geographically unique (Weeks, 1977: 91). Yet ascriptions of asexuality were kept rigidly in place and the actively sexual woman was a social pariah because she was acting against gender norms. As desire was seen as irrefutably a masculine province, a woman expressing desire was aspiring to masculine prerogatives and privileges. One reason why the woman could not be seen to express an autonomous desire was of course because she lacked a penis. Her clitoris, a 'vestigial' or inferior penis, was not seen as an autonomous site of pleasure because sex was determined by the presence of a male's penis. Sex for a woman was for the purposes of reproduction or of serving the man's sexual pleasure, not her own. When women's capacity to experience sexual pleasure was entertained, the sexologists set up a glorification of heterosexuality and motherhood, thereby confirming the primacy of heterosexuality, which Sheila Jeffreys defines as 'the organising principle of male supremacy' (Jeffreys, 1989: 24). The sexologists also influenced the attitude to and of lesbians, through pathologization.

Carroll Smith-Rosenberg suggests that the new women in the early twentieth century adopted the sexologists' language because the acknow-ledgement of their desire had to take place 'in a language meaningful within the hegemonical discourse' (Smith-Rosenberg, 1985: 265). Some women were 'scared into retreat' by ascriptions of pathology, while others internalized the imagings of themselves as freaks, perverts and monsters (Faderman, 1981: 340).

Newton refers to the concept of 'gender dysphoria', the feeling of gender identity being out of sync with the possession of a body thought to have the wrong genitalia (Newton, 1984: 292). This points to the precarious formulation of founding gender norms on genitalia, and yet this is precisely what we do with gender systems. I myself have no problem with the 'fixity' of my own female genital configurations, in that I am happy to inhabit a woman's body. It is the apparent fixity of gendered ascriptions that feminists wish to challenge. I would like it to be a *fait accompli* that I can express desire as a woman, for a woman, with a woman, without having to think of myself as abnormal, or see myself as having usurped male privileges. To adopt what is ours by right, that is, an assertion of active female desire, should not be seen as usurpation but as an enactment of our equal subjectivities.

The readings of butch and femme confirm for me that a lesbian identity is still seen very much as belonging to the realm of a feminist usurpation of masculine privileges. I am arguing that certain 'prerogatives' should be ours by right, and not merely by reappropriation. Rosa Ainley states, 'For straight society, lesbian is synonymous with butch' (Ainley, 1995: 145). This not only replicates the phallocentric order, but also delimits the lesbian by default, so that the butch is a failed man because she is not a real man and the femme is a failed woman because her desires are not for a real man. So the readings go. Ainley considers the view that the butch is 'playing with it, rather than being it', that butch and femme are about the performativity of gender (*ibid.*: 152). Although Ainley is aware of the 'danger' that this is a 'pseudo-theoretical way of saying butch on the streets, femme in the sheets', she is hopeful that there is 'room for optimism here' (*ibid.*). I am not sure. My feeling is that there is little novelty in the apparent reworking of gender here. Taking on certain roles in relation to a masculinist framework is not radical for me. Imitating the paradigms of phallocentrism may be seen as radical by some, but I see such behaviour as reproducing the very precepts we are supposedly trying to challenge.

Cherry Smyth poses some key questions about the ambiguities surrounding the issues of performance as a playing with gender:

> Are lesbians reasserting, rather than subverting, a dominant male sexuality? Do lesbians have to appropriate phallocentric images of sexuality in order to represent an active sexual arousal and autonomy because there is no such obvious symbol in lesbian sex? (Smyth, 1992: 44)

What is central is the problem that there is no signifier of desire other than the phallus. Smyth argues that the lesbian appropriation of phallocentric desire is not so much a replication of male sexuality as it is a 'self-conscious parody' (*ibid.*). I can only reiterate my view that the intention of parody may be transgressive, but the form of its enactment very much plays into the strategies of the dominant order's ability to co-opt our oppositional practices. Smyth quotes Elizabeth Wilson, 'Nor is transgression per se radical' (Wilson, quoted by Smyth, 1992: 46). Therefore to deploy a medium of transgression that can be used against us to reinforce what we want to resist is surely playing a dangerous game. In taking this stand, I myself am playing into a hand dealt by others, a stand where we resist the phallicization of desire and the masculinization of active sexual expression. I agree with Wilson that 'there could be an adult sexual identity that was constructed around a different symbolic differentiator' than the phallus (E. Wilson, 1981: 173).

Let us now briefly recap on narrative in relation to desire. Judith Mayne reminds us that Oedipal desire, which she reads as 'the desire to become like the father', suggests that classical cinema addresses a male subject (Mayne, 1993: 23). Because cinema as narrative addresses a subject, 'the subject becomes a narrative effect', that is, the subject is addressed as a position of coherence, and this subject is also positioned by the codes and conventions of the unfolding cinematic event (*ibid.*: 25–6). We have seen that in fact classical narrative cinema has allowed the woman spectator the possibility of plural positionalities whereby we do not merely passively absorb our objectifications. Although, as Christine Gledhill says, classical narrative is 'predicated on the safety of an already known closure' (Gledhill, 1978a: 44), it is through the process of arriving at different meanings that we can receive the text as both what positions us and is positioned by us. Imagings of active lesbian desire can have the effect of rewriting narrative and desire. As spectators we can be less concerned to achieve knowledge as mastery, where we do not demand of the narrative that it tell us everything we might want to know. Penley refers to how epistemology, as the desire to know, can slip into epistemophilia, in which knowledge is a perversion (Penley, 1989: 19). I think it is preferable to be accepting of gaps rather than attempt to compensate through the manifestation of controlling behaviours.

Lesbian cinematic narratives can also rewrite the female as a subject of desire, thereby achieving what has eluded us for so long. De Lauretis refers to female desire as located in the place and time of 'nowhere' and 'now' (de Lauretis, 1984: 99). I would want to reformulate lesbian desire as 'now-here', the here and now of an active sexual expression and an equal autonomous subjectivity. Not that female desire is new, it is ancient. What is new is that effectively, for the first time possibly since prehistory, we have in certain metropolitan and global centres the opportunity to reformulate female desire outside of its territorially defined phallocentric frame of reference.

According to Lacan and Julia Kristeva, the only place for the social subject other than the acceptance of the phallocentric order is in psychosis. Certainly I know that psychosis can be an extreme form of psychic protest at the tenacity with which the social order maintains its dominance despite being founded on fraudulent formulations. However, I think it is possible to work within the symbolic order while resisting its phallocentric foundation without falling into psychosis. A non-patriarchal symbolic order is what we have to strive for, despite its apparent contradictions. I agree with Rose that the linkage of the symbolic order with the phallus as signifier of desire is not inevitable, that it is an 'open' question as to why symbolization as the subject's social structuration should be linked to the phallus as privilege (Rose, 1982: 56).

Although I do not want to deny the permeance of the phallocentric order, I do question its patently fraudulent basis. Psychosis can be a place of last resort. But a better formulation is of course the occupation of oppositional positionalities that remain in contact with the project to destabilize certain practices without falling into psychosis. We have to walk on wire, balancing between the acceptance of an order which dictates a predetermined sociality, and the resistance to the nihilism of this order, where we reconstitute our subjectivities within an articulation of contesting positionalities.

I end with a joke from a Marx Brothers film, where they are examining a contract. One asks, 'What about the sanity clause?' and the other brother replies, 'There ain't no Santy Claus.' If only this could be the case.

Notes

1. Jacqueline Rose (1982: 32).
2. I made my first attempt to write a short story in 1987, which was eventually published as the title story of *In and Out of Time*, an anthology of lesbian feminist fiction edited by Patricia Duncker and published in 1990 by Onlywomen Press. This story featured the two central protagonists going in and out of lyrics and prose and also intercutting between points of view, all without one word of dialogue. I was most interested in this intercutting, seeing it as a means of breaking up the narrative while retaining narrative cohesion. Even though I was very experimental in what I was attempting, taking risks that would ruin most narratives, I think the story was successful precisely because I concentrated on making it work as a piece of narrative. During the course of this story I expanded on ideas I have had about how pop/rock could benefit from the lure of narrative, as a way of structuring CDs around the concept of relationships as they unfold.

PART TWO

Subtext

5

Lesbian Representations
from Text to Screen

Reworking the Received: *The Color Purple* and *Fried Green Tomatoes*

The first thing you do is to forget that i'm Black.
Second, you must never forget that i'm Black.

Pat Parker[1]

The novels *The Color Purple* by Alice Walker and *Fried Green Tomatoes at the Whistle Stop Café* by Fannie Flagg both have an explicit lesbian content, but the film versions do not. The presence of lesbian sexual desire in the written texts has been deliberately erased in the screen versions, possibly because the film industry has until recently been reluctant to grant screen space to something as progressive and disruptive as lesbian identity. The films, however, do raise some useful questions concerning black subjectivity and the viability of alternative family groupings. Reworking the logic of the received, we will delve into historical material on the African-American subject to demonstrate the doublethink of racist ideologies. The family as an institution will also be examined to suggest that alternative social groupings can successfully regender masculinities and femininities as fluid.

To move from a verbal text to a visual screen medium involves a necessary modification of materials, a reshaping of them according to the demands of differing media. The first rule is compression (Peary and Shatzkin, 1977: 5–6). With the aim of refiguring a large text into economically functional visual units, entire sequences and characters are left out, the timeframe can change, the plot can be altered and dialogue is often condensed in key places. These are established conventions in the compression of literary texts into workable screen versions, so the omission of lesbian desire can be achieved easily for the purposes of cutting down the larger scope of a novel into the smaller screen version. Lesbian desire is simply left out as the unspeakable, the ineffable.

I think the lesbian desire in the novels has been taken out of their screen versions because it is too radical, almost a final frontier, where a lesbian identity is seen as the ultimate mark of women's alterity, our radical otherness. Rather than discuss in detail the question of lesbian desire in these screen versions, where it has been relegated to a subtextual function, I will widen the argument to show how racial and familial ideologies are reworked in these films. The film texts rewrite the black subject, while working through the stereotypes of us as servants and sexual servicers, and they rewrite the family in terms of the feminine economy, seen here in alternative envisionings of household groupings. Both are progressive projects, and I think the film-makers might have thought that to posit a lesbian identity too explicitly would be going too far. The exposure of racism and the bonding of women in alternative family structures were probably seen as sufficiently radical, without alienating audiences not then ready to acknowledge lesbian desire. This mirrors the processes of politicization that have taken place around the discourses of race and gender, where black women are slowly being recognized as specifically disadvantaged. Discourses around dissident sexualities have still to catch up in the quest for legitimation. And the omission of lesbian desire in the transition from the text to the screen shows that mainstream cinema has been slow to acknowledge the impact of lesbian identity, preferring as it does here to sidestep the issue by masking it with other concerns.

Here I would like to offer a brief critique of psychoanalysis, while remaining indebted to what it can productively provide for the understanding of sexed identities and the unconscious. We need to be aware that 'there is a very distinct danger that psychoanalysis can be used to blur any serious engagement with political-cultural issues' (Johnston, 1985: 70). This danger of an apolitical stand is aggravated by the tendency to overlook 'socio-economic factors', which Christian Metz points to as 'the weakness of Freud's sociological efforts' (Metz, 1982: 24). Certainly, the problems of positing universal psychic structures without accounting for political-cultural issues and socio-economic conditions present a serious drawback to the readings that psychoanalysis can make. Biodun Iginla points out how psychoanalysis 'cannot theorize historical, political or social specificity: the oedipal ur-paradigm folds all of material history into a transhistorical "family romance"' (Iginla, 1992: 33).

Black and white feminists have taken issue with some of the findings of psychoanalysis, and I wish now to explore the subject of the family, taking as a starting point the objection to certain family structures being seen as universal. Jane Gaines finds 'the Freudian scenario' to be 'incongruous' with the 'racial and sexual relations' in African-American history, where to 'use a psychoanalytic model to explain Black family relations' is to 'force an erroneous universalisation, and inadvertently reaffirm white middle-class norms' (Gaines, 1986: 198). Gaines references the deployment of historical accounts to demonstrate that the black male during Recon-struction followed the model of the white patriarch by learning how to dominate, and that patriarchal relations, initially foreign, were introduced into the African-American community historically (*ibid.*: 203).

Several black feminist commentators have documented the introduction of sexual antagonism as a result of the white American imposition of its own norms onto African-American ways of relating. Toni Cade records how African men and women in Africa, prior to enslavement and colonialism, shared domestic, hunting and warrior activities, where 'communities were equalitarian' (Cade, 1970: 103). Women were active in all spheres, and Cade finds no evidence in her readings to suggest that they were emasculating their men. What she does find is evidence of how 'the European white was confused and alarmed' by this equality, trying to undermine its effectivity by 'creating wedges between the men and women' (*ibid.*: 104).

Angela Davis also documents the egalitarianism between black men and women under slavery, when black women were primarily equal workers and black men 'could not be candidates' for the position of family patriarch (Davis, 1981: 5, 8). Davis emphasizes that the importance of a domestic family life for slaves was due to it being 'the only space where they could truly experience themselves as human beings' (*ibid.*: 16–17). She reiterates that 'sexual equality' characterized relations in the black family under slavery (*ibid.*: 18).

Patricia Hill Collins also documents that 'African-Americans' relation-ship to the slave political economy made it unlikely that either patriarchal or matriarchal domination could take root' (Collins, 1990: 52). Changes came about afterwards, when, 'during Reconstruction, the Black family, modelled after the white bourgeois household, was constituted defensively in an effort to preserve the race' (Gaines, 1986: 203).

Although the reasons for forming such families were as a resistance to the dehumanizing processes of slavery and racism, the adoption of white bourgeois models only served to alienate many black men and women from each other. Michele Wallace also records how this antagonism took place as a result of African-American men's acceptance of white American standards of family and gender norms (Wallace, 1992: 24). As Gaines points out, this historical introduction of male supremacism into black familial relations is a refutation of universalist claims of patriarchy as being ubiquitously in place (Gaines, 1986: 203). So we see that false universalizations can serve apolitical ends, can deny cultural influence and underestimate the impact of the socio-economic conditions we operate within.

Returning briefly to the subject of psychoanalysis, we see that black subjectivities pose a challenge to some of the paradigms psychoanalysis offers. Mary Ann Doane suggests that, from the point of view of exclusion, neglect, and an active tension, psychoanalysis 'cannot be *applied* to issues of racial difference but must be radically destabilized by them' (Doane, 1991: 216; original emphasis). If we are to proceed to draw on the findings of psychoanalysis, we must selectively take what is beneficial to our understanding. Having critiqued psychoanalysis for the dangers it can pose, I must assert that I have also benefited enormously from my readings of this subject, that certain findings have illuminated my understanding, say, of sexed identities and the unconscious, or desire and repression. I am fortunate to be able to do this, a black subject dabbling with 'white issues', but in fact I see some of these issues as relevant and beneficial to all subjects.

The Color Purple as a film is an example of carefully structured visual representations of women-bonding that take place in the immediate context of male brutality, and the larger context of the historical facts of slavery and colonialism. By showing the bonding between the women as a source of power and enablement, we are affirmed as active subjects who have agency. The autonomy and self-determination achieved by the women is a welcome model for us, all the more so because they are black women triumphing in an assertion of identity. Their presence at the end asserts female strength and solidarity, and conventional family values are apparently refigured to frame an alternative feminine economy. But this feminine economy is seen ultimately to depend on blood ties for its validation. Although these women attain their self-determination, their moment of success is only after much struggle, pain and suffering, and their autonomy is seen in the context not of lesbian desire, but of its omission.

Fried Green Tomatoes is also a story of lesbian desire that has to be suppressed filmically, so that this desire becomes subsumed under the ostensible messages of friendship, family, finding a female voice. This omission of the subject of lesbian desire is an attempt to contain it, to mitigate the threat of a feminine economy which would seek to destabilize the phallocentric culture, and replace it with pluralism and the privileging of suppressed voices.

The Color Purple begins with its central theme, the bonding between two sisters, Celie and Nettie. Whoopi Goldberg plays Celie, who is sexually abused by the man she knows as her father. By the time she is fourteen she has given birth to two children fathered by him, who are taken away from her at birth. He also sexually harasses her sister Nettie. Celie marries Mr―― in an arranged and loveless union. Nettie temporarily shelters with them but is forced to leave when Mr―― throws her out for resisting his sexual demands on her. The sisters promise to write to each other, but Celie does not hear from Nettie.

Mr―― has a mistress, Shug, with whom Celie is fascinated. Shug is a woman of the world, who has independence and sexual autonomy, but she suffers from her father's rejection. She is a blues singer, and sings a song publicly addressed to Celie. This is followed by a seduction scene of sorts, but anything explicit beyond a few kisses is eclipsed by a pan to a wind-chime, shimmering, supposedly to signify lesbian desire.

Through the agency of Shug, Celie receives a letter from Nettie, who is alive in Africa with Celie's two children. Celie discovers a cache of dozens of letters from Nettie, which Mr―― had hidden from her. Strengthened by this discovery, and embittered by Mr――'s treatment of her, Celie leaves Mr―― and goes to Memphis to live with Shug. She inherits a house and sets up business. Shug is reconciled with her preacher father. But something is still missing for Celie, until she is reunited with Nettie and her children.

The need for these reunions suggests that lesbian desire is insufficient on its own to sustain an identity, and that it is through family bonding with blood-members that one can feel fully the sense of self, recognized and validated by blood ties rather than socially formed bondings. I would suggest that this emphasis on family as 'blood' is a way of displacing the threat of lesbian desire, of containing the potential effectivity of lesbian identity. Though we see a feminine economy at work in the family that Celie and Shug establish together, its emphasis is lessened by the importance placed on 'biological' family. What is primarily being validated is not a family premised on 'pretended' and socially formed links, but on 'kin' as a bonding of blood.

Much of Celie's suffering is telescoped visually, through violence and blood, so that this imaging of pain is sometimes simple and reductive. From the early scene of Celie in childbirth, the result of rape, to the beatings she suffers from Mr____, we see how male brutality operates to oppress women. To conclude from this that it is the brutality of black men that is being exposed is to read only a fraction of both book and film. Male brutality exists not in a void, but in the context of patriarchal misogyny. And the violence of black men exists here in the context of the African-American experience of slavery, a violence aggravated by the ascription of a non-humanity, by which black subjects are literally seen as being outside the category of 'human'. If a subject is constructed as sub-human, as effectively an animal, then being the brute or the beast will be the apparent reading of that subject.

Not that we can deny the brutality of the black men in the film. The effects of their very oppressive treatment are conveyed in highly charged scenes. As a result of the mass exposure to film audiences of this abuse, Alice Walker has come under attack from black men who think she is colluding with white supremacism in portraying them as brutes. She has been accused on many fronts, and she reports that she found it 'hardest to tolerate the charge' that she hates black men (Walker, 1996: 23). Clearly such an accusation is a complete misreading, especially given Walker's generosity in redeeming Mr____ despite his brutal behaviour. Her vision does not centre on revenge or punishment, hatred and banishment, but on redemption, inclusion, on the need for transformation and the forgiveness that follows.

bell hooks points out that the negative response to the film has less to do with accurate representations and more with the concern of parading 'one's dirty laundry in public' (hooks, 1990: 70). The accusation was that the film damages black men by exposing what should be left private and secret, that violence and abuse should not be publicly admitted. Airing issues of abuse among black people is seen as a 'betrayal of racial solidarity', but as Andrea Stuart points out, black male writers' negative representations of black women are not 'interpreted as a treachery against the race' (Stuart, 1988: 61). To challenge violence and abuse, we do need to know the extent to which black men have internalized the dynamics of the oppressor, so that they can stop replicating it in their adopted behaviours. Walker understands how this brutality comes about, but she refuses to accept or excuse it. She will only forgive it if a change in such behaviours invites redemption. Although she replays certain stereotypes, it is important to see the representation of black male brutality in *The Color Purple* in the context of the history of slavery and colonialism with its culture of violence. For this reason I will give a potted overview of this history, one which needs to be rewritten in the light of a reinterpretation of the black subject.

The first Africans to arrive in America came in 1619 to Virginia, as indentured servants (Giddings, 1984: 33–4; Stetson, 1982: 71–2). Erlene Stetson records how the rights of black subjects were systematically eroded through legislation intent on exploiting their labour. A series of statutes were passed about 'Negroes', who were no longer called Africans, and by 1705 the General Assembly of Virginia decreed that 'all Negro, mulatto and Indian slaves' were now 'in the same category as livestock and household furniture, wagons and goods' (quoted by Stetson, 1982: 72).

The horrors of slavery were perpetrated in the name of civilization. When the Europeans instituted slavery, setting up trading companies going to Africa to kidnap black subjects who would be transported under inhuman conditions into enslavement, they had to manufacture a rationale to disguise the brutality and theft taking place. 'The Europeans justified their barbarous behaviour by turning logic on its head, arguing that they were "civilised" while the Africans were "savages"' (Curtis, 1984: 42). Although such a rationale depended on white supremacist ideologies for its justification, the British interest in exploiting other peoples was of course motivated by capital. 'The key to England's prosperity was the trade with the colonies, and in particular the trade in African slaves' (*ibid.*: 41). Although profitable at the time, the system could not hold. For one thing, the slave revolution in St Dominique (now Haiti) under the leadership of Toussaint L'Ouverture showed that black insurrection was striking terror into the hearts of the Europeans (Bryan *et al.*, 1985: 9–10). Additionally, 'independent pirates' in the African slave trade had 'displaced the seemingly more genteel trading companies' so that the European nation-states legislated to make slavery illegal (Jeffries, 1992: 156). There was a gradual awareness of the horrors entailed in the slave trade that even hypocritical doublethink could not justify. The work of the Abolitionists was also a factor, but as Beverley Bryan *et al.* point out, it was more the growing 'unprofitability of the system' that forced Britain to abolish the slave trade (Bryan *et al.*, 1985: 10). This began in 1808, with an Act of Parliament in 1833 that was ratified the following year (*ibid.*).

In America, Abolition had taken place in the North by 1830, but in the South, slavery became 'domesticated' after 1830. Paula Giddings reports how the white slave master passed as benevolent family patriarch under whom the slaves were supposedly happy to be infantilized as loyal and obedient (Giddings, 1984: 41–2). Although slavery was eventually abolished in the South, the period of Reconstruction was soon followed by the passing of Jim Crow laws which established overt discrimination as part of the social structure. Unemployment or pauper wages, social disadvantage and disempowerment, and the threat or reality of Ku Klux

Klan atrocities made it almost impossible for black subjects to achieve their autonomy. Racist ideologies were deliberately developed. An example was the claim of the American school of craniometry that African people's differently sized skulls were proof of black people's inferiority to whites. Such 'scientific' findings helped establish race as an analytic category later in the nineteenth century. 'The extent to which this American cultural feat served to earn the accolades of Europe cannot be overstated' (Jeffries, 1992: 156).

The white culture was so determined to justify its oppressive practices that there was no self-awareness of the hypocrisy of its mission. There is no doubt about the presence of a hypocritical doublethink in racist ideologies, which on the one hand maintain supremacist claims of a superior and civilized culture, and on the other demonstrate their barbarity in violating black subjects for the purposes of profit. There are other examples of this doublethink, which takes the form of projecting onto the black culture those negative and socially undesirable character-istics that white subjects possess but try to disavow. For instance, whites deny their own violence by projecting it onto black people, so that 'mugging' is seen as an activity predominantly carried out by black males, while in fact the violence in racist attacks has a long history but is given less of a profile.

Yet another example of this hypocritical doublethink is in the persistent myth of the black man as a rapist, a 'sexual brute', and of the black woman as promiscuous, an 'exotic whore' (Bryan *et al.*, 1985: 213). Davis has demonstrated how the myth of the black rapist was a 'distinctly political invention' to justify the lynching of black men (Davis, 1981: 184–5). It was a white supremacist ploy to discourage relations across race and gender, and served to terrorize black people. In fact, not one instance of a rape of a white woman by a black man was publicly recorded during the course of the American Civil War, a time when white women would presumably have been at particular risk (*ibid.*: 184). The myth of the black rapist was a distortion of facts, as was the myth of the black woman as sexually promiscuous. White men lynched black men for supposedly assaulting white women. The truth was, white men *raped* black women as a matter of course, and disguised their violence with a doublethink. Some commentators see the violation of black women by white men as examples of 'desire'. But we know that rape is not about desire, certainly not about affection, but about terrorization and control. The violence perpetrated by whites against blacks is truly barbaric and brutal, but white history would have us believe otherwise, and its racist ideologies are still deeply entrenched.

It seems appropriate here to expand on how I am identifying myself as black when I am Asian, and when the cultural, historical and geopolitical experiences between our peoples are so divergent. The differential dynamics of identification are complex. For instance, how can I be British and Asian, a British Asian, when British carries 'white' and Asian carries 'black'? Similarly with Black British, which is seen as a contradiction in terms. However, to borrow from Walt Whitman, we are vast, we contain multitudes, and it is the plurality of our identifications that gives us the adaptability necessary to negotiate our different positionalities. I would like to be able to incorporate and access different parts of my identity with equal facility, including offering the formulation of my identity as an Asian black who is British. The apparent tautology is really a clarification, that I identify myself as an Asian who identifies as black. It is worth doing this in a way which spells things out, because I know personally the phenomenon whereby some Asian subjects do not identify as Asian, much less as black, because they have been whitewashed and have become white-minded. To claim I am an Asian black who is British is to call on multiculturalism and summon different parts of my identity. Such a label enables me to assert my Asianness with the pride of cultural enrichment and diversity. It enables me to identify with black people and to see that African-American struggles speak to all people of colour. And it enables me to enjoy my British status as a subject who resides in Britain where I am exposed to a particular set of geopolitical positionings. I am aware in all this incorporation of different identities that I cannot speak from certain positions, but I know these positions speak to me. For instance, as an Asian I cannot share in the same way the experience of living as an African or Caribbean subject. Nor for that matter can I share the same subjectivity as Native-American, Asian-American, or South East Asian subjects. If that were not enough, my identity as Asian does not mean I am guaranteed access to the many positionings held by those from the Indian subcontinent. So I do not of course claim to be speaking for the black experience in all its diversity, no matter how strong the pressure put on individual black subjects to represent our plural voices. However, I am speaking as a black subject who identifies with the spirit and the substance of black resistance against white domination. I closely identify with the word 'black' as an indicator of my politics, as an expression of my solidarity and not merely a jumping on the bandwagon of black as beautiful. Although I am Asian, we share commonalities such as a similar legacy of colonialism and systemic racism, and to allow individual differences to destroy our greater solidarity would be foolishly divisive.

I am aware that the identity of 'Black British' has referred to black subjects who are thought to be 'confused about their cultural identity' (Zhana, 1988: 203). This confusion, to borrow from Paul Gilroy's title of *There Ain't No Black in the Union Jack*, occurs because the terms 'black' and 'British' are seen to be mutually exclusive, or at least incompatible. Although I am proud of being a black subject, and although this gives me a capacity to be critical of British history, I wish not to deny the geopolitical shaping of my positionings in the context of an Asian subject living in London. Therefore I access black British Asian with equal facility.

Amina Mama writes of Asians identifying ourselves as black because of a shared history, of indentured labour which has parallels to slavery, of colonial domination, and racism (Mama, 1984: 23). However, there are many debates on what we call ourselves, and sometimes these centre on gradations of skin colour, or what Claudette Williams has called 'colourism' (Williams, quoted by Mama, 1995: 151–2). Savitri Hensman points out that when black lesbians have organized groups and met at conferences, 'who was and was not Black was often on the top of the agenda' (Hensman, 1995: 24). Some subjects of African descent assert a greater experience of racism because they are darker than Asians, and hence they do not wish to address Asians as blacks (*ibid.*: 35). Meanwhile some Asians do not wish to identify as black because of internalizing racial prejudice against people of African descent, while other Asians want more specific terms to signify their separate experiences (*ibid.*).

Although 'colourism', prejudice, and national pride have served to keep peoples apart, I agree with the view that it would be productive to band together under a diaspora identity, which Mama defines as 'more about establishing an international racial unity than about nationhood' (Mama, 1995: 106). As Hensman says, 'unity is not the same as uniformity' (Hensman, 1995: 50). While it is beneficial to strive for solidarity, this does not preclude our self-locations and identifications in more specific geo-histories. Da Choong is 'partial to Women of Colour' as a term of identification because it refers to our 'diversity as well as commonality of experience' (Choong, quoted by Mason-John and Khambatta, 1993: 37). Although I prefer black and Asian, 'colour' is of course the key, where mixed-race subjects must also be able to find a voice. It has also been debated whether white Irish and Jewish subjects should be included under the banner of black. I draw a line at this, wanting to differentiate between the ethnic and the racial. If we did not do this, we would have to include some white European subjects resident in Britain as largely suffering from the same forms of social exclusion so prevalent in this society. Although the exclusion may be similar, I do not think of such subjects as black. I do not want to endorse the practices of exclusion, but I do wish to define racism as closely related to 'colour', where white supremacy dictates a differential treatment of black and white subjects.

Racist ideologies have dehumanized and demonized the black subject, creating a category of 'blackness' as other, pathological, dangerous, a social problem. We are excluded by ascriptions of animality, or at least derogated by ascriptions of our cultural inferiority. At no point is 'whiteness' rendered problematic. On the contrary, it is seen as the norm against which blackness is judged, just as the woman is the 'minus-male' to the male as norm. As Hazel Carby has suggested, and as is being adopted by some white subjects, one position would be for whites to acknowledge that they too are constituted as 'racialized' subjects, where 'it is important to think about the invention of the category of whiteness', which would interrogate itself on its naturalized status (Carby, 1992: 193). hooks also favours 'the production of a discourse on race that interrogates whiteness' (hooks, 1990: 54) with the aim of achieving the 'deconstruction of the category "whiteness"' (hooks, 1992: 12). This is in the context of 'descriptions of Whiteness' being 'absent due to denial of imperialism', which Claire Pajaczkowska and Lola Young find in European history (Pajaczkowska and Young, 1993: 202). They question why the white identity is 'so resistant to self awareness' (*ibid.*), and they too report the finding that the white subject disavows the undesirable aspects of its own identity by projecting these aspects onto black subjects (*ibid.*: 203). We would like white subjects to reassess themselves as they reread black subjectivities. To the question, 'What can the white man say to the black woman?', Walker suggests that reparation must be made for the black lives lost to white male brutality, and she ends her poem with the words, 'We are listening' (Walker, 1995: 93–8). We could add to this, we are still waiting.

By exposing racism as the dominant discourse that disempowers black subjects through the oppressive treatment we receive from whites, we see that it is not just black men, but white men and women, who operate in such a culture of violence, the heritage of colonialism. So, in exposing the false ethics of racist discourses, the sub-plot of Sophia and Harpo in *The Color Purple* assumes a crucial function. When Celie tells her stepson Harpo to beat his wife Sophia to keep her in line, it shows she has completely internalized the dynamics of domination. She accepts her marital enslavement in the hope of a heaven and a hereafter. Sophia is more concerned about fighting back in the present, but she too is beaten into submission. She is imprisoned for years, separated from her family, and forced into servitude to the mayor's wife, the white woman responsible for her loss of spirit and freedom. Only years later, when Celie stands up for herself, is Sophia able to reclaim her strength and later return to Harpo on the terms of an equity she always wanted with a partner. From fighter to victim to victor, Sophia represents different faces of the woman.

The central relationship between Celie and Shug shifts away from passion to companionship and the lesbian desire between them is underplayed. I have already suggested that this is to mitigate its threat by subsuming its importance to that of blood ties, family primarily as biological kin rather than the social households of pretended 'families'. To this end, the relationship between the sisters is crucial. Nettie reinforces kin not as 'fictive' but as factually based on known blood ties. Her separation from Celie is emotionally wrenching as she is physically thrown out and is effectively erased for years because of Mr___'s machinations. To learn of her survival, and of her reunion with Celie's children, is a vital reaffirmation of the strength we associate with black women, and this is not just about blood-bonding. When we learn of her story, told through letters written over the years which are visually telescoped as Celie reads them, we receive images of Africa, with its beauty, its struggles and strengths. Nettie is living in Olinka, a fictional African village which is nevertheless a comment on the reality of colonialism. The village is destroyed so that a road can be built, and we see how armed force protects capital and profit at the cost of lives and homes. Colonialism thrives on dispossession and displacement. The history of slavery, with its rendering of black subjects as chattel without subjectivities, and the history of colonialism, with its exploitation of peoples, economies and resources, shows the real foundation of European and American wealth and power, based not on being civilized but on the instituting of brutal regimes. The links are there for us to make. Just as we have received images of black male brutality, so too we can see the culture of violence in colonialism operating to maintain white supremacy. Black male brutality is seen to result from a macro-structure of misogyny and violence, put into place in prehistory and further practised in the history of white male imperialism. And I agree with Kathleen Cleaver who apportions blame for violence and abuse not on black men but on colonialism (Giddings, 1984: 323).

Nettie's presence in Africa widens our vision to incorporate considerations of the African-American experience in the context of colonialism. However, her most important function is to confirm that 'family' is more meaningful than 'fictive kin' or the pretended 'families' of chosen members. The reunion of the two sisters is highly emotional, and I find this impact is due less to blood ties than to their having had pre-Oedipal contact. By this I mean that when there is some contact with a pre-Oedipal state, not only as a mother–daughter dyad but a sister–sister dyad, the closeness of this contact can account for the privileged space given to family members. Because they are coincidentally present at the time of pre-Oedipal states, and hence have a primary contact as yet unmediated by the social order, there is something rich and intimate in this contact. I would like to think this has less to do with 'blood', and more with the material facts of a shared childhood, with the first recognitions and love that sisters can bring.

While the reunion between Celie and Nettie and her children is integral to the book, Shug's rejection by and eventual reunion with her preacher father was written into the screenplay. I think this was done to soften the implications of the feminine economy that Celie and Shug have established, living independently in a household together, sharing, caring, defying the conventional norms of the family. Shug must be made subject to the name of the father, especially as Celie is revealed to be outside the law of the father, as when she discovers that the man she knew as her father did not biologically sire her. The implications of incest are underplayed by this revelation, but nevertheless it would have been psychically very scarring for Celie to think of herself as a victim of incestuous sexual abuse. (Compare this with Faye Dunaway in *Chinatown*, where she is both 'mother' and 'sister' to her daughter by her biological father.) In the book, when Celie discovers the truth of her parentage, with both father and mother dead, 'Shug say, Us each other's peoples now, and kiss me' (Walker, 1983a: 156).

Celie is a survivor. From the start she is fixated with Shug. Her first contact is as a servicer – she cooks for her, bathes her, cares for her. When Shug recognizes her, effectively by returning her love, Celie is empowered and validated. Shug is the first person to love Celie besides Nettie, and this is a powerful affirmation for Celie. But the representation of their lesbian love affair as it takes place in the book is completely transformed into minor relevance in the film.

Shug first openly recognizes Celie at Harpo's jukejoint, where she sings an ambiguous song publicly dedicated to her. This could be a lesbian lyric, but it could also be a sexually innocent declaration of friendship:

Sister, you've been on my mind
O sister, we're two of a kind
So sister, I'm keeping my eyes on you.

Later, Shug gets Celie to dress up, but Celie is still shy about smiling, and covers her face with her hands in nervousness. When Shug tells her she is beautiful, and kisses her, Celie smiles without trying to hide her face. She is obviously waiting for more. Another kiss from Shug, Celie smiles broadly, then ventures a quick peck back. The women touch each other's shoulders, and kiss again. But instead of spelling out their desire with more sexual detail, further representations of their sexual contact are disallowed. In her memoirs where Walker recounts the process of making the film and its aftermath, she says she regrets 'that Shug and Celie don't have the erotic, sensuous relationship they deserve' (Walker, 1996: 41).

Rather than explore lesbian desire, the film displaces it by emphasizing family ties as blood-bonding. This is evident in Celie's reunion with Nettie and her children, a necessary factor for the text's happy conclusion. Shug's reunion with her father is of a different nature. Jacqueline Bobo does not find this reunion to be a containment of Shug's power as an autonomous woman, as critics have suggested (Bobo, 1992: 72). It seems to me more a sub-plot mirroring of an endorsement of family as blood, of kin as essential. As I have already argued, I think this is due to the apparent dangers of a lesbian identity being too radical, so that the presence of lesbian desire has to be removed and replaced with a stronger emphasis on family as kin. This demonstrates a misrecognition of lesbian desire, and an ill-informed anticipation of its unacceptability to film audiences. In an *Omnibus* programme on her work, Alice Walker said Steven Spielberg was 'embarrassed' by the lesbian content.[2] I find this shyness or reluctance to be misplaced, and in fact I think lesbian desire is the next frontier for films to push beyond the barriers of current representations of women.

The bonding between the women in *Fried Green Tomatoes*, in the form of setting up alternative households in a feminine economy, is also achieved at the cost of omitting lesbian desire. This is no mere accident, but a deliberate suppression due probably to a wish to maintain an apparent credibility for middle-of-the-road audiences, who are thought to be frightened by the explicit representation of lesbian desire.

The story of what happened at the Whistle Stop Café is told to Evelyn, a present-day married woman who is having a menopausal mid-life crisis. It takes the form of intercutting between the present narration and a past flashback of sorts. Evelyn discovers her own voice through hearing this story, told to her by the elderly Mrs Threadgoode, of a central relationship between two women, Idgie and Ruth. They are all white women. The story involves the murder of Ruth's husband, for which Idgie stood trial.

The subtext tells us there is a clear motif of lesbian desire, but any explicit reference is completely omitted from the film.

Idgie and Ruth are close friends, but Ruth is obliged to marry a brutal woman-beating man. Eventually Idgie rescues her and brings her home, Ruth has a baby son, and the two women set up the café. There is danger from the Ku Klux Klan because Idgie and Ruth serve black subjects at the café and will not be deterred from doing so. Ruth's husband returns to kidnap the baby, but he is killed by a blow from an unseen assailant. Some temporal disjuncture in the editing suggests Idgie might be responsible for his death. She eventually goes on trial for his murder but is acquitted, along with Big George, her trusted black male servant. Ruth dies of cancer and leaves her son in Idgie's care. In the present-day narrative, Evelyn decides to shelter the homeless Mrs Threadgoode in the spirit of a woman-bonding solidarity.

Repeatedly, the values of friendship rather than desire are what get communicated. This is acceptable of course, especially as it results in a reworking of familial ideologies where the primary bonds are not of blood, marriage, and family as kin, but of freely chosen partnerships, friendships, relationships. The four central women are or become feminists in the sense of asserting themselves as subjects of their own destinies, and there is a paralleling between the past and present-day narratives, with Ruth and Evelyn finding their voices through the agency of Idgie and Mrs Threadgoode. Gender is also reworked, not as fixed but as a shifting of fluid masculinities and femininities.

Evelyn is the middle-aged menopausal woman who is anxious to save her marriage with Ed, a well-meaning but insensitive man obsessed with watching sports programmes on television. Evelyn goes to self-assertion classes to reclaim the power of women, but it is only in meeting Mrs Threadgoode that she finds the solidarity of bonding with women. By hearing of Idgie and Ruth through Mrs Threadgoode's narration, and through Mrs Threadgoode herself as a model, Evelyn finds her own voice. She becomes health-conscious and gets a job. Her friendship with Mrs Threadgoode empowers her to access her feelings, much the same way as Ruth is empowered by Idgie's love to defend herself and renounce passivity. When Mrs Threadgoode discovers that her house has been demolished because it was condemned property, Evelyn persuades her to go live with her and Ed, in what will be a refigured domestic economy. The film ends with Mrs Threadgoode telling Evelyn that the most important thing in life is 'friends, best friends.' This reinforces the absence of lesbian desire.

Idgie and Ruth first meet when Idgie is still a little girl, and they are both helpless witnesses to the death of Idgie's beloved brother, who is also Ruth's beau. Idgie is devastated by her brother's death and her mourning carries into her adulthood. She has wild tomboy ways, she hunts, fishes, fights and gambles like the rest of the boys, she is uncontrollable. When Ruth comes to stay for the summer, they become close and share lawless adventures distributing food supplies to dispossessed people from a moving train. When Idgie risks her life for Ruth by getting her some fresh honey from a dangerously active bee's nest, Ruth calls her a bee charmer. Idgie is devastated when Ruth leaves at the end of the summer to marry Frank Bennett.

Idgie is troubled by her brother's death and Ruth's marriage, and this is imaged in terms of her playing with gender. From an early age she refuses to wear dresses, and her tomboy ways persist into adulthood in a way which at first seems uncritical of gendering. Her masculinities are seen as a sign of grieving, and at first are pathologized. However, when the 'feminine' Ruth proves just as resilient and courageous as Idgie, we see the two engage in a re-gendered partnership, not about butch or femme, but as a fluid exchange of masculinities and femininities incorporated in both of them. Drawing on Idgie's example, Ruth renounces passivity to protect her child.

The narrative of the film is very much centred around the death of Frank Bennett and Idgie's subsequent trial. I find it to be an obvious contrivance, done for reasons of sensationalism. I do not think the mystery of his death is particularly suspenseful. But what is interesting about the trial is that potentially the subject of lesbian desire could come up, for the prosecution to pathologize the defendants. Clearly it is no secret that Ruth and Idgie share a home together. However, no hint of this desire surfaces. When the prosecutor asks Ruth why she left her husband for Idgie, thereby violating the sacred bonds of family, she responds: 'Because she's the best friend I ever had and I love her.' Ruth's love, or lesbian desire, is immediately masked under the values of friendship. Beyond a small murmur in the courtroom, this arouses little of the furore it would if it were read in the context of lesbian desire.

What I find to be a strength of the film resides in its representations of a feminine economy with its progressive reworking of 'family'. First, such an economy entails sharing, giving, exchanging; it is not about appropriation or exploitation. Second, a family formed on socially bonded links is to me a more progressive grouping than one formed on blood ties ratified through marriage. Paula Gunn Allen recounts the principle of bonding among Native American peoples as based on 'spiritual kinship', which is 'at least as important a factor as "blood"' (1986: 110). I see this as a model worth emulating. In the film, family includes black subjects, Big George and Sipsey. Idgie is not tempted by the offer to escape trial. She cannot let Big George take the rap and knows she has to stand trial herself because of white jurors' alacrity in hanging black subjects. So, effectively, she risks her life again, in loyalty to her 'pretended' family.

The film is also strong on reworking masculinities and femininities, for instance by exposing Bennett's violence and Ed's insensitivity to women as the unacceptable faces of a misogynist culture. Bennett is killed and Ed is converted. Idgie transcends dichotomies of gender, by incorporating the best of both, masculine autonomy and a feminine economy. Ruth and Evelyn, conventionally 'feminine', both renounce the passivity of their gendered ascriptions, and attain separate voices. And Mrs Threadgoode too, self-sacrificing and loyal, is rewarded. She is not killed off (as in the book), but given a home and a new lease of life with her friendship with Evelyn. 'Femininities' which encapsulate autonomy and self-assertion emerge as triumphant for having negotiated gender not as a fixed category, but as a system offering fluctuating possibilities. The problematics of a femininity based on self-denial, and a masculinity based on aggression, are renegotiated by reinscribing the one and rejecting the other, whereby femininity incorporates autonomy, and masculinity is divested of its more damaged and destructive properties.

The project of destabilizing gender as a fixed category, and instituting fluctuation and fluidity as a more healthy objective, could indeed be achieved through the family refigured by the feminine economy, where gendered subjectivity is re-gendered non-phallocentrically. It seems appropriate here to offer a brief overview of 'the family', both as fiction and fact.

As fiction, the prototypical family is constituted through heterosexual marriage ratified in law and through genetic offspring. It consists of a male breadwinner who works in the public sphere of production, and a female domestic who runs the household in the private sphere of the home. While the male assumes responsibility for financing the household through productive labour, the female has to service the male sexually, has to reproduce future labour by having and raising children, and has to maintain the household. In this fictional model, the woman does not work outside the home.

The question has been posed as to whose interests are being served by the woman's labour in this configuration of the family. The Marxist explanation pinpoints capitalism, while the feminist arguments locate patriarchy as benefiting from women's labour. I think there is evidence to support both explanations, and I agree with the sociological formulation that there is a 'functional fit between the nuclear family and industrial society' (Barrett and McIntosh, 1982: 85–6) which controls women's labour to service the phallocentric order and to reproduce future workers as well as consumers.

I think patriarchy and capitalism have parallel mechanisms in how they appropriate the woman's labour, which for me is most starkly represented in the erasure of the woman's name, not only for herself but for her children. Consider how the worker is invisible in the product of labour. So too the woman, who conceives, carries and cares for the child, who enculturates it more than the male in my opinion, so too this very same woman forgoes her identity as signified symbolically in her own name. When the woman loses her name on marriage, this is a complete appropriation of her labour, a denial of her effectivity, and an erasure of her visibility. Her own 'labour' is obliterated symbolically in having children who also do not bear her name, and this again is a stark example of male appropriation, of a denial of the woman's agency. Such an appropriation maintains the fiction of the woman's ineffectivity under phallocentrism.

By exploding this fiction and exposing the myth of woman's ineffectivity we can begin to redress the inequities of the phallocentric culture. A major site for this transformation lies in the family, both by exposing its fictions, and by benefiting from some of its factual conditions.

One fiction is that the prototypical family as described so far in this section is a natural, inevitable and universal phenomenon. This is to deny the comparatively recent emergence of the family as it has come to be idealized. Linda Nicholson makes the point that recent studies on the family have traced similarities between ancient and modern family forms, but that these 'reflect historical, and not natural, social divisions' (Nicholson, 1986: 107). She clarifies that 'while the category of "family" is not limited to the modern period, it is not universal either' (*ibid.*). Historically, the nuclear family in its current form is said to have evolved with the Eurocentric bourgeoisie in the eighteenth century. As the bourgeoisie gained economic and political power, becoming the dominant group by the end of the eighteenth century, it was able to institute a hegemonic hold through prescriptive definitions of the prototypical family, to the extent that the working class also adopted this ideological family form. Although this 'embourgeoisement' of the working class was more for reasons of its own internal demands than an imitation of the middle class, Mark Poster sees this adoption by the working class of middle-class family forms as one of the bourgeoisie's most powerful political achievements (Poster, 1978: 196).

The class position of the family was determined by the status of the male breadwinner, and increasingly this status was reflected in whether the woman worked or not. Class differences separated women from each other, and it is a fiction to say that women do not have a long history in the labour force, a fiction that denies the facts of the labour of black and working-class women. By the nineteenth century, while white middle-class women were isolated in the home, encouraged to be the idle and perfectly self-sacrificing 'Angel in the house', who typified the Victorian model of the presentable woman, black and working-class women laboured without any of the luxuries of surplus time or wealth (Phillips, 1987: 38–9). It was envisaged that the emergence of women in the labour force would lead to their emancipation, but black and working-class women were the first to know that our presence in the work force was not of itself liberating. However, this presence was a precedent for the later entrance of middle-class women into the labour force, even though this has also not been an adequate answer to our inequality, given the lack of actual equal pay, where two decades of legislation, including on equal opportunities, have had little effect.

What is encouraging about the prototypical family is that its ficticity is being exposed. In fact, the model family of male breadwinner, female domestic, and legitimate offspring cohabiting in one household has differed across class, culture and time, and its idealization as natural and transhistorical is a false denial of the facts. In 1986, only 7 per cent of American households corresponded to this model of a nuclear family (Judith Stacey, 1992: 93). This is not a breakdown of the family but a reworking of it.

While I am in favour of maintaining family bonds, I am fortunate because in my own experience these links have been restructured in alternative formulations different from the ones usually received through family. hooks also wants to support family life, while eradicating 'the abusive dimensions created by sexist oppression without devaluing it' (hooks, 1984: 37). We do not want to 'smash the family' as much as we want to reconstitute it. Calls to dismantle the family by white feminists disregard the social, economic and political forces also operating on the family, as if it were some reducible entity that could be isolated and eradicated. In India and other Third World countries, for example, 'there are few if any alternatives to a family based household at present', and Ursula Sharma reports that white Western feminists' emphasis 'on sexual individualism and autonomy from men' has been 'unrealistic' in the context of the economic and social organization of certain cultures (Sharma, 1986: 197–8). We do not need to destroy the family as much as to reconstitute it, especially in relation to the woman's autonomy with reference to gendered subjectivity.

Because gendered subjectivity is primarily learned in the family, a refiguration of the family would offer the possibilities of renegotiating both how the mother is perceived and gender is received by the child. Michèle Barrett suggests that we distinguish 'between the construction of gender within *families*, and the social construction of gender within an *ideology of familialism*', and she locates the latter as more operative (Barrett, 1980: 206; original emphases). That is, it is not so much family members themselves who coerce gender-response in stereotypical ways, but the ideologies prevailing external to families about what their ideal form and functions are (*ibid.*: 205). If we can reshape ideologies of familialism to transform the perception and the reception of the mother, we may be able to achieve family forms which are not an oppressive site of hierarchy and domination, but a supportive location for love, recognition and respect.

I have discussed elsewhere the necessity of seeing the mother as an autonomous subject, by according her the identity of her own name as a prerequisite for an alternative social order. The black woman as mother and other also offers liberating possibilities. As mother, the black woman was historically ahead of her time by having women-headed households not necessarily connected with males through marriage, and this model now serves other women who have placed male presence on the periphery. Collins references hooks on how 'othermothers' are equally responsible for child care, reducing exclusivity and the notion of children as 'property' (Collins, 1990: 119–23; cf. hooks, 1984: 144). Collins argues that we need an 'analysis of motherhood that debunks' white men's myths of the '"matriarch" and black men's myths of the "superstrong Black mother"', and she recognizes that while we cope with race, gender and class oppressions, we cannot escape them (1990: 117, 133). However, our struggle testifies to our strength and autonomy. If the child can see the mother and the other mother as equally unmarked and unbound, as both autonomous, this is already to rework the trajectories that desire takes, to re-envision the gendering of subjectivities. To incorporate gender in fluidity, we would need to borrow the best of masculinities and femininities, drawing on autonomy as well as relational strengths, and reconstituting the subject as a permanently shifting site of gendered attributes, determined by a renegotiated sense of self. We need to transcend gender as a fixed category.

Both *The Color Purple* and *Fried Green Tomatoes* rework racial and familial ideologies. In *The Color Purple*, racist stereotypes of black women as servants and sexual servicers are replayed through Celie and Shug, but such stereotypes are re-imaged to represent the woman as eventually triumphant. Similarly, in *Fried Green Tomatoes*, familial ideologies are reworked to frame a feminine economy, with a shared household composed of fictive kin, in which masculinities and femininities are renegotiated in alternative versions of gendered subjectivities. Both films show children being raised by other mothers, Nettie the sister and Idgie the partner, in ways that could liberate biological mothers from the demands of a desire for their exclusive attention. In order to liberate the mother, we need to recognize her as an autonomous subject and not as a maternal function. The emphasis given to black subjectivity also differentiates these films in that such a treatment is so rare in Hollywood. Though *Fried Green Tomatoes* is a mostly white view of black subjects, it is at least sympathetic, and better than the otherwise near-complete silence around black presence. *The Color Purple* is also unusual, in that it was the first venture of near-epic scope given by Hollywood to a predominantly black experience, one which consulted carefully with Alice Walker, and which attempted to convey the complexity of black subjectivity seen through a black perspective. From this point of view, radical ideas are being represented in ways acceptable to mainstream audiences. The projects of reworking racial and familial ideologies are laudable and certainly necessary, even though they are presented in the films at the cost of omitting lesbian desire. Given that the written texts hold an explicit though not emphatic content of lesbian desire, this omission is severe. I think the reasons for this decision were based on mistaken ideas of the unacceptability of lesbian desire on screen. Time is already telling that mass audiences are ready for such representations.

To repeat the two lines from Pat Parker which began this chapter:

The first thing you do is to forget that i'm Black.
Second, you must never forget that i'm Black.

These lines convey to me with their economical acumen the heart of the apparent dilemma between equality and difference. The two lines speak respectively of equality and otherness, of sameness and difference. The compatibility of these two conditions must be established if we are to move beyond false dilemmas. In fact, a synthesis of the two positions would be a step forward. While I myself am in favour of radical change and a recognition of difference, I see this project as an unfolding process which takes place in time, moving from the reality of now to a future transformation of social subjectivities. We can only go into a future out of a present based on the past. To suppose otherwise is to argue in a void. Therefore I am prepared to acknowledge the tenacity with which the existing social order perpetuates itself, and I prefer to work within it to effect change, rather than fall into psychosis as a sign of my revulsion and protest at its inequities. I sympathize with the liberal feminist insight that seeks transformation in the context of existing social conditions, not because I want to stay within these conditions, but because they constitute the symbolic order as it is. My understanding is that it would involve less a compromise and more a cooperation between positions to include the ideals of equality with the reality of difference. As a radical feminist who wants real change, I prefer not the vacuum of some mythic future to be arrived at mysteriously, but theoretical strategies for social transformation that take their point of departure from existing conditions. I would like to see the dismantlement of the symbolic order as it currently stands, not by denying its permeance, but by disallowing its phallocentrism to dominate our lives.

I think it is a false division to set up equality and difference as polarities. We must incorporate both as mutually compatible. The black subject must of course insist on both our equality and our difference, and this enables a precedent for female subjects to also insist on our equality with men at the same time as we maintain the right to our difference from men. We need a transformation of the social order that will acknowledge and not suppress the facts of pluralism. We want equal rights but on different terms.

We must insist on equality *and* difference. To be obvious, black subjects are equal: we breathe, we bleed in the same ways, we are as human and as valuable as whites. To deny us our equality is tantamount to persisting in notions of our non-humanity, as if we were sub-subjects, sub-human and savage. To be granted our equality in more than tokenistic and lip-service gestures is the least we require. But our equality does not preclude our difference, and indeed we need to celebrate our differences as the mark of cultural diversity and creative strengths in establishing a plurality of voices.

The vision of a black feminist politics promises the possibility of inclusion with respect, not exclusion with indifference. As Collins finds, 'the primary guiding principle of Black feminism is a recurring humanist vision' (Collins, 1990: 37). Collins qualifies that this use of the term *humanist* has an Afrocentric historical context separate from the Eurocentric version, and she quotes Margaret Walker on how 'it is only in terms of humanism that society can redeem itself' (Walker, quoted by

Collins, 1990: 40). The term 'humanism' has shifted historically several times to signify different belief systems. Here, I read it in senses derived from the root, that of being human and part of the human race, as Margaret Walker reads it. I see the human race as capable of realizing its value and potential for productive achievement and sometimes creative genius. I see 'humanism' also as that which acts on the humane impulse of benevolence, and on a principle of humanitarianism. Finally, I see humanism as the belief system that can 'humanize' the black subject, literally read us as equal humans and not as the animals and lesser beings we have been considered.

Not surprisingly, given the internalization of endemic racism, black women have been divided amongst ourselves, whether across colours or cultures, class and creed. Audre Lorde talks about the critical way some black women can approach other black women. 'How are you judging me? As Black as you? Blacker than you? Not Black enough? Whichever, I am going to be found wanting in some way' (Lorde, 1984: 170). Lorde recommends that we accord each other some respect in our encounters to enable our mutual empowerment (*ibid.*: 174–5). Such a view finds double favour given the multiple ways we have been denied recognition and respect.

Collins documents several positions of an 'ethic of caring' which she finds characterizes African-American culture (Collins, 1990: 216). June Jordan's vision of a feminist movement involves the inclusion of children and men (Jordan, 1989: 65). This not only recognizes children as equal subjects, but also does not bar men from inclusion, provided their behaviour merits it. These black feminist principles are repeated in black women's literature. 'The capacity to forgive is much emphasised in black women's novels' (Stuart, 1988: 67). It is the inclusion of Mr___ in *The Color Purple* that I found very moving in the screenplay that Walker wrote. Not used, this screenplay figures Celie making a quilt of her life history.[3] When Mr___, abandoned because of his abusive behaviour, discovers this quilt at the end, he sees it is unfinished and 'the blank ending intrigues him' (Walker, 1996: 114). In that blank space is written the possibility of redemption and not exclusion, forgiveness and not punishment. It is in the spirit of this inclusion that Lorde writes, 'we must allow each other our differences at the same time as we recognize our sameness' (Lorde, 1984: 142).

Equality requires recognition of sameness, but this is not enough, for we must also recognize the difference of the other. Difference takes work. All the securities of identifying with sameness are destabilized when confronted with difference. Difference needs an entirely new framework, an alternative mindset, of questing, openness, an alertness to the other who does not merely mirror or echo the self. Black subjects can and do recognize difference. Lorde has also written about how oppressed peoples have to observe the oppressors in order to survive, and she questions whether our energies in teaching the oppressor about our own experience could not be better redirected toward redefining ourselves (Lorde, 1984: 114–15). Whatever the route, black subjects must be accorded our subjectivity and our agency, so we can rework racist ideologies and replace them with ethical values of an actual and not pretended equality. The aim to redress racist ideologies must work in concert with the struggle to eradicate other oppressive regimes. One such struggle would be the project to attain a reworking of gendered subjectivities, so that masculinities and femininities are renegotiated to divest us of destructive aggressiveness, and to reaffirm relational capabilities. The lesbian identity is particularly privileged in allowing for such a re-gendering. If we can build on our capacity to reinvent ourselves in alternative social groupings, with progressively reworked racial and familial ideologies, we will be able to reconstitute the subject in a climate that recognizes equality and difference as co-existing in a necessary compatibility.

Notes

1. Pat Parker, 'For the white person who wants to know how to be my friend' (1978a: 13).

2. *Omnibus* on 'Alice Walker and *The Color Purple*', transmitted on BBC1 in May 1986.

3. I think the decision not to include in the film Alice Walker's idea of a quilt was a missed opportunity to convey Celie's subjectivity. The quilt could well have been a visually appropriate and historically authentic imaging of her life history.

6

Lesbians Come out on Celluloid

Rage and Trauma as Subtext:
Lianna on *Thin Ice* Listens to *Nocturne*

Coming to voice is an act of resistance. Speaking becomes . . . a rite of passage where one moves from being object to being subject. Only as subjects can we speak.

bell hooks[1]

Lianna, *Thin Ice* and *Nocturne* reflect on the theme of coming out in the context of homophobia, actual and internalized, real and not imagined. I will discuss material in relation to the family and mothering, especially the black family, and give some consideration to our pathologization, including that of the Asian family. Coming out is never done in a void, but in the context of familial, social and institutional pressures, and I will also discuss the issue of homophobia. I suggest that while we aspire to social cohesion we should not blame the family for its breakdown, nor support the pathologization of the black subject, because the problems we encounter are in the main social and not personal, to be addressed collectively and not individualized as endogenous and personal pathology.

The process of coming out voluntarily, or even its unintended disclosure, can follow a route from rage to recognition, from trauma to triumph. While analysing the narrative of these films by concentrating on the theme of coming out, I hope to endorse the disclosure of a lesbian identity as a vital life decision, with its rejection of dishonesty and doublelife playing. A lesbian identity proudly out is a sign of strength and courage in the context of heterosexism and homophobia, and it also affirms integrity, credibility, honesty. If it is fused with a feminist analysis, such an identity can provide the framework for functioning as politicized subjects who are alert to the need for social transformation. The rage of the lesbian can be directed towards the struggle for change, and the trauma many of us have been through can be seen not as personal pathology but as the inevitable response to a sick social system. While we do have to come to terms with our personal histories of rage and trauma, it is helpful to see them as a symptomatic outcome of a social order that cannot accommodate all people as having equal subjectivities. Although I will follow the film-makers' emphasis on personal rage and trauma in these films, I hope these can be seen not as some endogenous pathology where our own psyches are at fault, but in the context of the failures of the current social order.

'A lesbian is the rage of all women condensed to the point of explosion' (Radicalesbians, quoted by Becker *et al.*, 1981: 303). The New York Radicalesbians who offer this definition of a lesbian explain this rage in the context of our disempowerment as women under patriarchy. As lesbians we are more likely to realize how oppressive the social and symbolic order is, which is a view shared by all groups on the margins. I will go further to suggest that rage also reflects a lack of recognition, through exclusion and the denial of expression. I would want to emphasize that rage is to be encouraged in women, precisely because we have traditionally been denied the right to feel it, it being seen as 'unfeminine' and therefore unnatural. Similarly, the experience of trauma is something that women undergo, not just as extreme occurrences (abuse, rape, violence), but as a commonplace condition in our contact with a social order that denies us our equal subjectivities. I see trauma as a form of blockage, that which impedes and oppresses us, barring many of us from functioning fully. I differ from Laplanche and Pontalis who define trauma in the singular as 'an event in the subject's life defined by its intensity' (Laplanche and Pontalis, quoted by Pajaczkowska and Young, 1993: 199). I think that which is traumatizing can be plural and recurring, with different degrees of intensity. They further define trauma as characterized 'by the subject's inability to respond adequately to it', with the result that the subject feels disrupted, psychically and otherwise, possibly permanently (*ibid.*).

Kaja Silverman opens up the term by describing a formulation of trauma 'as the rupture of an order which aspires to closure' because of 'a force directed toward disruption and disintegration' (Silverman, 1990: 116). That which is traumatizing serves to disrupt our semblance of self-control, whereby we cannot process our experiences but are damaged psychically by their intensity. I will suggest that rage and trauma coincide for many women, where we feel enraged by our derogation and are in daily contact with practices that attempt to block, silence and disempower our efforts to experience our autonomy. This situation also characterizes much of the experience of the black subject under racist discourses.

Although I begin with concepts taken from psychoanalysis, I wish to continue with a very brief critique of it. Mary Ann Doane suggests that psychoanalysis can 'be seen as a quite elaborate form of ethnography – as a writing of the ethnicity of the white Western psyche' (Doane, 1991: 211). The characteristic theme of such a psyche has been to set up the phallus as ultimate signifier while erasing the mother. Marianne Hirsch documents this erasure of the mother, and she refers to the 'repeated process of *othering* the mother' (Hirsch, 1989: 136; original emphasis). She argues that 'so long as the figure of the mother is excluded from theory *psychoanalytic feminism* cannot become a *feminist psychoanalysis*' (*ibid.*: 12; original emphases). What we need of course is a theoretical framework which includes the mother as a woman with autonomous desires, self-determined and not dictated to by fraudulent definitions. Perhaps the most blatant example of the mother's suppression is the obliteration of her maiden name on marriage.[2]

I would like to extrapolate from psychoanalysis what we can appropriate for feminist ends, especially drawing on what we can learn of the unconscious as a site of contradictions, and as a place of alterity, what Constance Penley refers to as its 'radical otherness' (Penley, 1989: xvi). This brings me to a now familiar theme, that of the advantages of a decentred subjectivity, fragmented and fractured in its postmodern guise, not the whole or unitary self of the modernist position. Black feminists have expressed their doubts about the viability of such decentred positionings. bell hooks wonders:

> Should we not be suspicious of postmodern critiques of the 'subject' when they surface at a historical moment when many subjugated people feel themselves coming to voice for the first time. (hooks, 1990: 28)

Nancy Hartsock asks a similar question:

> Why is it that just at the moment when so many of us who have been silenced begin to demand the right to name ourselves, to act as subjects rather than objects of history, that just then the concept of subjecthood becomes problematic? (Hartsock, 1990: 163)

I do see the dangers of adopting a sense of self as fragmented when the dominant discourse can render this position into a further marginality, by concentrating on contradictions as evidence of ineffectuality. However, our multiple subjectivities do involve the contradictions of plural positionalities, and black subjects especially are aware of the necessity of negotiating these contradictions. In the words of Cherríe Moraga and Gloria Anzaldúa, 'We learned to live with these contradictions. This is the root of our radicalism' (Moraga and Anzaldúa, 1983: 5). Bonnie Zimmerman references this position as a 'double vision' which 'disfranchised groups have had to adopt . . . for survival' (Zimmerman, 1981: 203). Rather than being frightened of our fracturations, we can take strength from the 'double vision' they enable. These fracturations echo the fragmentation of the divided psyche and a split ego, but they need not preclude personal cohesion or social action.

> Although the subject of the unconscious is divided, this does not mean that the social subject (which functions at a different level) cannot be cohesive, or at least cohesive enough to be able to enter into political groupings as a result of (more or less) conscious decision-making. (Penley, 1989: xviii)

A fractured psyche and a fragmented identity need not prevent us from being functional subjects and I do not think such a subjectivity is a disadvantage, given that we have to operate under conditions of loss as well as oppression.

As we will be looking at issues of mental health in some detail later in this chapter, I will venture into a brief preamble on how health has impacted on our lives as a medium of oppression as well as a site for resistance. As Beverly Smith says, an exploration of the subject enables black women to see 'how we are broken physically and mentally in this oppressive society', allowing us also to celebrate 'how we have struggled and survived' (1982: 103). Smith argues that the facts clearly indicate that 'our political position as Black women affects our health' (*ibid*.: 105). She suggests that our mental health has been affected due to centuries of being at the receiving end of brutally oppressive practices (*ibid*.: 108). In conjunction with our experience of endemic racism, I would suggest that the higher incidence of severe poverty among black subjects is the modality through which we are controlled and constrained. June Jordan suggests that 'we, Black women, subsist among the most tenuous and least likely economic conditions for survival' (Jordan, 1989: 85). Added to the hardships of impoverishment and deprivation is the stress we have to negotiate daily as black subjects. As women we are also defined by ridiculous prescriptions of femininity, which in its most reactionary version is the prototype of very unhealthy behaviour, including infantilization, excessive dependence, lack of subjectivity and so on. It is not surprising that many women respond with depression as the main symptom of their suppressed rage at the dissatisfaction with their lives and relationships. Suman Fernando finds that in depression, the female/male ratio is approximately three to one (Fernando, 1986: 112).

Hilary Allen makes the point that mental health statistics indicate that 'women are mentally sicker than men' (1986: 85). This is 'embarrassing' but it is also a testimony to 'women's suffering', which serves with other factors 'as a function of women's social oppression' (*ibid.*: 86). There is a suggestion that as we suffer more from challenges to our mental health, this is indicative of other modalities of oppression which we as women are more likely to experience in multiple forms.

Lianna is the story of a thirty-three-year-old white mother and wife. Her husband teaches English and film at a small-town college, and it seems that Lianna gave up her own studies to marry him because of the tension in being both his partner and his student. Lianna goes to night classes, where she meets a woman lecturer with whom she becomes sexually involved. This is a first for her, and the film charts the beginning of her lesbian identity by concentrating on how she comes out.

Lianna's husband Dick is a bitter teacher, good at what he does but lacking humanity because he is so preoccupied by his own advancement and selfish impulses. A clear parallel is set up between him and Ruth, Lianna's lover, as they vie in rivalry and competition. Ruth is already a professor, in child psychology, which Dick sees as an easy ride, an indication of his jealousy and insecurity due to his lack of tenure at the college. Although he teaches in the English department, his main interest is in film. He resents that Lianna should prefer to spend time on her own studies rather than help him with his film research. He is also resentful that Lianna prefers to go to Ruth's class rather than to one of the faculty parties to promote his career. He has sex with a research student at one such party, and Lianna comes on them by chance. She confronts him that evening, and it emerges that he has slept with other women students before.

While Dick is away at a film convention, Lianna is seduced by Ruth. On Dick's return, Lianna comes out and he feels threatened. He tells her she is still fucking her lecturers; she tells him he is still fucking his students. He says that at least they are 'the right sex'. He is enraged when she effectively tells him she has never loved him, but that she loves Ruth. He throws her out of the house. Dick sinks from deplorable to despicable behaviour, threatening Lianna over the custody of the children. In the end he is broken, as the film department head post he wanted is given to a male rival, and he is confined to teaching only English with no tenure.

His bitterness is of his own making, but it will probably destroy him as internal rancour does.

So Lianna's first coming out occurs in the context of the hostility of homophobia, its self-righteous appeal to heterosex as 'the right sex', and its hatred of dissident sexual identities and the alternatives they offer. This is the position that Dick effectively plays as husband (whose name signifies a penis).

Ruth (whose name signifies regret) also compounds the difficulties Lianna faces, first by her closet status and then by her rejection of Lianna for a previous long-term partner. Ultimately, I am critical of Ruth's lack of responsibility towards Lianna, and I do not think she is worthy of Lianna's love.

Let us now look in more detail at how Lianna comes out. From the start she is in awe of Ruth in her role as professor, holder of knowledge and the promise of empowerment. As teacher, Ruth is in the position of 'the subject supposed to know' – she has power because she is presumed to hold knowledge (Penley, 1989: 168). Of course such a dynamic has its foundation in inequality, even though Ruth stresses to her class that she has as much to learn from her students as they do from her. Lianna offers to do some research work for her and they meet for dinner at Ruth's place. Dick is away at a convention.

While drinking and talking, Lianna and Ruth get closer. Eventually they are on the sofa exchanging fantasies, then talking about crushes. Lianna comes out about an adolescent lesbian experience and Ruth kisses her. Lianna kisses her back. This is followed by a sex scene with blue-gel lighting, set to a mainly inaudible whispering voice-over. I heard some French in this erotic soundtrack, 'Dis moi des mots d'amour' (speak to me in the language of love). After the love-making scene, the women very credibly run through that first moment of physical contact. At Lianna's questioning, Ruth admits that she was terrified when she kissed Lianna in case it was not welcome and her advances would become public knowledge. Lianna asks her why she took the risk. Ruth says because she wanted her that much. Lianna says she is glad.

In terms of the first good initiation, it is of course a source of joy to discover lesbian sex. But the question arises as to whether Ruth should have been more responsible, and more careful about what she was starting, especially as Lianna is both a younger student as well as a novice to lesbian sex. By long-standing tradition, the first sexual partner is often seen as significant, and when that first partnering involves lesbian sex, the explosiveness of the experience and the intensity of it make the encounter overcharged. Hence Ruth comes to be endowed as holding the power of the first completion, one we may continue to seek from the memory of its intensity.

What is frustrating for Lianna is that their desire has to be secret because of society's homophobia. The women cannot display desire or even affection openly. At a scene in a swimming pool, Lianna says she would like to kiss Ruth, who says they cannot there: 'It's part of the package'. Lianna starts making verbal love to Ruth, and I am reminded of the scene from Martin Sherman's play *Bent*, where the two men have to use their erotic imagination to make love because they are physically constrained from doing so. Here, there is no physical constraint on desire being enacted, but it must be behind closed doors, so that the subterfuge of heterosex as 'the right sex' can be maintained.

This subterfuge in hiding lesbian desire is evident in Ruth's closet behaviour. As a child psychology teacher who needs parents' support, she is terrified that the small-town mentality of homophobia can threaten her work. For me, Ruth loses all respect in a later scene when they are in bed. She starts by saying that Lianna should not address her as Ruth in class. She says it is not about authority or distance. Effectively it is her closet fear for her career. Then she tells Lianna she does not want her to do the research work for her now that they are lovers. To an extent this is correct not to want to replicate their inequality on another dimension. But this rejection of Lianna's offer of labour is in the context of her unsuccessfully looking for work, where the withdrawal of the project is another financial setback. If that were not enough, Ruth then announces to Lianna that 'There's a woman back home'. The question is raised about Ruth going back to her.

I find such behaviour verges on the irresponsible, where Ruth does not accept the accountability of her actions in relation to Lianna. However, Ruth is not a villain, she merely misreads the lesbian desire she has set in motion. She announces in a class that she will be away visiting her department head, a brutal way of letting Lianna know her plans. It turns out the department head is the lover back home. Lianna's rage starts to surface.

At a later explosive encounter between them, Ruth offers that one can be in love with more than one person at a time, to which Lianna counters 'You're the only one I've ever been in love with.' This is a key exchange, and I will return to its implications for desire. Lianna's rage has emerged, she tells Ruth she got her into this, that the moment she told her she loved her Ruth started backing away, how could she do that to her. Her rage is justified. But Ruth remains credible as someone who is mistaken, not as some heartbreaker villain. She tells Lianna that sometimes straight women sleep with lesbians out of curiosity, that she could not have known what would happen. So she is guilty of misreading the impact of lesbian desire, of starting something she cannot honour. Ultimately she is irresponsible in not recognizing Lianna's love as equivalent to the love for the first object, the m/other who contains the child. I think this is a serious miscalculation, especially given that the subject of child psychology must have taught Ruth something about mother–daughter dyads, and how they get replicated in lesbian relationships.

Their last love-making scene, prior to Ruth leaving to return to her previous lover, is intercut with a dance performance where a man and a woman enact desire and displeasure, intimacy and antagonism. This conveys both the recognition and the rage in lesbian desire, here made more poignant by it being the last instance of their sexual contact together.

It is worth going over the process of Lianna's coming out again, in relation to the other characters, to demonstrate the place of rage and recognition in this process. Her friend Sandy immediately knows that Lianna has a crush on Ruth, and this is OK, a same-sex crush is normal. However, after the seduction, when Lianna tells Sandy about Ruth, Sandy is incredulous, as if acting on lesbian desire is inconceivable to her. Lianna tells her 'It happens', a classic understatement.

Lianna is mostly open about her new-found lesbian sexuality. At first she is scared when Ruth takes her to a women-only club, but she eventually settles to some dancing without inhibition. Her coming out propels her into finding a place to live and a job at a supermarket check-out. She tells Ruth she always wanted a room of her own, a reminder that she studied English through a literary reference to Virginia Woolf's *A Room of One's Own* (the title of which omits the access Woolf had to an inheritance to enable her to support her space). At her new residence, Lianna meets a woman in the laundry room and comes out. She says 'I'm gay', to which the other woman replies, 'I'm Sheila.' This is possibly the film's funniest moment, indicating both Lianna's courage in coming out and the nervousness, uncertainty, as well as pleasure at being out.

Lianna is almost completely isolated and goes back to the women-only club, where a woman called Cindy starts talking to her. They go back to Cindy's place, and make love. It is a step forward for Lianna to assert her identity as lesbian separately from Ruth. Her discovery of her sexuality enables her to identify with women in a new spirit of a shared commonality brought about by same-gender status. 'Lianna learns to look' (Merck, 1987: 172). But she is still isolated, and we see real-time images of her lonely existence. When Ruth returns temporarily, she says she feels a lot of pressure from Lianna, who says she is isolated. Ruth says there are other women Lianna can talk to, but Lianna says she does not want a support system, she wants Ruth. Ruth tries to tell her Lianna loves women, not just her, but for the moment Lianna is fixated on just Ruth.

Ruth reminds Lianna that to be lesbian is to desire women, and, what is more, that desire is not fixed but can incorporate different objects. I agree with this in principle, but what Ruth is misreading is the impact of the first lesbian partner as the desired object. The first lesbian partner who shares the intimate space of same-sex mergence has endowed in her all the promise of the completion we seek from the phallic mother. Ruth fails dismally to recognize her responsibility to Lianna.

The rage that Ruth activates in Lianna at her abandonment is countered by the recognition that she receives elsewhere. Barring Dick the homophobic husband, all the other characters are supportive of Lianna's lesbianism, and her two children also accept it. Lianna's close friend Sandy, a resolutely heterosexual woman, has to work through her homophobia. At one point she remembers with aversion that she walked with Lianna holding hands in public, to comfort her when she was in a state, as if this is some kind of contamination. Sandy is temporarily in a muddle about lesbian desire. She does not understand or approve of it, but she still loves Lianna and tells her so. The film ends with the two of them publicly hugging in the park, a confirmation that female friendship can be celebrated, that Sandy recognizes Lianna as an equal though different subject of desire.

We can read into the ending that Lianna will work through the trauma of her first rejection, that she will move to a position of triumph as her lesbian desire is met by partners more worthy of her love, who can receive it fully with recognition, and without a rejection of the rage it can also bring up.

Lianna is a mother, and her two children are not hostile to her new-found lesbian sexuality. Although I do not address her identity as a mother in any detail, the film confirms how maternal status is marginalized. This is very much in keeping with the dominant readings of the mother, for example, 'Mothers don't write, they are written . . . ' (Susan Rubin Suleiman, quoted by Elizabeth Wright, 1990: 145; original emphasis). Mothers are silent in their own voices, reported but not agentic, their rage suppressed. I think much of the mother's rage is due to her not being recognized as a subject in her own right. Adrienne Rich differentiates motherhood as 'experience' and as 'institution'. Experience involves the potential relationship to reproduction and children, and can be a source of celebration. The institution, however, characterized by male control, is a site of contestation (A. Rich, 1976: 13). This is a helpful distinction which clarifies the tensions between the celebration and the derogation of mothering. While many women can and do enjoy their positions as mothers, this capacity for reproduction can also be the site of their bodily subjugation, where the woman's labour is appropriated, her name often obscured, her subjectivity submerged, and her desire seen to be invested in phallic identifications.

Nancy Chodorow attempts to posit explanations for why women reproduce reproduction by suggesting a cyclical model of gender, where women want to mother because of their capacity for relational contact. She sees that boy children are more differentiated by their mothers, individuated earlier so they can take part in the world of work where there will be less space for affective relations. 'Boys come to define themselves as more separate and distinct' (Chodorow, 1978: 169). Girl children tend to be kept in greater degrees of mergence. They are individuated less and later, so that they 'come to define themselves more in relation to others' (ibid.: 93). Chodorow deduces from this that 'the basic feminine sense of self is connected to the world, the basic masculine sense of self is separate' (ibid.: 169). Of course, it is precisely this capacity for the relational that can become distorted by seeing the woman as only mature as a mother. Moreover, this same capacity has served to designate the woman as self-sacrificial, wanting an autonomy to which she can no longer aspire, because autonomy is seen as a masculine prerogative.

Parveen Adams references Donald Winnicott's concept of the 'good-enough' mother, one who can meet the demands of the child appropriately (Adams, 1983: 318). She makes the important point that 'the child's psychic health is not in the gift of the mother' (ibid.: 319). For one thing, 'no child-rearing practice can guarantee normality', for 'that would be to abolish the unconscious' (ibid.).

On the subject of mothering, Hirsch finds that we 'need to transform more radically the paradigms within which we think', and this would involve transcending 'patriarchal myths and perceptions' (Hirsch, 1981: 221). Rather than pathologize the mother or blame the family for social incohesion, we could engage in the instituting of a political climate which has a need, as Elizabeth Wilson argues, 'for social solutions to the oppression we experience as private' (1981: 174).

Thin Ice is the story of two young women skaters, one black and the other white, who meet in London, start a partnership, fall out, and then reconnect in New York to win a gold medal together at the Gay Games. It remains a sweet and funny film despite treating the serious subjects of suicide and trauma, homophobia and rage. The sense of camaraderie in the lesbian and gay community emerges, and friends are welcoming and supportive of each other across race and age, gender and sexuality. There are villains of a minor sort in the persons of a neurotic sister and a predatory brother-in-law, but they are rendered comic and not sinister. The predominant feeling we get is lighthearted pleasure as the two women triumph at the end, and what we can read is the continuation of their relationship as it develops to incorporate both lust and love.

For the purposes of this chapter, I will focus on the movement from rage to recognition, trauma to triumph, as it takes place in the film's narrative. Natalie, the young white woman, has been previously traumatized by the shotgun suicide of her father. That this is still very present in her psyche is cleverly conveyed when this past event is re-enacted in a dream she has, cut in a way to show its shock as still immediate and painful. Natalie has no friends, she does not go out and she is obsessed with her skating lessons. Although her mother is supportive of her, her sister Fiona is self-obsessed and jealous of Natalie, and her brother-in-law Charles is a reactionary bigot. Natalie has to endure bickering about money, babysitting her niece for her sister, and unwelcome advances from Charles. She is living in her sister's house, working in her sister's shop, fending off her sister's husband, and is desperate to get out of this domestic prison. Enter Steffi in her life.

Steffi is a young black woman skater and an out lesbian. Her previous black woman lover, who was also her skating partner, has left her and she has to find another partner to take part in the Gay Games. She actively seeks Natalie out as a skating partner, but she makes the mistake of not revealing that she and a gay friend Greg have a commission from the *Observer* for a story on the skating couple. This is because the story has to have a romantic angle with the two of them as lovers, and Natalie is apparently straight. This deception is the complication that leads to rage in their relationship.

The previous trauma and the present rage could be a recipe for an explosive relationship, but Natalie's coming out is also a working through of trauma and rage, so that the relationship can develop. There are three central exchanges between them that lead to the resolution of rage and the laying to rest of trauma. First the seduction, then the falling out, then the reconnecting.

The seduction takes place at a country cottage belonging to Greg's ex-lover. When out walking in the woods, Natalie is traumatized by some shotgun shots which bring up the memory of her father's suicide. She comes out to Steffi about this incident, and Steffi is comforting. This then is an initial intimacy of sharing trauma through its relation. That evening, Natalie asks Steffi about her previous lesbian partner, and the subject of love is raised. I would venture to suggest that Natalie is falling in love and that at this stage, Steffi is about to act on lust. They practise their dance routine for Greg, who leaves the room because it is becoming clear that they are awaking to their mutual desire. They hug, hold each other, dance, then Steffi leads Natalie away. But the next morning, Steffi is less forthcoming, and she pretends to be asleep when Natalie tries to wake her, thereby denying Natalie's desire on the first night's morning after.

When Natalie finds out about the *Observer* story, the rage she feels has a justifiable reason in deception and what seems betrayal. 'You used me', she tells Steffi, that classic line of rage at abuse. Her first act of lesbian sex has become treacherous and not joyous, and in another classic line she says, 'Don't touch me', something we can sometimes say when we most want to be held safely. Although Steffi tries to clarify what is happening, Natalie is unable to trust her, and pulls out of the partnership.

The resolution takes place in New York, after the performance that wins them a gold medal and international media coverage. This victory validates their partnership, even though there is no suspense about whether they will win, and no surprise when they do. The resolution we are looking for is not to be found on the rink, but in their relationship. Natalie reminds Steffi that 'That night did happen', as if denying it took place could erase the subject of their desire. When Steffi says 'You're straight', Natalie replies 'Says who', a declaration more than an inter-rogation. They kiss publicly in Central Park. This is the first time we see them being passionately intimate, and the film ends with their participa-tion in the twenty-fifth Stonewall anniversary march as an affirmation of lesbian and gay identity proud to be out.

It is not Natalie's coming out in itself, as a white woman who dares sleep with a black lesbian, that causes a problem, because we are not always the source of the problems we face. Rather, it is the homophobia and racism in the reception to being lesbian and/or black that is at fault. By following the now accepted paradigm of placing racists and homophobes as themselves pathological, where it is their own sickness that they attempt to project onto us, we can relocate the black lesbian identity as healthy and affirmative. This is not to say that we have no share of pathology, as if we were separable from and innocent of our societies' sicknesses, but that we do not have a monopoly on pathology by virtue of our blackness and/or sexual dissidence. Whatever pathologies we may exhibit are not to be seen as solely of our own making, but the response to an unjust social order.

The racism and homophobia that Charles and Fiona exhibit, as Natalie's brother-in-law and sister, are conveyed without too much emphasis attached to their presence, so that they are ultimately ineffectual rather than threatening obstacles. Charles is a pompous rich man who seems to think his advances to Natalie are his prerogative as a brother-in-law. When Steffi storms in one evening and rushes up the stairs to see Natalie, he asks half incredulously, 'She was black, wasn't she?', as if he cannot believe that a black subject can enter his house. Fiona finds Natalie's lesbianism to be a personal act of spite against her, intended to embarrass her and her family, as if something as important as Natalie discovering her sexuality should be orchestrated to revolve around her, Fiona. Sibling rivalry is still present in their relationship, and the concluding frame of the film ends with Fiona seeing Natalie and Steffi on the cover of *Life* magazine, in horror at the publicity of her being openly out.

Natalie's movement from the trauma of her father's death to the triumph of discovering a lesbian identity also involves a path of rage to recognition. Although the deception that takes place is contrived, to create a complication that needs a resolution, we find it credible because it provides a narrative place for the rage that does emerge with lesbian mergence. In this case, the deception can be sorted out, and the rage is resolved for now through the mutual recognition and acting out of their desire.

Steffi is also credible as an ambitious skater who gets caught unawares emotionally with a white woman whom she thinks is straight. That Natalie is supposedly straight is another complication, so her coming out is a happy resolution. For Natalie, skating is more than 'a phase', her desire for Steffi is more than 'a crush', and the triumph of their winning coupled with the joy of reconnecting as lovers is the happy conclusion we want. Although Steffi is the initiator, I think it is Natalie's drama of coming out, by working through the trauma and rage, that forms the film's nucleus.

What is refreshing is that Steffi is not pathologized as the abnormal other, nor is she presented as the exotic erotic black woman luxuriating in promiscuous sex, both prototypes of how the black subject is received in white mythology. Although she is caught up in a deception, Steffi's desire for Natalie seems spontaneous, and only incidentally involves an element of emotional manipulation. Steffi sleeps with Natalie thinking she is straight, and she can be forgiven for not foreseeing the impact of this one act. Rather than follow the stereotype of presenting the black subject as pathological, it is Natalie as the white woman who has to work through her trauma and rage, with Steffi's agency.

The effect of this reversal of stereotypes is to turn the tables on the usual processes of pathologization. I would like to explore further how the black subject is pathologized, particularly in relation to our over-representation in mental health institutions, which I think has as much to do with white pathological behaviour as it does with the way black subjects can express our distress in social contexts that do not recognize our equal subjectivities.

The pathologization of the black subject is the legacy of slavery, colonialism, and the 'perfection of racist regimes' which Amina Mama argues still influence 'psychological discourses on black people' today (Mama, 1995: 39). Mama does not want to 'underestimate the institutional power of the discourse which construed black people as unquestionably mentally inferior and as exhibiting racially specific forms of pathology' (*ibid*.). Let us look at this racist discourse at work. Sander Gilman describes pathology in terms of the distinction between 'healthy' and 'sick' (Gilman, 1985: 23). Gilman says our conceptualization of the pathological is based on the vulnerability of the body to 'disease, pollution, corruption, and alteration', and of course death. 'The potential illness, age, and corruption of the self is projected onto others' (*ibid*.). Gilman suggests that 'it is because these forces actively lie within and are projected outside the self that the different is so readily defined as the pathological' (*ibid*.: 24). Gilman makes further links between pathology, sex and race, where 'physiognomy or skin color that is perceived as different is immediately associated with "pathology" and "sexuality"' (*ibid*.: 25).

The categorization of the black subject as endogenously pathological serves to both infantilize us and render us dangerous. I turn now to a related subject, that of the over-representation of black subjects in mental health institutions and the differential treatment we receive. Fernando reports the finding of one British study where 'Asians and West Indians were over-represented amongst compulsory detentions' (Fernando, 1988: 78). Kobena Mercer makes the point that misdiagnosis is often the key issue (Mercer, 1986: 115). Erica Wheeler references the statistics showing that black subjects are diagnosed as schizophrenic four to ten times more than their white counterparts. What is more, the initial diagnosis that black subjects are given is more likely to be revised than the one given to whites (Wheeler, 1994: 51). This high incidence of misdiagnosis is indeed disturbing, because obviously diagnosis affects the form of treatment to be administered.

In addition to the evidence of an over-diagnosis of schizophrenia and an overuse of compulsory detentions, Fernando provides evidence from British research that confirms an overuse of ECT and excessive transfer to locked wards for many black subjects (Fernando, 1988: 74). It is unsurprising therefore that most black subjects are never offered psychotherapy (Fernando, 1986: 146; Mercer, 1986: 116). Mercer confirms that this is an area not for healing but social control, and he references the 'linkages between policing, the prisons and psychiatry' (Mercer, 1986: 114–15). With other commentators, Mercer draws on the work of Roland Littlewood and Maurice Lipsedge, who argue that psychiatric practitioners should be able to differentiate 'between normal forms of cultural expression and signs of potential mental illness' (*ibid.*: 126). In other words, psychiatrists should not read their own white Eurocentric norms into different cultural behaviour. Because many of these psychiatrists have little understanding of other cultures, many black subjects can seem deranged when in fact their behaviour may be appropriate to their situation. Because of a lack of understanding of other cultures and because of an ignorance of the disease of schizophrenia itself, some psychiatrists can be quick to collapse their own ignorances by assigning them to a label which few understand.

Philip Rack confirms most of the above findings. He reports on the contradictory statistics on Asian admissions, where there is some doubt as to whether we feature prominently in compulsory detentions (Rack, 1982: 162). Rack also finds that the initial diagnosis given to Asians is often revised after in-patient observation (*ibid.*: 165). And he too emphasizes the cultural pitfalls in diagnosis and alerts us as to how black subjects are being pathologized for exhibiting culturally different behaviour.

Let us look briefly at the vexed question of whether racism actually causes mental health problems. Fernando examines some of the factors in the incidence of depression and suggests that 'racism is not just an added stress' for the black subject, but 'a pathogen that generates depression' (Fernando, 1986: 130). He finds that 'racism causes depression' because the condition of depression is connected to low self-esteem, loss and helplessness (*ibid.*: 133). I read these as poor morale, absence of protective shields, and the sense of powerlessness these engender, and I can see the logic of applying this paradigm to the experience of many black subjects who have been exposed over and over to oppressive practices, whether overtly brutal, or subtle and insidious.

Aggrey Burke reports similar findings and states that 'the evidence points to the conclusion that racism does lead to mental illness' (Burke,

1986: 124) through several mediums, including 'social deprivation', 'withholding care', 'humiliating Blacks' and 'by implementing methods of social/medical control' (*ibid.*: 154).

These authors offer convincing evidence that black subjects are more likely to be committed for treatment by compulsory detention orders under Section 136 of the 1983 Mental Health Act, that we are more likely to be misdiagnosed and given inappropriate treatment, and that labels such as those of schizophrenia are often assigned in ignorance of cultural differences. Added to this is the question of psychiatry as a system of social control and racism as an actual instigator of mental illness. It is worth making the point that although many black subjects can choose the language of mental illness to express our outrage at our disempowerment, this avenue of psychic protest is not our sole domain. There are many black subjects who escape the mental health system, although we are pathologized elsewhere, just as there are many white subjects who choose the language of mental disorder to express their disturbance.

I would like to conclude this section on a more affirmative argument from Mama, who finds that the notion of racism as damaging to black psyches only pathologizes millions of black subjects living in racist societies (Mama, 1995: 111). Mama reminds us that there is much 'more to black subjectivity than psychological damage' and she argues that 'racism can be seen as texturing subjectivity, rather than determining black social and emotional life' (*ibid.*). For me, this affirms how racism impacts on us without allowing it to dominate who we are. Black subjects are many things other than being black. Rather than codifying us as black = pathological = dangerous, we would seek a paradigm that includes blacks as equal subjects with plural multiplicities.

Nocturne is primarily a theatrical piece which economically conveys the complexity of lesbian desire, here as frustration. To enjoy what it offers, we have to extratext with theatre and go beyond the expectations of conventional cinema. By 'extratext' I mean the practice of fusing the conventions of different media into new syntheses. By incorporating some of the conventions of theatre within cinema, we can achieve new creative practices. With theatre we get more psychic drama and less action, more claustrophobia and less sensational activity, more characterization and fewer characters. Another difference is that the theatrical medium requires more carefully scripted dialogue, and more of it, than does an action film within the cinematic conventions of lots of action culminating in a grand finale. Those spectators who are frustrated in their reception of this film are missing the extratext, indeed are missing out on an experience that reworks film and opens it up to wider possibilities. Not confining but expansive, *Nocturne* offers hope and new beginnings, both in content and form.

The film begins with the central protagonist Marguerite, who has just attended her mother's funeral. Although the mother is physically dead, she remains as a psychic presence, and Marguerite has to lay her to rest, to break the bond that keeps her blocked in stasis. Marguerite returns to her mother's cottage, the place of her own childhood, where she had to study from home because of poor health. The adult Marguerite has memories that we receive in flashback. A narrative question is set up to suggest that Marguerite is a closet lesbian in quest of liberation, but in fact beyond this subtext there is another, to which we are given access through the flashbacks as well as by the agency of two young lesbians who arrive unexpectedly at the cottage.

The young Marguerite has a tutor, Miss Carpenter, a young working-class woman from the north of England who befriends the young girl. Her mother is a detached woman who knows all the social rules but lacks all the social graces, and we learn that she does not even know what Marguerite's favourite game is. One day when Miss Carpenter and Marguerite are caught in a rainstorm, and enter the mother's study drenched and dripping, Mrs Tyler the mother is transfixed by the tutor's wet clothes clinging sensuously to her skin. Rather than let them go and change into dry clothes, she asks totally inappropriate questions, including whether they had a satisfactory walk. Marguerite makes apparent the question's absurdity: 'It rained, mother.' We are alerted to there being something of a malfunction in Mrs Tyler's interpersonal skills.

Meanwhile, in the present, two young lesbians, black and white, erupt into Marguerite's life. They are runaway fugitives who end up stranded in the woods. Caught in a rainstorm, they burst into the room where Marguerite is, probably the study where she and Miss Carpenter burst in some twenty to thirty years ago, also drenched. Almost immediately, an unspoken arrangement is arrived at between Marguerite and the white lesbian Sal, who reads Marguerite's intentions with uncanny accuracy.

Sal knows that Marguerite needs to ritualistically enact something through her agency and that of her black lover Ria. When Marguerite gives them dry clothes to change into, Sal asks a series of key questions: 'How do we look? Will we do? What do you think?' Marguerite replies, 'I think you're just right.' These monosyllabic questions and statements have the effect of accessing a childhood register of language, where often the preferred words are of one syllable. 'How do we look?' refers to both the activity and passivity of looking.[3] The question 'Will we do?' has a subtextual function of relating to their use-value. Sal knows Marguerite needs them, and why she needs them is apparently because Marguerite is a closet lesbian who needs to confront what she has attempted to repress. But what has Marguerite repressed? What explanation is she seeking to find? Is it her lesbianism? Or is there something else she has to recover from the past, something tied up with her mother?

Marguerite remembers her first disobedience of her mother, when she refuses to play a difficult piece, one of Chopin's Nocturnes which she has not learned yet. The young girl is upset at having such demands made on her, and she exits to her bedroom where she hurls herself on the bed. From the wardrobe mirror in her room, we see Mrs Tyler reprimanding Miss Carpenter, reminding her she is a servant. Miss Carpenter replies she will remember that, provided Mrs Tyler does too. What does this suggest? It is clear that the moment is connected to the daughter's trauma.

The reason we have to use extratext with theatre to benefit fully from the film is that it is precisely the subtext of theatre that is being so cleverly reworked here. We have only to think of Chekhov and Ibsen, Tennessee Williams and Arthur Miller, Jean Anhouilh and Eugène Ionesco, Joe Orton and Harold Pinter, among many others, to remember how the theatrical medium depends on what is being said to convey complex and plural meanings. The unspoken text runs concurrently with the spoken, so that in this subtext we see the workings of interior processes.

The subtext is most apparent at the main dinner scene of this film, where it is clear that Marguerite is playing her mother, and that Sal and Ria represent Miss Carpenter and young Marguerite. They are all very drunk, the weather is very close and about to break, and there is tension as we do not know which way things will go. Marguerite/mother says that Ria is very privileged, 'You see, you've got it all on your side.' She then adds, 'The condiments, I mean', referring to the salt and pepper pots, thereby linking the psychic with the physical, in a way which allows the message of the subtext to come through in the mechanics of the overt text. Later, Marguerite says, 'I've never had what you had', it being clear that the subtext is sex. Because Marguerite has merged with her mother, we are at first unclear about whose desire it is that has been frustrated. Sal says to her, 'You never got any either, did you? That's your trouble, isn't it?', clarifying that it is both the mother and the daughter's desire that has been left unmet. But there is still the question of clarifying this frustration, and we learn of it in another flashback, in the form of a revelation to the daughter of her mother's lesbian desires.

This revelation takes place through the mediation of a mirror, rendering the vision obversely to convey its emotional impact at a remove, a kind of visual euphemism. Miss Carpenter has just tucked the young

Marguerite into bed and kissed her good night. She leaves the room, we see her in the mirror in the other room, she goes up to Mrs Tyler and touches her shoulder. Mrs Tyler turns around, she kisses Miss Carpenter on the lips, then she tells the young tutor to leave, to get out of the house. We can assume from this that Miss Carpenter has been sacked.

What else can we read from this exchange? Is it a first kiss, or the final one with a history of previous intimacy? What does it say about the frustration of desire? These questions seek answers in the form of explanations, and we know that the revelation of her mother's lesbian desires has given Marguerite access to repressed memories in a way which provides here a peaceful resolution to psychic drama.

At the end, Marguerite is freed of the grip of her mother's psychic hold on her. One has only to project and imagine the unhealthy household that constituted the site of the rest of Marguerite's childhood to be able to sympathize with the experience of psychic scarring that she undergoes. She has laid the ghost of her mother to rest by re-enacting the moment of trauma and coming to terms with it. From this point of view, she has greatly benefited from the agency of Sal and Ria, whose criminal behaviour of stealing goods from her is not really a betrayal of trust, more an aggressive seizing of the opportunity to gain what advantage they can from her. In Ria's case, their actions are a form of revenge as protest at her having been infantilized. They take her goods and make their getaway. But they have given herself back to her – she is intact and functioning. The ending suggests that she is unsurprised by their flight, moreover, that she is rested and recovered, even relieved, and certainly happy at the resolution of her trauma. What this film confirms for me among other things is that white subjects are just as vulnerable to the psychic disturbances that are seen to characterize the black family as endogenously pathological.

Turning now to the Asian family in Britain, one extreme stereotype has the father-husband as patriarchal despot, the mother-wife as passive and ignorant, and the young daughter as subject to an arranged marriage to a man twice her age whom she has never met before and whom she cannot refuse. I deliberately fuse all the worst images of Asian families into this one scenario, because it is often these images that strike the most terror as well as distaste. This scenario evokes an Asian man who has no awareness and who might resort to violence in the home. It evokes an Asian woman who is home-bound, and possibly uneducated to the point of illiteracy. And finally it calls up an image of a young Asian woman who has no choice but to marry, and no choice in whom she marries. I draw on this scenario to demonstrate the extremity of ignorance operating in such stereotypes. Errol Lawrence draws attention to the media myth-making that perpetuates such stereotypes. As Lawrence points out, such images fuel the notion of Asian 'barbarity' as compared to the 'superior' British freedoms of choosing one's own partner (Lawrence, 1982: 75). This is to ignore cultural differences as well as the degree of negotiation involved within and between families (*ibid*.: 75–6).

We find in this model of the Asian family a woman who is often stereotyped as 'passive', helplessly dependent and docile. Avtar Brah argues against this stereotype (Brah, 1993: 66), and she also finds these stereotypes rooted in discourses which 'pathologize Asian family life', again deflecting from 'racial, sexual and class inequalities' as the central cause of our problems (*ibid*.: 69). On the question of arranged marriages, unlike the stereotype of young women being forced to marry men against their will, Brah finds that there is 'negotiation between generations' (*ibid*.: 72). On the subject of resistance internal to the family, Brah reports that the level of 'intergenerational conflict' in Asian families corresponds to that of white families (*ibid*.: 74). Pratibha Parmar also wishes to discard the stereotype of young passive Asian women, who she finds 'have developed their own forms of resistance, articulate their own ideas about British society, and rely on their own historical cultural traditions as a means of support' (Parmar, 1982: 239).

Let us look further at the subject of the black family with reference to its repeated pathologization in racist discourses. Angela Davis confirms how the African-American family has been seen as pathological because it does not conform to the white American norm (Davis, 1984: 75). Davis argues that this alternative family is blamed for causing problems when in fact these problems are 'often directly attributable to the social, economic, and political promotion of racism' (*ibid*.). We have in this argument the two threads I am following in this chapter, that the black family is seen as pathological, thereby deflecting the responsibility for the lack of social cohesion onto black subjects, and not the oppressive social and symbolic order we operate in.

Davis details how the African tradition of family was not confined 'merely to biological parents and their progeny' but involved an extended family unit, 'a vital tradition' (*ibid*.). Patricia Hill Collins also confirms how these extended families were recreated in America from African paradigms to resist 'the dehumanizing effects of slavery' (Collins, 1990: 49). These families did not follow a patriarchal model of the man as breadwinner and the woman as housewife, because under slavery the man had no wage and the woman was an equal worker. Collins reports how the absence of patriarchal structures in black family life has been 'used as evidence for Black cultural inferiority' (*ibid*.: 75). Black women's 'failure' to subscribe to 'the cult of true womanhood' is seen 'as one fundamental source of Black cultural deficiency' (*ibid.*).

hooks points out that in fact many black men have been happy to stay at home and rear the children while their female partners have worked. This reflects the greater availability of jobs for black women than for men, but hooks makes the further point that it is 'a sexist standpoint' to think these men were emasculated, when many of them may have been glad to be spared the dubious privilege of working for an exploitative and racist white employer (hooks, 1992: 92–3).

Hazel Carby provides a similar analysis of the black family in Britain, which is seen as pathological (Carby, 1982: 215), and where black mothers are stigmatized because they are wage earners (*ibid.*: 219). Here too, 'the black family has been a site of political and cultural resistance to racism' (*ibid.*: 214). But rather than being seen as an affirmative site for the enculturation of oppositional positionings, the black family has been conceptualized as pathological, and Valerie Amos and Pratibha Parmar find that white feminists have not challenged this concept (Amos and Parmar, 1984: 9). Ann Phoenix finds that interpretations of studies and research 'locate pathology in black people while leaving social and political causes untheorized' (Phoenix, 1990: 121).

Let us now link up the black family with issues of homophobia and the false assertion that black communities are pathologically homophobic.

> The myth that Black families or people are more homophobic than whites should really be demolished, because really what is obvious is that the security links we need with our families/communities are stronger. (Shaila, 1984: 54)

This need to stay within family bondings and community connections is pronounced for black subjects, whose frequent sense of dislocation in this culture is countered by the grounding and support we can receive from certain quarters. Valerie Mason-John and Adowa Okorrowa make the point that 'The possibility of losing our families and communities can mean cultural bereavement' (Mason-John and Okorrowa, 1995: 81). So the family especially, as a site for strength and resistance, has a huge significance for the black subject who is lesbian, and frequently we are frightened that coming out may endanger our position. This is not because the black family is prone to be any more pathological than the white family. It is common knowledge that as black women we face a barrage of oppressive practices, and that to come out as lesbian as well can be seen as one difference too many to cope with. Here, I see that difference is equated with difficulty, so that when a lesbian comes out to her family, they will be aware of the additional oppression being taken on board. As Barbara Smith says, 'Heterosexual privilege is usually the only privilege that Black women have', and 'maintaining "straightness" is our last resort' (1977: 171).

Homophobia in the Asian community in Britain is little documented, even though it is of course a feature of the Asian lesbian experience here. Most Asian men do not have the same 'macho' sensibility attributed to African-American men, even though sexism and heterosexism predominate among unpoliticized Asian men. The Asian community also has to operate under the rules of *izzat* (family honour), *sharam* (shame and guilt) and *khandan* (standing in the community) (A. Wilson, 1978: 99, 104–5). Asian women specifically have to conduct themselves with honourable behaviour, and it is in this context that Asian lesbians are additionally stigmatized. This is partly why many of us are invisible. Although I could venture into a personal history of coming out as an Asian lesbian, I will concentrate on African-American women because of the greater availability of their writing on the subject of homophobia.

Cheryl Clarke finds that 'the lesbian has decolonized her body' (Clarke, 1983a: 128). I read this decolonization as an alternative positioning to the phallicization or hystericization of the female body. Clarke locates one version of homophobia in the context of the 1960s Black Power movement, where 'heterosexual and male superiority' were dominant ideologies (Clarke, 1983b: 198). She correctly sees the dangers of homophobia, which 'divides people as political allies' and 'perpetuates patriarchal domination' (*ibid.*: 207).

Ann Allen Shockley finds that homophobia in the black community is due to 'misinformation', 'animosity' and ignorance about us (Shockley, 1979: 84). Shockley also identifies the source of homophobia against black lesbians as resting on our posing a sexual threat to the 'Black male macho' (*ibid.*: 85). Lorraine Bethel also finds that 'for many people, fear of self-defined Black women is fear of lesbianism' (Bethel, 1982: 185). Davis endorses the making of connections, and finds that sexism and homophobia have the same roots in the economic and political institutions that perpetuate racism (Davis, 1984: 12).

Valerie Mason-John and Ann Khambatta offer evidence of how there have always been black lesbians and gay men (Mason-John and Khambatta, 1993: 19), a point that Barbara Smith confirms (Gomez and Smith, 1990: 48). Smith quotes from Shockley, 'Play it, but don't say it' (Shockley, quoted by Gomez and Smith, 1990: 49), where the black community can tolerate homosexual activity but not the political identity associated with it. In what is an echo of the turning of the tables on the pathologization of homosexuals, Smith sees homophobia as a form of 'arrested development' (Gomez and Smith, 1990: 47). But we must see this homophobia in terms of 'the heterosexist culture we live in' (Clarke, 1983b: 205). If black subjects are concerned about a homosexual identity among members of their family, it is often because of their perception of the added difficulties of sexual dissidence, and their awareness that this identity is multiply located as the target of oppressive practices.

To say that the black community is more homophobic than its white counterpart is to feed into ancient stereotypes. In the words of Linda Bellos, 'Saying that homophobia is more prevalent in the Black community is like saying there are more Black men who rape' (Bellos, quoted by Mason-John and Khambatta, 1993: 22). Such stereotyping would only serve racist ends. Although it is true that black lesbians can be 'caught between the racism of white women and the homophobia of their sisters' (Lorde, 1984: 122), this should not be taken as an indication that black communities exhibit a more pathological homophobia than white ones.

Black subjects do not have a monopoly on mental distress, although we are probably subjected to more stress. I think all subjects can be prey to psychic dysfunction to varying degrees, and I list some of the more obvious instances here: suicidal depression and hyperaggressiveness; multiple and dysfunctional personalities; hysteria and mania; dependency and addictions; narcissism and neurosis; paranoia and schizophrenia; dementia and delusions, hallucinations and voices; antisocial and psychopathic behaviours; perversion and abuse; catatonia and hyperactivity; autism, alienation, amnesia; compulsive and obsessional behaviours; eating and nervous disorders; phobias and anxieties; and so on. It would be a rare subject who cannot identify one to several of these forms of derangement as part of their psychic make-up. And I would suggest, without being alarmist, that if we are to avoid globally high incidences of mental disorder, which I see as a growing threat given the extent of dispossession and displacement many subjects undergo, we will need to transform sociality from its structuration in domination. I end with the rather ominous words from Pat Parker, 'and where will you be / when they come?' (Parker, 1978: 210).

Notes

1. bell hooks (1989: 12).
2. On the patronym, Leigh Gilmore refers to it as representing the subject's 'public identity'. The mother's maiden name is considered a private secret, a 'password' that banks can use to identify that a client is not an impostor (Gilmore, 1994: 88).
3. Cf. Teresa de Lauretis, 1994: 85.

7

Early Cinema Lesbians
in and out of the Closet

The Subtext Speaks the Unspeakable:
Rebecca Seeks *Queen Christina*
with Several *Maidens in Uniform*

A lesbian is . . . that which has been unspeakable about women.

Bertha Harris[1]

In this chapter we will look at the subtext of lesbian desire in *Rebecca,* *Queen Christina* and two versions of the German *Mädchen in Uniform,* in conjunction with an exploration of early representations of lesbian desire. We will also look at the lesbian as she has been historically positioned, which has involved attempts to suppress a category of experience, and we will make some links between colonialism and the suppression of subjects entailed by imperialist aggression.

According to Edith Becker *et al.,* subtexting has been the central 'viewing strategy' for lesbians, whose 'knowledge, suspicion or hope' of a lesbian orientation among the cast or crew of a film has allowed us to read lesbian (Becker *et al.,* 1981: 301). It is through gossip, as 'the official unrecorded history' of lesbians in film, that lesbians learn of these possible orientations (*ibid.*). I would suggest that even if the participants are all known to be resolutely heterosexual, we can still read between the lines, supplying lesbian meanings where the gaps in the text allow for such a space. But, as Becker *et al.* point out, 'subtextual readings can be erroneous' (*ibid.*: 302). I think meanings can only be infinite if there is a disconnection between text and subject. However, if one is to stay connected, one must have a correspondence between text and spectator which necessarily limits meanings. Therefore I agree that 'to be convincing', subtextual readings 'must remember to keep the film in sight' (*ibid.*).

Richard Dyer also talks about how we 'practise on movie images what Claude Lévi-Strauss has termed *"bricolage"*, that is, playing around with the elements available to us' for subtexting purposes (Dyer, 1977: 1). And as Cherry Smyth writes, subtexting, also known as reading against the grain, 'began as a wish for inclusion by marginalised, underrepresented people and ended up as a strategy essential for our survival' (Smyth, 1995: 123). Subtexting, here in the sense of supplying lesbian readings, has accordingly been the means of feeding our hunger for imagings of us. As Dagmar (a pseudonym) says, talking of lesbian representations in a *Jump Cut* interview, 'We're so starved' (quoted by Whitaker, 1981: 111). Jane Gaines also suggests that 'positing a lesbian spectator would significantly change the trajectory of the gaze' (Gaines, 1986: 200). So the coincidence of subtexting strategies with a lesbian look suggests that certain texts can allow us to respond with active and split spectating positions.

Let us briefly look at some early representations of homosexual desire. Vito Russo reports that 'the first film to discuss homosexuality openly', *Anders als die Anderen* (*Different from the Others*), was produced and released in 1919 as a result of the first gay liberation movement in pre-war Berlin (Russo, 1987: 19). Commenting on 'the obligatory suicide' at the end of the film of the first gay man on film, Russo notes how 'that would mark the fate of screen gays for years to come' (*ibid.*: 21). Although I begin with the example of the first gay man's film, I do it for landmark reasons, and will stay almost exclusively with lesbian films in this discussion.

Russo identifies the Countess Geschwitz, in the 1929 film *Die Büsche der Pandora* (*Pandora's Box*), as 'probably the first explicitly drawn lesbian character on film' (*ibid.*: 24). British censors excised the film's lesbian content by deleting the character of Geschwitz, and in the United States the initial version of the film that was released did not feature her, although she was later restored to future prints of the film (*ibid.*: 25).

Censorship was to become the major block in the representation of lesbians and gays. Although images of us were available, in the form of 'mannish' women and 'sissy' men, the US Motion Picture Code of 1934 banned references to homosexuality, making representations of us go underground, specifically in the subtext. This code was changed in 1961 and involved a battle against the Motion Picture Association of America, which announced after some confusion that 'homosexuality and other sexual aberrations may now be treated with care, discretion and restraint' (quoted by Russo, 1987: 121–2). The battle was waged on several fronts, and I will recount the impact of *The Children's Hour*, made in 1961.

Here, director William Wyler remade his 1936 version of *These Three*, the first film based on Lillian Hellman's play, and the lesbian content that had been erased from the first film version was now restored. Andrea Weiss recounts how United Artists put pressure on the Hays Office, which was responsible for implementing the code against 'sex perversion', and as a result of some active opposition, it was the code that was altered and not the film that had to be censored (Weiss, 1992: 69–70; Russo, 1987: 120–2).

The Children's Hour (aka *The Loudest Whisper*) ends with a devastating suicide. But this was to be expected. 'In twenty-two of twenty-eight films dealing with gay subjects from 1962 to 1978, major gay characters onscreen ended in suicide or violent death' (Russo, 1987: 52). In 1968, for instance, *The Fox* featured the death of the lesbian played by Sandy Dennis, while her lover exits into heterosex with a male partner. As Russo puts it, 'One lesbian is killed, the other cured' (*ibid*.: 164).

In Britain too, censorship operated to make representations of us a 'taboo' area until the early 1960s (Sheldon, 1987: 89). The first film to treat the subject of male homosexuality with respect was *Victim*, featuring Dirk Bogarde as a repressed homosexual who risks his career to break up a gang of blackmailers responsible for the suicide of a young man he was once attached to. Despite the closeted and traumatic status assigned to a homosexual identity in this film, it offers what was then a rare representation in its sensitivity. From those early moments of out representations, no longer closeted by censorship, grew the beginnings of what has now become a considerable body of film material on lesbians and gay men. But of course this did not evolve overnight, and I will trace earlier examples of lesbian representations, where the subtext speaks the unspeakable.

The haunting by the woman Rebecca, in Alfred Hitchcock's film *Rebecca*, represents the return of the repressed, namely the question of Rebecca's lesbian sexuality as it speaks in the subtext. My discussion will contrast this lesbian subtext with the main characters' happy heterosexuality. The unspoken speaks only to be vilified and destroyed, because it is itself seen as vile and destructive. The overt text of stable heterosexual coupling is complicated by the dead Rebecca, who returns to threaten the relationship. Manderley, the house itself, is haunted by Rebecca and in the end destroyed through her indirect agency.

The unnamed narrator, played by Joan Fontaine, makes an unexpected marriage to Maxim de Winter, handsome, rich and aristocratic, a recent widower said to be broken by the death of Rebecca in a sailing accident at Manderley. Played by Laurence Olivier, de Winter is phallic and fragile at the same time. He falls in love with the young Fontaine, who is clumsy, unconfident, unsophisticated but genuine. They marry and then go to Manderley, his large country house, imposing in its capacious evidence of wealth.

Fontaine meets Mrs Danvers, the housekeeper who is obsessed with Rebecca, her dead mistress. She is both servile and intimidating, conveying to Fontaine that it is Rebecca who still dominates the house with her presence. Mrs Danvers maintains Rebecca's bedroom suite exactly as it used to be, and I am reminded of Miss Haversham in *Great Expectations*. The dead Rebecca lives through Mrs Danvers, and the suggestion of a lesbian sexuality for both women is evident in the text, both of film and novel.

When Rebecca's body is discovered and brought up from the sea, Olivier confesses to Fontaine that he killed her. She insists it was an accident. The question of murder or suicide is brought up by the investigation. Rebecca's favourite cousin, played by George Sanders, gets Mrs Danvers to tell them the name and address of Rebecca's doctor in London, because he thinks she was pregnant with his child. On visiting the doctor, it is confirmed that Rebecca had terminal cancer, thereby establishing a motive for suicide. Olivier is cleared. On returning to Manderley that night, he realizes it is on fire. Mrs Danvers has set it ablaze and is herself consumed by the flames. Olivier and Fontaine are reunited, both safe after their ordeal. The dykes are dead. Long live the hets. Certainly that is my reading of the film's conclusion. The presence of lesbian desire suggested in the subtext must be destroyed so that heterosex can triumphantly proclaim its so-called normality as so-called right.

Let us look at the lesbian subtext again as it contrasts with the overt text of heterosexuality representing an ethical social order. It is precisely on the grounds of Rebecca's lack of ethics that any lesbian leanings are criticized and punished so severely.

The character of Mrs Danvers speaks the subtext of lesbian desire. Called affectionately by the name of 'Danny', she dotes on Rebecca, and is correctly said to be insanely jealous of Fontaine for supplanting the identity of Mrs de Winter, bitterly resentful that she is now the mistress of the house. This devotion bespeaks desire. In the bedroom scene where she fondles Rebecca's underwear, where she reconstructs the memory of Rebecca as vital and desirable, it is clear that she herself is haunted by the woman, whose death represents the repression of her lesbian desire. Later, she refers to the way Rebecca laughed at the lot of them, implying her male lovers, and thereby suggesting there was more to her sexual escapades.

163

This suggestion is confirmed by Olivier, who tells Fontaine he hated Rebecca, that they had a sham marriage with her being sexually promiscuous in London. Although a male presence is deliberately suggested for Rebecca's sexual activity, it is clear that there is a subtext in operation, one that spells lesbian desire.

We can see that Rebecca's crime is not her lesbian activity, but her attempt to bring about Olivier's downfall at her death, by provoking him to kill her. From this point of view, her lack of ethics is not based on lesbian desire, but on her moment of moral corruption at wanting to destroy life because her own is about to expire. However, the problematic considerations around her death are too easily resolved in the film, where Olivier is absolved of all guilt, including manslaughter. In the book, de Winter clearly commits a murder, and this had to be rewritten as an accident to meet the requirements of the Motion Picture Association Code, whose censorship stipulated that murder could not go unpunished. What is clear is that rewriting murder is preferable to speaking lesbian desire. Murder is absolved of guilt while lesbian desire must be punished by death.

With the burying of Rebecca and the burning of Mrs Danvers, the ghost of lesbian desire can be laid, and heterosex can emerge as the restoration of order. So the gauche but genuine Fontaine can fulfil the powerful, but tragic and troubled man with her love. She can help him through the haunting, and support him as he buries the dead. The inequalities of her being inexperienced and poor and him being considerably older and rich are ironed out in the act of sharing love, a common resolution in the traditions of Mills and Boon and Harlequin. I am also reminded of the ending of Charlotte Brontë's *Jane Eyre*, where it is again the agency of the first wife that must be suppressed, in the name of narrative expectations of a satisfying resolution. The right woman gets her man, although their manorial homes are burned down, and, in Jane's case, the man is maimed, a symbolic excision that levels the partners to share a greater equality. In *Rebecca*, Olivier is exorcized of the guilt of carrying the responsibility of murder, which haunts him and which could destroy him, just as Fontaine is released from her fears that Rebecca still lives in Olivier's heart. The ghost can go, and the restoration of order is achieved through the celebration of heterosex.

Weiss comments on how the film 'manages to convey both visually and narratively the sexual deviance of Rebecca de Winter while rendering her literally invisible' (Weiss, 1992: 53). This is achieved through Rebecca as haunting, threatening to return. Given Hitchcock's mastery at manipulating fear and suspense, I think his lack of interest in supernatural horror made him miss the opportunity of developing this haunting on a more mysterious basis. Rebecca's corpse at first is not recovered, and this could have added to the threat of her re-emergence as a rupturing of the heterosexual couple. Consider the famous bedroom scene when Mrs Danvers fondles Joan Fontaine's cheek with Rebecca's furs. There is a suggestion at the beginning of this scene of Rebecca's presence as a spectre, whose haunting includes the opening of windows where later Fontaine will be urged to commit suicide. There is in this central scene another example of the lesbian subtext, where Mrs Danvers tells Fontaine that Olivier lavished furs and expensive presents on Rebecca. On first reading we take this as signalling his heterosexual desires for her. But how are we to read this scene when Olivier himself tells us he loathed Rebecca? In the contradiction we see the potential for subtexting. If Olivier hated Rebecca, such gifts would be a confirmation of his maintaining the sham of their marriage, a sham because she could not return his heterosexual desire. Either Mrs Danvers is lying about the gifts, or there is in this contradiction a space to supply lesbian readings. I imagine the latter. Russo quotes Arthur Laurents, scriptwriter for Hitchcock's *Rope*, featuring two gay men, on how Hitchcock 'was interested in perverse sexuality of any kind, and he used it for dramatic tension' (Laurents, quoted by Russo, 1987: 94).

Mary Wings has analysed the film in relation to the book, and with reference to emerging biographical material on author Daphne du Maurier's lesbianism. She asks, 'Is the narrative of *Rebecca* an elaborate defence against homosexuality? Was *Rebecca* an inner drama related to du Maurier herself? Was killing Rebecca symbolically killing the lesbian impulse?' (Wings, 1994: 13). The question also arises as to what is being served by this subtext. Do we really want to claim Rebecca when her creator herself was so very troubled about her own sexuality, endorsing views of lesbianism as depraved and disgusting? Do we really want to identify with Mrs Danvers? I think not. Rebecca is unethical and Mrs Danvers is unbalanced: neither is a model we would particularly welcome. So the purpose of discussing the lesbian content in the subtext is not to celebrate that they are lesbian, but to see that as a starting point, as a posing of a possibility.

I have suggested elsewhere that by supplying lesbian desire to my reading of filmic texts that are not overtly lesbian, I am filling the gap of what is unrepresented by projecting my own lesbian desire. This has raised some questions from my editor, Jane Greenwood, whom I quote:

> Does this mean that a lesbian subtext can be read only by a lesbian who can supply that desire? Or can a straight woman (or man)

also recognise that subtext without supplying the desire? If so, what
are they supplying to come to that reading?[2]

I find this an illuminating interrogation of the mechanics of the subtext,
and I will explore these questions in conjunction with an analysis of
Queen Christina. This is an example of a film which lesbians have claimed
has a discernible lesbian subtext, a spectating position that I agree with.
What is interesting is that a male heterosexual spectator who has not
been politicized around certain discourses would probably protest our
claim to it as an unjustified pretension. We can account for this dichotomy
of spectatorial positions quite simply by being alert to the politics of desire
as inevitably impacting on our political positionings. As lesbians who can
be feminists, our desires and our politics place us in a separate space from
most men and many women, even those who have been politicized in
similar frames of oppression.

To return to Jane's questions, I think a lesbian subtext need not only
be a result of supplying lesbian desire from the lesbian position. Straight
women and men can be receptive to the subtext, and it is I think their
politicization that enables this receptivity to take place, separately of their
positioning in relation to identifications. Of course politicization in itself
is not a complete solution. Sometimes it can become a mask of adopting
the correct position because of what we know or are told constitutes the
correct line. And politicization is always the site of plural positionalities,
where no preordained 'rights' are attached to any single politics, only a
conviction that our own body of ethics and beliefs are the productive
vehicles for social action. Ethics are the key indicator of one's politics.
An ethics of caring and of exchange is about political inclusion, aligned
to the left, while the reactionary right is premised on a false ethics, based
on what I think are destructive values, such as expediency, exclusion,
exploitation. Although I think there are some subjects who may remain
unknowing of their political positions, or confused in them, their politics
will probably coincide with whatever body of ethics they have incorporated into their identities.

So I would argue that male and female heterosexuals can read the
lesbian subtext in certain films by supplying their politicization to the
text. Although subtexts can be subjective and even unable to prove, it is
the politics one brings to the text that can determine meanings. To return
to the film, a male spectator who insists on its heterosexual content is
probably unpoliticized around the discourses of desire, gender and
sexuality. He might protest that Queen Christina's desire is exclusively
heterosexual because the loved object is a man. Let us deconstruct this

position. First, it is to read desire as singular, not plural, and second, it presupposes that the gender of the love object is always unchanging, as if a heterosexual identity were a fixed entity not subject to alteration. Such a reading fixes the object of desire in a grip of permanence, when we know that the object can be transitory.

I will summarize the film and refer only to key scenes. Greta Garbo plays Queen Christina of Sweden, who came to the throne as a young girl. She has suffered from her country's history of warfare, with her father dying in battle and her own reign troubled by years of war. She is a woman of culture who reads Molière and appreciates Velázquez. She represents the female values of peace and reconstruction, and she is able to quell bloodthirsty calls for war. Rather than persist in male values of aggression, she initiates alliances with other European monarchs.

She is unmarried and there is pressure for her to provide an heir to the throne. The Lord Treasurer pursues her, the people clamour for her marriage to an elderly national hero who is her cousin, and the King of Spain proposes to her, but she resists them all, and becomes infatuated with the Spanish ambassador, Antonio. At the end, she abdicates from the throne so she can live in Spain with him. When he is killed after a duel, she sails away regardless from the throne of Sweden to the beginnings of a life unmarred by public pressure. She has allowed desire and not duty to determine how she will live, and she has the autonomy to achieve her ends.

Let us look more closely at the question of Queen Christina's desire, with reference to two relationships. First there is Countess Ebba, a rare woman in a court dominated by male presence. We have the famous kiss on the lips at their first meeting, too brief for some, but enough to convey lesbian desire. We read from this kiss that it is not a first kiss, there have been other kisses, and from that we can read there have been other women as well, also with kisses. Why is this so important? Because it spells the possibility of lesbian desire.

A kiss is just a kiss. But in the context of a blanket censorship of representations of lesbian desire, that kiss comes to signify all that cannot be said elsewhere, the unspoken text of the film resident in its subtext. Here, lesbian desire supplies clarity to the reading. There is, for instance, an ambiguity about their previous relationship which emerges in the way the two women have a misunderstanding and temporarily fall out. We again read in lesbian desire to explain the extent of the rage Christina feels at Countess Ebba's apparent betrayal.

I do not wish to deny that heterosexual desire also operates in the film, but I do wish to deconstruct it. Antonio, the male love object, can himself be deconstructed to question heterosexual desire as inevitably phallic. It is precisely his feminization that makes him attractive to Christina. He is cultured, enjoys talking, is a romantic who can negotiate emotions, all the attributes that the other men in Christina's life so sadly lack. I would suggest that his feminization raises questions about the logic of heterosex. Do heterosexuals all and always have intercourse? Is the necessary definition of who they are predicated on there being penile penetration, possibly in the missionary position, with mutual orgasm the ultimate goal/grail they seek? I would prefer to apply the philosophical position of 'necessary doubt' that Colin Wilson explores in an unusual detective novel of that name. Just as lesbian history has been preoccupied with the question of whether 'we did it', so the representation of heterosex can also raise the question of 'did they do it?' By applying the same necessary doubt to the heterosexual representation of Christina's desire, we can see that its apparent endorsement of the phallic is really a feminization of the phallic. We have considered how Antonio is feminized though he is not effeminate. In the same way, Christina is phallicized, her male costume and her status as sovereign invest her with power, but she herself can be seen as transcending gender, incorporating the best of masculinities and femininities.

Echoing a line from the film, where Christina says 'It is possible to feel nostalgia for a place one has never seen', Russo finds that the film 'created in gay people a nostalgia for something they had never seen onscreen' (Russo, 1987: 65). Rather than confirming the heterosexual order, Weiss finds that the ending offers the possibility of subtextual readings, with 'her inscrutable Garbo face contradicting the aims of narrative closure' (Weiss, 1992: 46). Weiss confirms that while heterosexual spectators might affirm a heterosexual conclusion, lesbian spectators would see the ending as 'rejecting the heterosexual social order' (ibid.).

Lillian Faderman's historical documentation supports a lesbian reading of Christina's desire. Her 'masculine dress and sexual advances to women were recorded' in the letters of her numerous contemporaries in Paris, where she lived for a while after her abdication (Faderman, 1981: 55). Faderman argues that this instance of known lesbian activity in the seventeenth century was acceptable insofar as Christina evaded punishment due to her 'exalted birth' (ibid.), where her royal status and wealth gave her a freedom not widely available to women.

The film's ending reminds me of the ending of Charlotte Brontë's *Villette*, where the hardy heroine Lucy Snowe has survived to become an autonomous subject, and faces the future alone on the death of a male love object. We know Lucy will suffer emotionally from this loss. But both she and Christina have attained an autonomy by escaping the constraints that serve to subordinate them, and they are freed to act as subjects of their own desire. The subtext of lesbian desire speaks in Queen Christina's need to transgress the parameters of what others find acceptable behaviour, and in her transgression of the social order that dictates a desire she cannot meet, we see the beginnings of alternative practices around sexuality and sociality. Unlike most women of her epoch, she is freed to follow the transgressive pleasures of lesbian desire, independently of family pressure, a male partner, the demands of marriage and children, or debilitating financial constraints. Autonomy indeed. One that speaks to all subjects, especially black lesbians, who have been divested of our claims to an equal subjectivity, and whose attempts to achieve and maintain our autonomy are always under threat.

In one key exchange, Antonio asks Christina if she believes in a 'great love'. She says she believes in its 'possibility' but not in its 'existence'. This for me crystallizes the 'activity' versus 'identity' debate, where the possibility of acting on lesbian desire has always been there, but the existence of a lesbian identity is only a recent phenomenon, and still only relatively accessible to some of us.

I will now explore the subject of lesbian history by initially differentiating between acts of lesbian sex and instances of lesbian identity. As Rosa Ainley asks, 'Is it what we are or what we do?' (Ainley, 1995: 25). John D'Emilio makes the distinction between act and identity, so that 'homosexual *behavior* . . . is different from homosexual *identity*' (D'Emilio, 1984: 144; original emphases). Jeffrey Weeks also differentiates between the two, where homosexual behaviour is 'universal' while a homosexual identity is 'historically specific' (Weeks, 1977: 3). While we can acknowledge that we have always been here, our identifications as homosexual and lesbian have only recently become possible, and only in some geographical and cultural locations.

I agree with commentators who argue that it was the political impact of first-wave feminisms which enabled women to aspire to equality in the nineteenth century and that their seizing of educational and employment opportunities gave them an independence from men. 'The New Woman challenged existing gender relations and the distribution of power' (Smith-Rosenberg, 1985: 265). Carroll Smith-Rosenberg appropriates the term 'New Woman' and applies it to the middle- and upper-middle-class white American women who were born in the second half of the nineteenth century and whose achievements spelt 'the symbolic death of that earlier female subject, the refined and confined Victorian lady' (*ibid.*). This effectively meant the demise of the asexuality ascribed to women from the eighteenth century, when 'a good woman' was 'sexually dormant', an idea that the nineteenth century dictated 'with a vengeance' (Faderman, 1981: 154). Faderman records how many women had intimate friendships which were socially acceptable because they were seen as a good training ground for marriage, and mere preliminaries to a heterosexual partnership. Although these women would openly express their undying love for their female friends, although 'they might kiss, fondle each other, sleep together', Faderman suggests that for the majority, their intimacy would not have been sexual in the sense of involving genital contact (*ibid*.: 16). Such an argument is premised on the ascriptions of the woman's incapacity to experience desire.

It was in the nineteenth century, around the time that women were gaining some small social ascendance, that theories came to be formulated where 'the sexual is discovered as a key to the social' (Weeks, 1985: 74). In 1869, the word 'homosexual' was coined by a Hungarian, Karoly Maria Benkert (Weeks, 1977: 3). This was the same year that Carl von Westphal defined the female homosexual as a 'congenital invert', who was abnormal because of 'hereditary degeneration and neurosis' (Faderman, 1981: 239). Richard von Krafft-Ebing concurred that homosexuality was 'an inherited diseased condition' and 'a functional sign of degeneration' (Krafft-Ebing, quoted by Faderman, 1981: 241).

There has been some controversy over the 'naming' that was taking place in the sexologists' discourse. Weeks suggests that the categorizations and classifications of homosexual behaviour were meant to explain the behaviour and not to create it (Weeks, 1985: 94). He also argues that although the power of defining others that the sexologists held meant that homosexual subjects internalized these definitions, there was also a place for challenge (*ibid*.: 95). Most feminist commentators have found that the work of the sexologists was not so much liberating as morbidifying, where the pathologization of lesbians meant we had to adopt self-imagings of ourselves as perverts.

Havelock Ellis followed the lead and found that female homosexuality was pathological (Faderman, 1981: 241). He distinguished between the 'true invert', the real lesbian, and the pseudo-lesbian, the heterosexual woman who had temporarily given in to her attractions for women but who could be seduced back into the heterosexual fold. As Smith-Rosenberg points out, this made the 'true' lesbian or 'congenital invert' appear 'as a woman on the make, sexually and racially dangerous' (Smith-Rosenberg, 1985: 270).

Ellis saw the women's movement as having the result of increasing female insanity and female criminality, and creating the conditions for an increase in female homosexuality (Faderman, 1981: 242; Smith-Rosenberg, 1985: 271). In 1910, the feminist movement became more militant and in 1911 Edward Carpenter confirmed the links between feminism and lesbianism (Faderman, 1981: 337). By the 1920s, accusations of lesbianism were used to discredit independent women and the work they were doing (Smith-Rosenberg, 1985: 272). Smith-Rosenberg argues that the second generation of New Women learned no sexual language from their foremothers, and had no alternative but to accept the sexual discourse of the sexologists, although this now classified them as perverts if they expressed a desire outside of marriage and motherhood (*ibid*.: 273). As Celia Kitzinger says, 'The effect of the new science of sexology was to scare women back into marriage and conformity with fears of abnormality' (Kitzinger, 1987: 42).

Let us look at lesbianism in relation to law in Europe. Weeks reports that lesbians are absent from West European criminal codes, with the exception of one ineffectual piece of legislation in Germany (Weeks, 1977: 4–5). Weeks records the attempt by Parliament to criminalize lesbians in 1921. The House of Commons passed a clause which would have extended the 1885 Labouchère Amendment on male homosexuality to lesbians. Members of the House of Lords were alarmed that such a law would draw attention to what 999 out of 1,000 women would never have heard of, and they rejected the clause, which was not raised again (*ibid*.: 106–7). Some seven years later, in 1928, with the publicity generated by the prosecution of Radclyffe Hall's *The Well of Loneliness* under the Obscene Publications Act of 1857, lesbianism was put on the map in a way which the Lords had tried to forestall (*ibid*.: 108–9; cf. Bland, 1983: 21). We see in these efforts an attempt to suppress knowledge and render a category of experience invisible. Adrienne Rich's important essay 'Compulsory Heterosexuality and Lesbian Existence' details the main ways lesbian existence has been denied, through repression and invisibility. She categorizes some of the ways the institution of heterosexuality has been maintained, through a vast machinery of male power over women (A. Rich, 1980: 218–19). She challenges the presumptions of heterosexuality and argues that 'a feminist critique of compulsory heterosexual orientation for women is long overdue' (*ibid*.: 213).

To return to the question of activity versus identity, although from the early twentieth century there was some space, albeit limited, for lesbians to identify themselves, it seems bizarre to think that lesbian activity would only have emerged then. Evidence from Africa, Asia, and Native America suggests that lesbian activity had long been taking place (Gomez and

Smith, 1990: 48; Mason-John and Khambatta, 1993: 19–20; P. G. Allen, 1986: 107). Although white women in the nineteenth century were seen as asexual, I think this lack of interest for some was in heterosex, and that they may well have found sexual pleasures together. Faderman recounts that the phenomenon of romantic friendships used the language of heterosexual love, but she finds that these relationships 'were probably often without a realized genital component' (Faderman, 1981: 72). I prefer to think that some women may well have had a sufficiently independent subjectivity to realize sexual pleasures together, although 'genital connection is hard to prove' (Jeffreys, 1993: 8). Sheila Jeffreys argues that we need not transpose 'a contemporary lesbian identity or a determinedly non-genital one' onto these earlier women but may keep the question open (Jeffreys, 1989: 27). If I express my preference for there having been genital contact, this is not because I deny the sexual nature of intimacies such as kissing, caressing and cuddling, but because I see it as an affirmation of the intellectual and imaginative leap that feminists must make in order to remain at the vanguard of progressive movements in the face of perpetual backlash.

It is in the context of a lack of autonomy, of acute powerlessness, that the first cinema speakings of lesbian desire were heard. In the two versions of *Mädchen in Uniform* (*Maidens in Uniform*) that I now discuss, the subtext of lesbian desire erupts to the surface of the overt text, indeed it is this outing that constitutes the crime. Same-sex crushes in the girls' boarding schools are acknowledged by staff and students alike, even tolerated. But a lesbian desire that dares name itself, that publicly announces its possibility, must be ejected and suppressed. B. Ruby Rich refers to the 1931 original version as the 'first truly radical lesbian film' (1981: 102), and she states 'It is the *naming* of that which may well be known, this claiming of what is felt by the public speaking of its name, that is expressly forbidden' (*ibid.*: 110; original emphasis). In her analysis, Rich locates the film as originating in Germany's Weimar Republic when women, lesbians and gays had a brief blossoming of political activity before the emergence of the Nazis under Hitler. She documents how pre-war Berlin was known for its libertarian attitudes to sexual activity, 'the Berlin with dozens of gay and lesbian bars and journals' (*ibid.*: 100). Dyer agrees that Berlin 'probably deserved its reputation as the sex capital of the world' (Dyer, 1990: 8). He points out that *Different from Others* (1919) and *Maidens* (1931), the first gay and lesbian films, were made more or less at the beginning and end of the Weimar Republic respectively (*ibid.*: 7), and that this was in the context of 'a general openness about sexuality in German cinema' (*ibid.*: 8).

While *Mädchen* is clearly a lesbian film, Rich has found that its reputation as 'an antiauthoritarian and prophetically antifascist film' has obscured its lesbian content (B. R. Rich, 1981: 101), and her reading puts lesbianism back on the map as 'the film's properly central subject' (*ibid.*: 102). Caroline Sheldon also found that critics have emphasized the film's antifascism, 'burying the lesbianism of its content' (Sheldon, 1977: 21). A film which nearly disappeared because of Nazi suppression, in the 1970s it was rediscovered and 'embraced by lesbian viewers who were thrilled to see such a strong proclamation of erotic desire between women' (Weiss, 1992: 9).

What *Mädchen* evidences is the regulation of desire, a policing of it through regimentation and control. The first images of young women in identical school uniform, marching in line with heads bowed, shows militarism at work, compounded by endless regulations, a starvation diet, black-mark books and the threat of punishment. The young girls' own clothes are taken away, they are not allowed to keep money, and they are forbidden personal books. Outings are a rarity. This regime of discipline is in conjunction with images of phallic power in statues of male national heroes, deep staircases, imposing buildings, steeples, clock towers and churches, all resonant of male power and all resounding to the ringing of bells marking time as regulation. The Spartan regime is insisted on by the school's headmistress, who believes affection is a luxury, preferring authority and terror in the way she rules. Such institutions do exist, and in this case its militarism is founded on its being a school for soldiers' children, some poor, some orphaned, and all defenceless.

Manuela arrives as a new girl, and within minutes she meets Ilse, a rebellious young woman who jokingly warns her not to fall in love with her teacher, Fräulein Elisabeth von Bernburg, with whom many of the young women are infatuated. When we first see the teacher we know why immediately, as she has presence and beauty, affection and attitude. Manuela is understandably charmed, and falls under the teacher's spell immediately. In class the two are aware of each other, and Manuela's desire is evident in the nervous way she forgets her lessons when interrogated, even though she has prepared them. Manuela comes out to von Bernburg about her desire. She loves her and wants to come to her at night, but there is such a distance between them. The Fräulein counters that she cannot make exceptions or the other girls would be jealous. She does admit that she thinks of Manuela often.

So lesbian desire is out. But when it is expressed publicly in the spirit of defiance and resists attempts to repress it, this lesbian desire becomes a crime. After the performance of a school play in which Manuela dressed as a man makes verbal love to a woman, the girls get drunk on some potent punch. Manuela announces to all the girls present that the Fräulein cares for her. She is heard by the headmistress, who is scandalized at the way lesbian desire has spoken the unspeakable. In Dyer's words, 'it makes that experience public. It is a coming out' (Dyer, 1990: 29). The headmistress wants to expel her, but due to a contrivance, she decides instead that Manuela is to be punished by being isolated by the girls, who are ordered to ignore her. But the girls refuse to ostracize Manuela, and their refusal to obey this order is the first direct disobedience that they commit in solidarity. It is this agency that saves Manuela from dying in a suicide attempt. The films ends with a lack of closure or completion, as we wonder what will happen now that lesbian desire is out. Will the Fräulein leave the school, as she tells the headmistress? Will Manuela be able to recover from the loss?

Manuela's crime is that she declares her lesbian desire openly, she speaks the unspeakable. She is looking for explanations, definitions, some accounting of her desire, but all the Fräulein can say is, 'You are not allowed to love me . . . so much.' To Manuela's question 'Why not?', she is told, 'You must go now', and this dismissal of her desire makes her decide to attempt suicide. Throughout the film there is some excellent intercutting of material, and at the precise moment of the suicide attempt, the Fräulein is telepathically aware of Manuela's danger, indicating a degree of mergence.

I would like to consider the film's treatment of lesbian desire, not as spoken but as subtext, from the point of view of the Fräulein's desire. While the overt text names lesbian desire, the subtext also supports it, by suggesting that the Fräulein too is a subject of lesbian desire, that she too actively desires Manuela. When the teacher first sees the young new pupil, she is of course in a position of considerable power, and this is conveyed to us by her positioning as voyeur. To begin with, she sees Manuela but is not seen by her. Her gaze is of the observer unobserved, and in the power of her look we read the impact she has as a potential m/other, the object who can complete the self. The Fräulein must know how the girls are fixated on her, and she cannot be surprised at Manuela's attraction. What makes her also an implicit desirous subject is that she is seduced by Manuela's attraction for her, precisely because the young girl's desire is so explicit. The phenomenon of attraction by one can lead to the seduction of the other. The teacher knows Manuela has no mother, and can probably understand how she herself has come to stand in for the m/other. I agree with Dyer that 'the mother–daughter quality of the relationship only makes it more lesbian, not less' (Dyer, 1990: 40). In knowing she is the object of love and desire, might the teacher also want to return what she receives in an economy of mutual giving?

Let us consider the subject of lesbian desire further, with the kiss. It takes place during a ritual enacted each night at lights out, when the teacher kisses each girl good night on the forehead, something they value as precious, a token acknowledgement of their desire for her.[3] When Manuela's turn comes round and she desires more, the teacher kisses her on the lips, her hands seductively touching her neck. It is significant that there is no response of outcry or jealousy in the dormitory at this kiss, which helps render it innocent. However, for a lesbian spectator at a historical point in cinema where lesbian desire is only just beginning to be accessed in the mainstream, this one kiss is enough to speak volumes about our hunger for images that endorse our desire.

When we consider this kiss in the context of film-making codes of censorship, which account for our invisibility in the majority of films until the 1960s, and our pathologization in the few that did refer to our sexualities until recently, we can read the possibility of desire not just being named, but being returned. The teacher defends Manuela's desire to the headmistress: 'What you call sins I call the great spirit of love, in all its forms.' Significantly, this line had to be deleted to satisfy Hollywood censors (Russo, 1987: 58; Weiss, 1992: 11). Like the headmistress, they would not tolerate 'revolutionary ideas'. The teacher in a sense is a revolutionary, who stands by her set of alternative practices despite the prohibitions of the prevailing discourse. She wants equality with her pupils, not authority and distance. She wants trust and affection, not discipline and punishment. She is appreciated because she gets good results, but her methods are criticized. However, although I read her as a desirous subject, she too is controlled by the ethos that would suppress lesbian desire. Rich makes the important point that the teacher is an agent of control, insofar as the girls' desire and adoration for her from a distance serve to divert them from acting on desire more intimately with the other girls who are more accessible to them, and who might return their desire (B. R. Rich, 1981: 106). The teacher acts to focus their desire by being the safe object that carries it without returning it. Although we can read desire in her response to Manuela and her resistance to the headmistress, it is a closet desire, residing in the subtext. It is Manuela's desire that speaks out, that seeks confirmation in the absence of available explanations.

Russo details how American censors first refused to allow *Mädchen* to be screened, and then accepted a revised version, where cuts were agreed to obscure the relationship between Manuela and von Bernburg (Russo, 1987: 56–8). Russo reports how the censors cut out the lesbianism, how the critics did not see it, and how 'anyone who still saw it was labeled a pervert' (*ibid.*: 58). As Weiss says of this, linking it to the conditions of censorship that were maintained for some thirty years, 'lesbianism would be tolerated as subtext but any spoken pronouncement of desire, like Manuela's for Fräulein von Bernburg, was "expressly forbidden"' (Weiss, 1992: 11).

Sheldon documents how there were two versions of the film, with different endings, one a rescue, the other a suicide (Sheldon, 1977: 21). That Manuela is prevented from killing herself is a powerful endorsement of lesbian desire, and I agree with Rich that 'Manuela's rescue at the end represents a social legitimation of her passion' (B. R. Rich, 1981: 113). Rich celebrates the fact that the film ends with a 'provisional' victory, but as she notes, the ominous encroachment of the outside order threatens this victory (*ibid.*: 116). Given what was to follow with the rise of the Nazis and the horrors of the Holocaust, Rich concludes that we cannot afford to ignore or repeat history now (*ibid.*: 126). I agree that at this critical juncture of a new millennium, we need to learn from the past so we can avert the same mistakes as we proceed into the future.

Now, to link up some of this material with the subject of colonialism, in order to make clear the connections between diverse practices that attempt to suppress categories of experience by imposing and instituting oppressive regimes. These practices involve hypocrisy and deceit. For instance, Liam O'Dowd references 'the duplicity of the European bourgeoisie' (O'Dowd, 1990: 32). He quotes Aimé Césaire on Europe's response to the horrors of the Holocaust, where the unforgivable crime was the

> crime against the white man, the humiliation of the white man, and the fact that he (Hitler) applied to Europe colonialist procedures which until then had been reserved exclusively for the Arabs of Algeria, the coolies of India and the blacks of Africa.
> (Césaire, quoted by O'Dowd, 1990: 32)

This linking of the Nazi atrocities with the atrocities of slavery and imperialism serves to contextualize them as belonging to similar paradigms of oppression, namely persecution and exploitation. Albert Memmi also links colonialism with fascism, where 'colonialism is one variety of fascism' (Memmi, 1957: 128–9). He refutes the simplistic assertion that colonialism had beneficial effects on the colonized (*ibid.*: 178–9). A. Sivanandan is also clear that 'colonialism perverts the economy of the colonies to its own ends' (Sivanandan, 1982: 102), a point with which Amrit Wilson concurs (1978: 10).

And yet, despite historical evidence to the contrary, racist ideologies persist in maintaining a doublethink over their savage practices, which are projected onto the colonized. Homi Bhabha confirms that the object of colonial discourse is to see the native as degenerate so as to justify domination (Bhabha, 1994: 70). Avtar Brah reports that 'the Raj was legitimated by the ideology of the "civilizing mission"' (Brah, 1993: 69). Rozina Visram documents how it was seen as the 'moral duty' of this mission to reform India's 'barbaric' practices (Visram, 1986: 6). The British were convinced that they were 'culturally and racially superior' to their colonized subjects (*ibid.*). Because the status of women is taken as an indicator of a society's level of civilization, the British saw women's low status in India 'as another example of the backwardness of Indian civilisation' (Visram, 1992: 12). In the name of progressive reform carried out to save us from our backward practices, British rule sought to carry out social improvements for women. For instance, reforms were carried out around suttee, which was an example of atrocity against women, one which received widespread condemnation. However, the issue of suttee was confined to a tiny part of the population and reform affected only a few women. There were other serious questions to address, but in fact there was 'an erosion in the position of women' as a result of so-called reforms (*ibid.*: 12–14).

Kumari Jayawardena also confirms that the reform movement in India was based on assumptions that 'social reform and female education' were useful insofar as they would 'preserve the patriarchal family system' (Jayawardena, 1986: 79). The function of education, for instance, was to make women into good homemakers (*ibid.*: 88). In India and elsewhere, the ideal of monogamy was exalted for the purpose of turning bourgeois women into good housewives (*ibid.*: 15).

Hazel Carby confirms that 'far from introducing more "progressive" or liberating sex/gender social relations', colonialism 'sedimented racist and sexist norms' (Carby, 1982: 226). She suggests that women in Britain benefited 'from the economic exploitation of the colonies' in different degrees (*ibid.*: 221–2). Anne McClintock endorses this view by finding that white women were 'ambiguously complicit' with colonialism (McClintock, 1995: 6). Amina Mama refers to how, in the early 1980s, she 'coined the term "imperial feminism" to indicate the much-denied historical participation of white women in the colonial and racial domination of black people' (Mama, 1995: 12). The consensus of these commentators is that white women have not yet adequately addressed their complicity or even compliance with the project of imperialism. Valerie Amos and Pratibha Parmar also challenge white feminists, whose 'herstory' suffers from 'the same form of historical amnesia of white male historians, by ignoring the fundamental ways in which white women have benefited from the oppression of Black people' (Amos and Parmar, 1984: 5). This 'historical amnesia' extends to our own histories of struggle, so that 'the fact that Black people were said to have no history conveniently stripped them of a whole tradition of struggle' (*ibid.*: 10).

One way for racist ideologies to address these colonial projections and falsifications would be of course to recognize them in that guise. That would be a beginning and would entail a rewriting of history which has already begun. Such a reinterpretation necessitates the prioritizing of black women's voices and the acknowledgement of our contributions. Parita Trivedi writes, 'The role of women in revolutionary forms of protest is not acknowledged enough' (Trivedi, 1984: 42). Jayawardena confirms that women in India had 'another tradition of militancy' (Jayawardena, 1986: 108), which took the form of active resistance to the British presence. These women, hundreds and thousands of whom were imprisoned and harassed, are mainly nameless. Even the many women who were known for their acts of resistance occupy only the 'footnotes of history' while male heroes dominate the national consciousness (*ibid.*: 23). In a similar omission in African-American history, black male slaves have been celebrated while black women slaves are rendered invisible in their 'multiple jeopardy' (Stetson, 1982: 62). As the memorable title indicates, *All the Women Are White, All the Blacks Are Men, But Some of Us Are Brave*. Despite our erasure, black women are brave and valuable, and we seek inclusion. We do not wish to dominate through evoking guilt nor do we invite victim-blaming. We seek inclusion in a way which would allow us to articulate a social order where we recognise that All of Us Are Brave. This would entail the eradication of oppressive structures that seek to suppress our subjectivities.

The connections are there for us to make. Just as the horrors of slavery and colonialism came home to Europe with the Nazi atrocities, so the same forces are at work in the oppression of subjects today. Just one facet of this entire fabric of false history and brutal practices can be found in the condition of women today. It is the same process at work that aims to render women ineffectual and lesbians invisible. We really cannot afford to keep on making the same mistakes.

Mädchen in Uniform was remade in 1958. The threat of fascism had become a concrete danger with the rise of the Nazis, and the Second

World War was still recent history. The first film's anti-fascist look at militarism is reconfirmed in the second film, and the regimentation of behaviour, the policing of desire, the punishing of transgression, are similar to both texts. I will concentrate on some of the differences in the two films, to show how the declaration of desire speaks the unspeakable even more explicitly in the later film.

The evocation of girls' boarding-school life in this version has incorporated the same characteristics of such a life, where fighting, rivalry and jealousy among girls exist just as much as affection, intimacy and loyalty between them. Moreover, the overt text is lesbian desire. There is no misunderstanding or confusion about Manuela's declaration of love for Fräulein von Bernburg. What I have read as the subtext of the teacher's desire in the first film is spelled out clearly in this film, where her sexuality as active and desirous is a development on the earlier Fräulein's more sexually neutral persona.

The major differences between the two films centre around the kiss and the ending, so I will concentrate on what these differences convey. The outing of lesbian desire has moved from the subtext to the surface text, where it is the teacher's desire that is under scrutiny, not just Manuela's, as an active hungering for lesbian pleasure.

For one thing, the kiss is completely different, showing a historical shift away from innocence to guilt, from affection to desire. Is the crime the fact that lesbian desire can dare speak itself? Or is it the possibility of lesbian desire not merely being spoken but being returned that constitutes too much of a threat? In the earlier film, this kiss took place in the dormitory and was received by the other girls as lacking signification, which indicates that lesbian desire is still in the subtext. In the later film, the kiss is different: it is in private and subject to concealment. It evokes a brief eroticism that spells active lesbian desire.

Manuela acts as Romeo in the scene where he first meets Juliet at the ball, and they exchange their first kiss. She is alone in the room with the Fräulein, who reads Juliet's lines. On cue, Manuela kisses her, on the lips, and the moment is charged with desire. I definitely read that the teacher returns the lesbian desire in those lips. Later, when Manuela is on stage performing the same line, she kisses Juliet in the prescribed place, and this is met with audience approval. Because Manuela is divested of her uniform which represents her subjugation, because she is in the costume of a male and has the sanction of performance to stand across gender, she can liberate lesbian desire with a public kiss. It is interesting to remember that Elizabethan actors were all males, so that Juliet would have been played by a young man and homoeroticism would have been understood in a kiss. Here this is given a gender twist by making all the actors female, so that it becomes lesbian desire we can read in the kiss.

The ending of the film also provides a stark contrast insofar as the headmistress is somewhat redeemed and implores that the Fräulein stay with them. But the teacher knows this would be an untenable position, and I think this is because she is aware of her own desire. She leaves so that Manuela can recover without the problematic of her presence speaking a desire she cannot act upon. We can read that Manuela will survive without the Fräulein, and we can hope that what she has spoken as a possibility can find reciprocation with an actual other subject of lesbian desire. What could be a possibility can be translated into a reality so that the possibility of lesbian desire can lead toward an eventual lesbian identity. Because Manuela's desire is out, because it has been spoken, it has become speakable, and can be respoken, and returned.

Let us look briefly at the institution of girls' boarding-schools. Rich refers to them as the 'Achilles' heel of patriarchy' (B. R. Rich, 1981: 105). Sheldon calls them 'those notorious hotbeds of adolescent lesbianism!!' (Sheldon, 1977: 16). Rosemary Auchmuty reports how Ellis had considered such same-sex places as creating 'the ideal conditions for lesbianism to flourish' (Auchmuty, 1992: 136–7). Martha Vicinus reports that there were many slang words for a crush in the late nineteenth and early twentieth centuries to describe the phenomenon in girls' boarding-schools, including 'rave', 'spoon', 'smash' and 'flame' (Vicinus, 1985: 47). She argues that 'the rave flourished on a paradox of fulfillment through unrequited love', where distance fuelled desire (ibid.: 51). Vicinus finds that relationships between teachers and students would probably have remained on the level of spiritual communion. Because of the ascription of female asexuality, there were no suspicions of sexual activity despite the commonplace incidence of shared beds. Auchmuty reports that in 1924, references to sharing beds in boarding-school stories were still admissible because it was seen as innocent, where girls 'tuck in' together (Auchmuty, 1992: 114). Such references were omitted in later editions because of the pathologization of lesbians that had taken place (ibid.). Auchmuty finds that the appeal of these girls' boarding-school stories is in their offering, 'in a patriarchal society, a rare vision of a women-only world' (ibid.: 15).

More recently, we have gratefully enjoyed visual imagings of us and have gladly received what is now becoming a proliferation of lesbian representations in film. Mainstream cinema is only slowly waking up to this 'new' phenomenon. Art cinema has had a more sustained interest in lesbianism because of its greater ease in treating subjects of a sexual nature.

Since the 1970s, independent lesbian film-makers like Barbara Hammer and Jan Oxenberg have built up a prolific repertoire of lesbian imagings outside the mainstream. And of course, lesbians in pornography for heterosexual men have been what Dyer calls a 'commonplace' (Dyer, 1977: 2). Russo confirms that lesbian activity in pornography is a mere preliminary to the '"real" event', heterosex (Russo, 1987: 6). Sheldon notes how the avant-garde tradition has concentrated on male homosexuality, while lesbians have been relegated to pornography (Sheldon, 1977: 8).

Admittedly, representations of lesbians have changed, and for the better if we take the issue of visibility as a primary concern. However, certain dangers attach to this interest in lesbians in film. But I think possibly a major myth is being dismantled, where 'lesbianism is usually shown as an aberration, an individual psycho-social problem' (*ibid*.: 5). This is now being recast, so that lesbianism is represented as a healthy and not a sick desire. To redefine lesbian desire in affirmative terms would be a central concern in responsible representations of us. In this framework, what Teresa de Lauretis calls 'an aesthetic of reception' is of crucial importance, 'where the spectator is the film's primary concern', allowing for an audience to be 'envisaged in its heterogeneity and otherness from the text' (de Lauretis, 1987: 141). We have seen how this shifts the emphasis of producing meaning away from the text and onto the spectator, and this to me is an acknowledgement of activities such as subtexting as valid spectatorial positions.

As lesbians gain more media attention and screen space, it is important to maximize on the inroads we have made. We have to remember that where we are now is a legacy of some twenty-five to thirty years of campaigning, of creating spaces to be safely out in, of fighting for visibility and refusing the internalization of hatred, monstrosity and perversion. Although lesbians have always been here, much of our history has been written out, and it is only in the last few decades that we have so far successfully documented our existence in significant numbers. The terms of Clause 28 in the Local Government Bill of 1988 against the 'promotion of homosexuality' in schools by local authorities had the effect of making the lesbian and gay community rally forth in mass mobilizing. Although the Clause was passed, and became Section 28 of the Local Government Act 1988, it was seen by some gay activists as the possible scoring of 'an own goal' by its supporters (quoted by Smyth, 1992: 16). It served to publicize our presence nationally and internationally, and there was a sense that if we were provoking such reactionary legislation, we must indeed be posing a radical threat.

From the Gay Liberation Front to the Campaign for Homosexual Equality, from Stonewall (1969) to DAFT (Dykes and Faggots Together), from Stonewall to OutRage!, from Lesbian Strength to Pride, from Lesbian Nation to Queer Nation, from LABIA (Lesbians Answer Back In Anger) to FROCS (Faggots Rooting Out Closeted Sexuality), from *Outwrite* to Sisterwrite, from *Out on Tuesday* to *Dyke TV*, from ACT UP to the Lesbian Avengers, from the London Lesbian and Gay Centre to the Black Lesbian and Gay Centre, from Shakti to Zamimass, lesbians and gay men have met, merged and mobilized around the issue of sexual identity, among others. In the 1990s, queer is now here as an assertion of difference as well as an inclusion of different identities. No longer just about gay, lesbian, dyke, the term 'queer' incorporates bisexuals, transvestites and transsexuals in what is theoretically a move in the direction of solidarity. Although there is a danger that inclusion more often results in an exclusion of difference, queer promises not to court assimilation. If this is for the purposes of transformation, I think this is a viable positioning. If it is for the purposes of transgression for the sake of shock value, without the objective of social transformation, its radical edge will have been foreclosed and it too will risk its own recuperation, where its reclamation of the radical could be co-opted within the dominant order.

To conclude with de Lauretis, she affirms the productive conjunction between feminism and film practice and suggests that we are now closer to being able 'to construct the terms of reference of another measure of desire and the conditions of visibility for a different social subject' (de Lauretis, 1984: 155). I would want to urge all subjects to see that while we are subjected, we are also capable of agentic capacities, specifically with reference to making changes, beginning with ourselves and working outwards. To borrow from Yeats, the centre will not hold. What we need is a dramatic global transformation before the social fabric can aspire to some semblance of cohesion, and before all subjects can insist on our rights, precisely the right to an equal subjectivity.

Notes

1. Bertha Harris, quoted by Bonnie Zimmerman (1981: 193).
2. From a letter from Jane Greenwood to me dated 14 September 1995.
3. Martha Vicinus reports how admired teachers had 'social permission' to kiss girls good night, a tradition operating at schools such as Roedean (Vicinus, 1985: 52).

8

Lesbian Spectating of Film

Extratext, Subtext, Intertext, Interdiscourse:
Desperately Seeking Susan at the *Bagdad Café*
Looking for *Salmonberries* and *Fire*

Theories of representation may have to come to terms with discursive formations of the social, cultural and textual.

Annette Kuhn[1]

In this examination of spectating positions in *Desperately Seeking Susan*, *Bagdad Café* and *Salmonberries*, I will offer instances of extratexting, subtexting and intertexting to demonstrate the usefulness of such devices for reading cinematic texts. Discursive constructions of the subject take place on a terrain of contestation and struggle, and I will suggest that it is through the interdiscursive, or meeting-points between different discursive practices, that we can acknowledge the plural specificities of the social subject. I also discuss *Fire* in relation to the position of the Indian lesbian.

To begin, we need to clarify the distinction between the spectator as 'subject' and as 'viewer', which Judith Mayne separates as 'position' and 'person' respectively (Mayne, 1993: 8). 'Subject' corresponds to the way s/he is positioned in relation to the cinematic codes and conventions s/he receives. The assumption has been to see such a subject as largely 'passive'. The concept of 'person', conversely, corresponds to the actual subject, whose multiple subjectivities and plural positionings enable a more 'active' reception of the cinematic text. Mayne is clear that these positions are overlapping rather than discrete. She points out that the preoccupation with the binarisms of 'critique' versus 'celebration', or of 'critical' versus 'complacent' readings do not unproblematically refer to demarcated positions of active against passive spectating, of contestation against ideological indoctrination (*ibid*.: 4). I agree with this view of spectating positions, especially when Mayne argues that the capacity for negotiated meanings is the key to viewing strategies (*ibid*.: 93). I also concur with Mayne's view that 'meanings are both assigned and created' (*ibid*.: 81), that is, the cinematic apparatus addresses the spectator in definable ways, and the spectator as a social subject receives this address according to our own social and cultural specificities.

Annette Kuhn also differentiates between the spectator as 'subject' and as 'social audience' (Kuhn, 1992: 305). The position of 'subject' belongs to structuralist and early semiotic theory which saw the text in terms of its internal operations, as a set of structures and conventions that locate the spectator as fixed with a limited response. The second position, that of a 'social audience', refers to the post-structuralist focus on the spectator as the site of multiple positionings. This refocused attention on the spectator's plural subjectivity allows us to receive film as a playing with process and not just from a position of passivity. This shift emphasizes the importance of the receiving subject as autonomous as well as addressable by the text.

More on spectating in relation to definitions of the textual. Kuhn defines textual analysis as initially 'uncovering processes and structures at work in a text' with the aim of exposing its ideological operations which have been rendered invisible (Kuhn, 1982: 84). Kuhn sees textual analysis as founded on a concept 'of texts as constructs, as structured by the work of ideology, while at the same time naturalising that work', where 'de-naturalisation' renders the ideology of the text 'visible and thus open to critical examination' (*ibid*.).

A criticism, among several that are levelled at textual analysis, is that it 'relies too exclusively on the formal and technical aspects of the cinema', and that it 'ignores the complex nature of the cinematic institution' (Mayne, 1993: 105). In positing a spectator positioned by the formal properties of the text, textual analysis ignores the fact that the spectator in the institution of cinema is an autonomous subject with differing social specificities. In emphasizing structuring devices and practices of codification to reveal the ideological operations of a text, we are in danger of not accounting for the social subject who is receiving the text. However, textual analysis can deploy a structuralist attention to systems and encodings, as well as a deconstructive reading of symptoms and gaps, absences and cracks, otherwise known as indicating the aporia or lacunas of a text. This latter approach implies active spectating to me. So a textual analysis that does not preclude the receiving subject, but allows them to access their uniquely positioned subjectivities, is potentially a medium of analysis that could benefit from the detail of the text as well as the plurality of positions brought by the subject receiving that text.

Rather than staying with 'the old dichotomy of text and context' (Mayne, 1993: 105), which Mayne locates as a criticism against textual analysis, such analysis could draw on the benefits of active spectating positions through attention to formal detail. Kuhn is in favour of breaking out of the binaries that polarize text and context, asserting that 'we must abandon the dualistic thinking' that creates 'the text-context dichotomy' (Kuhn, 1988: 5).

As Christine Gledhill argues, if we are solely concerned with 'the cinematic production of meaning', we are in danger of delimiting the subject, where 'women as defined in other social practices' than the cinema are erased (Gledhill, 1978a: 19). Although attention to 'textual production' is a 'critical shift from interpretation of meaning to an investigation of the means of its production', we must not deny the specificities of the spectator as constituted by social practices other than the cinema (*ibid.*). Therefore textual analysis can only be beneficial if it offers both a method of reading cinematic languages and a medium for subjective response in those readings.

It is helpful to remember that there is no fixed unitary position of spectatorship, where response is uniform and where subjectivity is stable. We spectate across gender, across race and sexuality, class and culture, age and ability, and our different geopolitical and other positionings result in diverse spectating responses. We cannot accord the status of stability to a shifting arena of multiple discourses, because they are operating crosscurrently and constitute subjectivities in infinite syntheses of interdiscursive positionings.

The position of the lesbian spectator of mainstream film is one where we are usually denied any direct representation of lesbian desire. We have seen that a strategy open to us is to supply a resistant position of spectatorship and read in the desire at the margins of the film. This is to subtext, which I will explore further. I will also read lesbian desire as extratext, which I will suggest can take us beyond the constraints of genre into an analysis of multiple discourses. And I will also intertext, comparing the treatment of lesbian desire in two texts authored by the same director, where this intertexting will reveal that lesbian desire is on the fringe of the representable.

The extratext is sometimes confused with the intertext. The latter I see as a staying within genres, and I will return to this. For now, by 'extratext' I mean that which is outside the text, outside the genre as well as the discernible ambit of that text, but which still resonates in the text as an additional commentary on its machinery. The extratext can alert us to the arbitrary rules of genre, by stretching them, by creating new syntheses of generic forms, new complementarities to replace old conventions. Extratexting involves rediscovering the rules of genre, reworking them so there is a blurring of boundaries between different genres, which allows us to play with the differing expectations we bring to diverse media. This has the purpose of destabilizing our expectations of art products in the interest of inventiveness, so that new languages, new narrative questions, new anticipations can be arrived at.

The concept of the extratext has long been in operation. For example, the use of music in film, of illustrations and stills in books, of screens at rock events, and other instances of multimedia exercises are all examples of extratexting.[2] The emergence of CD ROM seems to be a confirmation of the impact of extratexting, and recent artistic developments seem to be tending to mix media forms in comfortable new syntheses. I certainly do not believe we have gone far enough to explore extratexting. For instance, I find it incredible that the selection of film soundtrack, either commissioned or pre-recorded, has often so little to offer the spectator in terms of a direct correlation between the filmed scene and the musical lyrics. I think this is a surprising oversight, given that generous film budgets could easily allow the commissioning of specific lyrics, while existing songs with pre-existing situations in the lyrics could be chosen with a better synchronization with the script-writers, who could write in more detailed references to the song, thereby extratexting in a way which many audiences would find pleasurable. More on that later.

Quite predictably, the extratexting I find in *Desperately Seeking Susan* relates to what Joni Mitchell has called 'stoking the star-maker machinery behind the popular song'. Namely, that it is Madonna as Madonna we read into Susan, streetwise New Yorker, tough, cool, wild, above all desirable. Lesbian desire for certain icons is at work here, but additionally it is Madonna's presence operating as a playful imaging of herself, a star in the music industry, who shocks, seduces and teases her audiences, who entices us with fantasies of her sexual availability and her offer of sensuous pleasures. This idea of the 'fact' of Madonna as the film's extratext may not seem to differ much from the effects of the star system, where it is the public's fascination for personal lives that makes stars the subject of mass audience speculation. I think here the difference is that we get pleasure from confusing the fictive with the factual, so that by reading Madonna as playing herself, whereby Susan is a facet of the Madonna persona, we are playing with the media of fiction and fact as texts that can complement each other as well as evolve new generic forms. I would like to suggest that actors could more frequently play themselves than they do, in fictive forms rather than just cameos, so that there is a referencing of the known of the star's persona, as well as an experimental exploration of their factual lives given in a fictional rendition. This is similar to docudrama, but the faction element of playing with fact and fiction gives it more potential for inventiveness. I think Madonna could have a much more successful film career if she would take scripts that centre on this 'factional' quality, where she is playing with who she is known to be. The film's extratext resides in Madonna playing Madonna, a cultural icon who feeds many an individual's fantasy of our self being the object whom she desires. This fantasy goes back to the early desire to be the exclusive object of the mother's desire.

Jackie Stacey's analysis of the film raises some crucial questions about desire and identification. She tells us that 'Susan is positioned as the classic feminine enigma; she is, however, investigated by another woman' (1988: 127). In investigating the 'interchange of feminine fascinations', Stacey says, 'This fascination is neither purely identification with the other woman, nor desire for her in the strictly erotic sense of the word' (*ibid.*: 115).

What I find is that there is also another agenda in operation, the search not for the other but for the self, the quest not to become like the other but to discover the autonomy of the self. This is narcissism in a positive sense. The film's device of mistaken identity enables Roberta, the subject who is doing the seeking, to adopt the identity of the object she is seeking. Roberta is a repressed and bored New Jersey housewife who is obsessed by her interest in Susan, a woman she has never met but whose life she follows through a series of personal ads in the newspaper between Susan and her male partner. Roberta contrives to see Susan for the first time, then follows and loses her, but manages to buy a jacket that Susan has exchanged at a boutique. This jacket now becomes the totem of their identities in mergence, temporarily, as others confuse Roberta for Susan. The shift into becoming Susan is brought about by Roberta's amnesia, where she attempts to find Susan to find herself. I think this quest to 'seek Susan' is precisely the quest to locate the self, to find an identity, get a life. Roberta is rewarded. By seeking and finding Susan, she is liberated from a stifling and emotionally empty lifestyle, and finds excitement, pleasure, and an equal sexual partner (though not Susan, and not a woman).

The film critiques 'heterosanct' ideals of monogamy, marriage and money, offering at the end a counterculture of open relationships and a fluid economy. Although there is no radical reworking of sexual politics, or of gendered ascriptions of femininity, the film is a charming exercise in extratexting, where I for one deliberately read Susan as Madonna, and in seeking Madonna/Susan with Roberta, I can both identify our similarities and locate our differences in a play with faction. As a woman spectator, I can enjoy the spectacle for the sake of untendentious pleasure, where I do not need the 'completion' offered by a sex scene because of my identifications or desires. My position of spectating allows me to scopophilically consume an icon of desirability, not to possess her or to identify with her as a resolution of my desire, but to enjoy the spectacle as innocently playing with fantasies for knowledge. If seeking Susan is to seek knowledge of her, and if to find that knowledge is the equivalent of possessing her, then already knowledge is less innocent, and has become guilty of premeditated demands. However, if we see that seeking Susan here is to seek the pleasure of seeing the enactment of a quest to discover the self, as a means of achieving autonomy and attaining liberation, the purpose of the search is less suspect. Of course, even in obtaining the object of the quest, that is, the self as self-determined, there is still a lack of completion, because even with the attainment of autonomy, identity remains precarious, and shifting positionalities deconstruct our pretensions to stability in the context of changing multiple discourses. I think this can be advantageous, insofar as it is the shifting subjectivity of the spectating position that allows for redefinitions of pleasure, not as completion but as a quest, a perpetual state of enquiry.

Let us look at the question of identifications in relation to desire. Richard Dyer tells us, 'A characteristic feature of gay/lesbian fantasy is the possibility of oscillation between wanting to be and wanting to have the object of desire' (Dyer, 1993: 88–90). And in interviews conducted with lesbian spectators, Claire Whitaker outlines how 'identify with', though intended to mean 'associate closely with', becomes interchangeable with 'love', the latter ranging from desire, to desire and affection, to affection (Whitaker, 1981: 106–7). In one interview, when asked about her identifications and attractions, Dagmar (a pseudonym) replies that 'the appeal is hard to put my finger on' (quoted by Whitaker, 1981: 109). This bespeaks a collapsing of identifications with desire.

Stacey would like to 'broaden the definition of desire but not to deny its erotic meanings', and she suggests 'that identification between femininities contains forms of homoerotic pleasure which have yet to be explored' (Jackie Stacey, 1994: 29). She speculates as to what might be 'beyond the psychoanalytic options of masculinisation or narcissism' in women's responses to representations of ourselves 'given the saturation of this culture with images of attractive femininity' (*ibid.*). She states, 'My argument is that cinematic "identification" does include some forms of desire. However, I am not suggesting the de-eroticisation of "desire", but rather the eroticisation of some forms of "identification"' (*ibid.*: 175).

I think that in eroticizing identifications one is in danger of paying too great a homage to desire as sexual. Despite an absence of a sexual aim, there are undoubtedly many same-sex relationships between women which are a source of much greater joy and support than those with male partners. I can understand the fascinations some heterosexual women have for other women, where attractions and identifications can and do take place, but in an absence of a lesbian framework or of any sexual contact. Here, gendered bonding is not about desire as a sexual aim, but about desire as an act of sociality and receptiveness between women. Teresa de Lauretis refers to this as 'homosocial', that is, 'woman-identified female bonding' (de Lauretis, 1994: 120). Homosocial relationships depend on social pleasures rather than sexual desires, and are as important and meaningful as sexual relationships. As a lesbian I have many non-sexual relationships with other women, including lesbians and hetero-sexual women, where desire does not figure as sexual but as social pleasure. That I am a lesbian who mixes with women does not of course necessitate that all my social contact will entail a sexual content.

De Lauretis writes 'on the confusion of desire with identification', and she wishes to benefit from the way psychoanalysis separates the two (de Lauretis, 1994: 116–17). She wants to maintain the distinction between ego-libido, or narcissism, and object-choice. That is, she wants to distinguish between wanting to be like or seeing oneself in the object, and feeling desire for the object.

> The distinction between object-libido and narcissistic or ego-libido is crucial here, for one is sexual and has to do with desire, wanting to have (the object), the other is desexualized and has to do with narcissistic identification, wanting to be or to be like or seeing oneself as (the object). (*ibid.*: 118)

De Lauretis finds it 'fairly incontrovertible' that ego-libido or narcissism are not 'to be confused with the object-choice component of *sexual* desire' (*ibid.*: 119; original emphasis). I find that there are linkages possible between narcissism and desire, despite the absence of a conscious sexual aim in the former. Here, in finding the 'self', I think that initial narcissistic processes can enable desire for the other. I think that narcissism is acceptable in this version, which challenges the usually negative view of it. Elizabeth Grosz quotes Freud on narcissists, seen to be mostly women, as those subjects who are 'plainly seeking *themselves* as a love object' (Freud, quoted by Grosz, 1990: 126; original emphasis). Grosz reports that 'the narcissistic woman strives to make her body into the phallus' (Grosz, 1990: 133). This woman wants to be the object of desire not out of desire for the other but out of a desire for the self. I would suggest that the woman preoccupied with narcissistic impulses is indeed unhealthy, especially in the phallicization of her body for the sake of wanting to be desired in conformity with phallocentric definitions of desire. However, narcissism also offers productive possibilities, and we could benefit from reclaiming some of its processes. Ellie Ragland-Sullivan reports that the Anglophone interpretation of narcissism follows Freud in seeing it as pathological (Ragland-Sullivan, 1992: 272). However, as she argues, 'without narcissism, we lack the necessary illusion of *being* from which we live by desiring and speaking' (*ibid.*: 273; original emphasis). To be a speaking social subject who can express her desire, the narcissist must be able to affirm herself as a subject. If her desire is not to remain regressed in infantile self-fixations, she must move to a position where she recognizes the other as a separate subject, who is not there merely to mirror her, but a subject with separate desires that do not always correspond to her own. As Nancy Chodorow says, for differentiation to take place, we need to recognize 'the separateness, or otherness, of the other' (Chodorow, 1989: 103). A narcissism that depends on being loved rather than being able to love, posits a 'false' self because it is predicated on the recognition by the other without even being able to bring a recognition of the other.

Let us briefly look at the question of a lesbian subtext again. By tradition, lesbian spectators have 'appropriated cinematic moments and read into them their own fantasies' (Weiss, 1992: 45). Additionally, grapevine gossip can contextualize certain imagings by allowing us to read lesbian desire between the lines, where 'a glance, a costume, a gesture, is enough to give the cue' for us to subtext (Becker *et al.*, 1981: 302). I think there are many moments in cinema of what Mayne calls a 'flirtation with lesbianism' (Mayne, 1993: 171), and I will cite three here, *Yentl* as extratext, *Julia* as subtext, and *Ghost* as intertext.

The lesbian content in *Yentl* is clear, involving Barbra Streisand crossdressed as a man. A contrivance brings about her marriage to a woman who loves her, but needless to say Streisand does not return this desire, because she loves the man who loves 'her' wife. All very funny for a while. What I extratext from this text is the discursive formation of sexed and gendered identities which are clearly being referenced. While the mainframe of the film remains staunchly heterosexual, the extratextual subjects of dissident sexualities, gender masquerade, and a fluid playing with marriage resonate for me in a way which enables my escape from the limits of heterosex to the plurality of other positionings.

In *Julia*, the subtext of lesbian desire explains the love and loyalty that Jane Fonda bears towards Vanessa Redgrave, and although it is given only a very brief reference, in a verbal hint of lesbianism which provokes Fonda to retaliate with a punch in dramatic response, this is all we need to confirm our reading.

In *Ghost* the famous near-kiss between Whoopi Goldberg and Demi Moore spells a moment of subtext as intertext. As Z. Isiling Nataf writes of this scene, 'Add to this the intertextual reference of Whoopi Goldberg's lesbian exchange . . . in . . . *The Color Purple*, and the circulation of lesbian desire runs riot in the scene' (Nataf, 1995: 70).

Let us now look at the suggestion of another lesbian subtext. *Bagdad Café* is a charming film, where the lesbian spectator can find lesbian desire suggested at the seams. This is again to see lesbian desire as untendentious, where we are not dependent on lesbian sex for cinematic satisfaction, because our identifications and our desires are engaged in pleasures that render the text a more innocent enterprise in our spectating. Pleasure is again about questing and less about completion.

The film brings together two very different women, a white European and a black American, both of whom have recently rejected their husbands. There is a mergence of sorts from their first meeting, and the synchronization of the soundtrack almost suggests that they have been waiting for this moment, that this was meant to happen. Jasmin the German woman has been abandoned in the desert by her husband, and arrives at Bagdad, which is a desert backwater on the edge of Las Vegas. She rents a room at the Bagdad Café Motel, which Brenda runs to support her family. Brenda is initially suspicious of Jasmin, who has walked out of the desert with no husband or car, only a suitcase of man's clothes. She cannot at first make sense of the mystery of Jasmin, another enigma. Jasmin transforms life at the café. She learns some basic magic tricks, and delights customers by producing crackers and other items apparently from nowhere. Soon the café is a roaring success, full of truck drivers who rendezvous there especially to see Jasmin and Brenda perform their magic.

The two women have to separate. Jasmin goes back to Germany because her tourist visa has lapsed and she has no work permit. The café is empty, the family is bereft, the magic has gone. Then Jasmin comes back, and there is a wonderfully emotional moment when the two women meet and embrace. An American male who is resident at the motel proposes to Jasmin so that she can have citizenship in the country, and the film ends with Jasmin's response, 'I'll talk it over with Brenda.' Cut to credits.

From the lesbian spectator's point of view, the subtext is not about lesbian desire for lesbian sex, but for the pleasure we receive in having representations of the woman as presence. This is not to reduce the woman to a maternal function, even though we may recognize that this presence promises a sense of the plenitude initially held by the mother. Here, two women engage in a woman-bonding which recognizes the other as equal, as autonomous in her desires, where what she lacks is not presence but status under patriarchy.

Let us see how the two women have equal subjectivities in the context of their differences. Brenda as the African-American woman is in the often repeated scenario of having to support a household as well as a male partner. She genuinely grieves at his leaving, even though she instigates his departure. Jasmin on the other hand is probably financially dependent on her husband, but has no regret at his departure. She prefers to walk a desert road going she knows not where rather than stay with him. Both women are at a point of crisis, and only a dramatic change of circumstance can save them.

This change takes the form of a literal transformation which Jasmin brings about. She begins with something as basic as cleaning Brenda's office, not only to express care for one's environment, but also to help Brenda take herself more seriously. Brenda's relationship with her family, fictive and otherwise, takes a dramatic turn with Jasmin's example, and rather than have a constant barrage of confrontational behaviour, the household becomes a unit of harmony. The two women's partnership of mutual support brings out the magic of both, and together they develop a repertoire of magic and performance that catapults the café into money-making success. Jasmin has found family, a home, work, above all a space for the assertion of her autonomous identity. The patriarchal order threatens to disrupt the woman-bonding through laws about citizenship, residence and work permits, but these are probably resolved when Jasmin is proposed to. When the film ends with Jasmin's classic line that she will make her decision dependent on what Brenda says, we can read that any marriage that takes place will be one of convenience under patriarchal law, and that the real marriage is the mergence of the women, not as sexual partners necessarily, but as two women who mutually recognize and support each other's presence and autonomy.

For the lesbian spectator, lesbian desire here is less concerned with lesbian sex and more engaged with the political positioning of putting women first. The ending, where any conventional marriage would be an understood arrangement, is a fluid reworking of the patriarchal order subverted from within, so that the relationship between the two women can cement into a fictive family unit in which both of them are equal partners. They have found community together, and together they make a community for others, so that in the exchange all participants find mutual benefit in a profitable and productive arrangement.

The subtext of the film suggests lesbian desire, not as sexual but as a longing for the sociality of the other woman's presence. In their mutual community, an affirmation of woman-bonding makes their equalities meet in mergence, while their differences maintain their boundaries as separate subjects. These differences revolve around their identities of race and nationality. As an African-American woman, Brenda's life experience has positioned her as other, and she probably perceives herself in these terms. Jasmin as a white European woman does have the privileges attached to white supremacism, but there is a deliberate levelling of her power. As a German woman in America, without permanent residence, without apparent income, operating in a foreign language in another culture, Jasmin is disadvantaged, and this disempowering of her is an othering that equalizes any privileges she has as a white subject. The two women empower each other precisely because they have equal sub-jectivities and differential positionings. We can subtext lesbian desire in their mutuality, but I do not find it disappointing that there is no imaging of this desire.

I now discuss black women in relation to feminism, to clarify how this too is a site of the interdiscursive. Feminism provides the terrain for competing subject positions, and, rather than attempt to close off this diversity, we could celebrate the plural that feminism contains. First, we must dispel the notion that black women cannot be feminists. Kumari Jayawardena reports that the word 'feminism' is not indicative of a recent Western phenomenon, but has been 'in common usage in Europe and elsewhere' since the nineteenth century, 'to signify agitation on issues concerning women' (Jayawardena, 1986: 2). Her book on Third World feminisms completely explodes the fiction that only European and North American women are politically active as feminists, and she traces some of the struggles that Third World women have been participating in, which have historically included the resistance to colonialism. The appropriation of feminism as somehow 'white' and 'Western' needs to be reworked, especially as I agree with Barbara Smith that 'racist white women cannot be said to be actually feminist' (1979: 50).

Looking at black women in relation to white feminism, we see we have been marginalized and rendered invisible (Carby, 1982: 213; Parmar,

1982: 236), in America as well as Britain. We were supposedly included under the blanket term of 'women' as oppressed, but of course as Audre Lorde states, 'the word *sisterhood*' pretends to 'a homogeneity of experience' which 'does not in fact exist' (Lorde, 1984: 116; original emphasis). The generic inclusion was really about an exclusion of difference. And the different is seen as the difficult. Lorde makes the point that white women did not wish to study black women's texts because we were 'too different', while these same women had no hesitation in absorbing Shakespeare and approaching Molière (*ibid.*: 117). Adrienne Rich has made a similar point (1979: 307). And a white woman admits that some organizations' attempts to include black women consist of the activity 'of sending out notices' (Pence, 1978: 46).

To relate this to the films discussed, I see *Susan* as confirmation of the exclusion of black women, who do not feature at all. *Bagdad Café* works on the inclusion of a black woman, and this is a big factor in my delight at the film. This inclusion for me is what feminism is about, the acknowledgement that we are all equal subjects acting in mutuality. I find that *Salmonberries* may attempt such an inclusion, but this takes the form of tokenism, which I see as the danger of feminism if appropriated by whites who are unpoliticized about their own racism, although they profess otherwise. Tokenism is more insidious than exclusion. Trinh T. Minh-ha refers to how we can 'become Someone's private zoo', and she writes on the phenomenon of tokenism in white subjects' attempts at inclusion (Minh-ha, 1989: 82–3). Midi Onodera also writes on how certain black women get taken up to represent the race, as when audiences want her 'to speak for all "producers of color"' (Onodera, 1995: 24).

Hazel Carby speculates on why black women are currently 'needed as cultural and political icons by the white middle class' and she suggests that this is a way of absolving guilt while maintaining social segregation (Carby, 1992: 192). While individual black women can of course express our opinions, we need to reiterate that we can represent only ourselves. When asked to define the role of black women, Toni Cade had to ask, because of the impossibility of representing the rich multiplicity of identity in one voice, 'What Black Woman did you have in mind?' (Cade, 1970: 101).

Let us now intertext with the film *Salmonberries*, also made by *Bagdad Café*'s Percy Adlon. Certain similarities in film-making style operate in both films, but lesbian desire, now outed, is unrepresentable as anything other than a source of frustration and failure.

Film-making techniques in both texts illustrate stylistic similarities that bespeak an authorial presence. My purpose in intertexting between the two films is to demonstrate that filmic strategies on their own are not enough, that strategies need more than an abstract concept. They need a concrete design to work. I will be suggesting that art without feeling, or direction without integrity in the design, can render some texts unworkable, no matter how well-intentioned their filmic languages are in an attempt to effect change.

Both films have an interrogative mode of questing, seeking, and this is to play skilfully with the use of camera to suggest and then to show, to set up an anticipation rather than supply an establishing shot. Such camera devices in the use of filmic languages locate the spectator as also questing, seeking to make sense and thereby interrogating our subject-ivities and activating our processes of intelligibility. The spectatorial positions we take are less passive and more self-conscious when we have to supply meanings to read interrogative texts. Both films have uncertain first images, unusual angles, disjuncture in temporal editing, intercutting, slow motion merging into real-time, and a pleasing play with lighting to suggest the uncanny. The effect of these devices is to create alert and active spectatorial positions in our reading of the texts.

This exercise in intertexting allows me to interrogate my own spectatorial positionings in my reception of the films, and I conclude that I prefer the subtextual suggestion of lesbian desire in *Bagdad Café* to the bleak treatment the outing of lesbian desire gets in *Salmonberries*. My displeasure at the latter film relates to crucial notions of narrative engagement, since I think it is preferable to hold the spectator than to alienate her with miscalculated filmic strategies.

Before looking at the film in more detail, a few words on the intertext. I use the term more in its 1970s usage, which is, as Mayne quotes Julia Kristeva, the identification of every text as a 'mosaic of citations' (Kristeva, quoted by Mayne, 1993: 64). Although the term now refers to an address to 'viewers across a wide range of texts' (Mayne, 1993: 64), I am working on the assumption that these texts will be within the same genre. That is how I clarify the distinction between the intertextual and the extratextual for the purposes of this chapter. So, proceeding on that limitation, we have to decide as creators and consumers 'what intertextual networks to assume' (Fischer, 1989: 4). Intertexting allows us not merely to compare and contrast in some self-referential but self-insulated analysis, but also to supply comment, whether on spectatorial fascinations or on authorial fixations, as consumers and producers of meaning. Nataf states, 'Inter-textuality is a very important way for lesbian, black and working-class spectators to bring their cultural experiences and discourses into the textual and symbolic exchanges with the mass media' (Nataf, 1995: 72).

I am intertexting differently here, in limiting the concept to texts of the same genre, but the principle is the same, that as a black lesbian spectator I will bring readings of previous texts to a product in ways particular to my positionings. I hope to show through intertexting how *Salmonberries* serves as an authorial example of one aspect of the malestream in film-making representations of lesbians. I will also extratext a little with the person of k.d. lang in the film, of whom Louise Allen writes in relation to her 'intertextual lesbian stardom' (1995: 70).

lang plays Kotzebue, a young androgynous lesbian working in Alaska, who falls in love with Roswitha, a German librarian. The film deals with a quest for origins and explanations. Kotzebue inhabits an outsider space, as she was abandoned at birth and her illegitimacy places her on the periphery of the social order. She is questing to discover her origins, and although she learns of her Native American roots, the frustration of her own lesbian desire leaves us in a void, as Kotzebue's fascination for a resolutely heterosexual woman is met with rejection.

During the course of the uneven narrative, Kotzebue buys two tickets to Berlin for herself and Roswitha, and there they are able to work through Roswitha's trauma at witnessing the shooting down of her husband years ago while trying to escape from East to West Berlin. Through the agency of Kotzebue, Roswitha is able to lay the ghost to rest.

That evening in their hotel room Kotzebue attempts to seduce Roswitha, and a long sequence details why Roswitha feels compelled to refuse. This is cut so that its duration appears to be over a long night, and it is punctuated to suggest that there can be no hope for lesbian desire at the gaps, that there is no space, no room, for such desire, as reasons for its rejection are so unremitting.

On considering some of the reasons for her rejection listed by Roswitha, we see a reworking of many a classic heterosexual line. First Roswitha recognizes that a lot is at stake, and that they have to be careful. This is to be responsible, and that is commendable. Next, lesbian desire is 'not me', and she could not sleep with Kotzebue and tell her that 'after the fact'. I suppose that is acceptable, and if Roswitha perceives her heterosexuality as fixed, we have to go along with that. She does assure Kotzebue that she does love her, that she has opened so many doors for them both. This could be a kind of teasing, to use love as a term while denying it sexual intimacy, but it confirms that social pleasures in bonding have an intensity that need not involve a sexual dimension. The ultimate in rejection lines is that the two women cannot risk what they have already, that their friendship is much too important for lesbian sex to get in the way. And so we have a conflict between Kotzebue's desire for sexual desire, and Roswitha's desire for a platonic friendship. The conflict is unresolvable. There is no meeting point where the different desires could be reconciled. Either they will sleep together or they will not. And whose wishes do we respect, Kotzebue's or Roswitha's?

The penultimate image of the film shows Kotzebue remembering their earlier ride in the snow, which is cut to the same lyric as in the previous scene, with the haunting chorus, 'I'd walk through snow barefoot, if you'd open up your door.' We might think this is it, we are going to end on a note of loss, reminiscence, lack. But no, the last image is of Roswitha's door, Kotzebue is knocking on it, requesting admittance. But on whose terms? Does the ending open up the hope for sexual lesbian desire? Or will Kotzebue have to accept the terms of friendship that Roswitha has so far preferred for their relationship?

I think that *Bagdad Café* works and *Salmonberries* does not, because the former has integrity and inventiveness, while the latter has only formula and frustration. As a lesbian spectator, I prefer the subtextual flirtation with lesbian desire to its being outed to meet with rejection and frustration. What could have been a cult project, possibly calling on k.d. to extratext with the film as herself, fails to move beyond the status of a curiosity-piece.

Allen refers to *Salmonberries'* 'weak portrayal of Native American identity' (L. Allen, 1995: 80), where 'blackness can be read in the film as undesirable' (*ibid.*: 82). This serves 'to devalue black lesbian experiences in popular lesbian representations of lesbian sexuality' (*ibid.*). This was indeed a missed opportunity, which 'enables white lesbian images to be consumed unproblematically' (*ibid.*: 80). Lola Young argues that we must identify how gender and sexuality can be seen 'as racialized discourses in the cinema' (Young, 1996: 13), and moreover 'that notions of femininity and feminism itself are intimately connected to slavery and colonialism' (*ibid.*: 15). By failing to acknowledge these connections, cinema disregards its complicity in the erasure of the black woman except as found in fixed images of white and black femininities, where white women are revered for their physical beauty, and where black women are largely confined to stereotypes, such as Eastern women's 'mystique' and African-American women's 'animalistic and voracious' sexual appetite (*ibid.*: 16, 21). What could have been an effort to address racial identity in a productive way is simply not attempted at all.

As music features prominently in these films, let us now briefly look at their use of musical scores. I think all three had enormous potential to deliver an inventive interpretation, but either these opportunities were missed or they lacked sufficient imagination. In *Susan*, there is a scene at a club where Madonna is dancing to one of her own early hits. The only links between the lyrics and the scene is that they refer to dancing. We need more imagination here. Could Madonna not have sung one of her own songs during the film, say with the band that her partner in the film is in? If the song had been scripted carefully, that would have allowed the lyrics to refer more closely to whatever scenario was taking place. This idea is explored more consciously in *Bagdad Café* and *Salmonberries*, where it is obvious that the songs have been written specifically in conjunction with the scripts. I find that *Bagdad Café* came closest to exploring the content of a lyric in conjunction with the filmic text. This was with the beautiful song, 'Calling You', where the haunting and melodic refrain is repeated to express the uncanny and telepathic attractions of the two women. In *Salmonberries*, because there has been no exploration of having lang extratext as herself, the fact that she co-wrote and sings the central song has a minimum impact, when it could have been used self-reflexively as a humorous reference to the 'fact' of k.d., another lesbian icon known for her desirability. Although it is an interesting positioning to locate her as a desirous subject, when she herself represents the desired object for many lesbians, the frustration of her desire feeds a frustration of the spectator's desire, because it is seen as outside the bounds of reciprocity.

In this chapter, to borrow from Leonard Cohen, first we take Manhattan and then we take Berlin, with Bagdad in between. The extratexting of Madonna in *Desperately Seeking Susan* as a persona playing herself, whose enigma we search to answer, has the effect of making our gaze one of questing. Desire is not given any sexual representation, and this is fine, as in *Bagdad Café*, where the overt text of putting women first, and its subtext of lesbian desire, are again about a desire for questing. But in *Salmonberries*, lesbian desire is spelt out only to be frustrated, which has the effect of foreclosing on celebration by favouring a denial of lesbian desire.

Turning to the question of how to reformulate film languages, Laura Mulvey had favoured 'a break with normal pleasurable expectations in order to conceive a new language of desire' (Mulvey, 1975: 59). I think that in order to proceed with such a project we can only work within the conditions open to us, so that, for instance, we retain some of the lures of narrative in cinematic languages while reformulating how desire is enacted and subjectivity embodied in the filmic text. One way of achieving the transformation of what constitutes the pleasurable is through a greater emphasis on intelligibility as a conscious and self-conscious mechanism. This I see as the main benefit from New Latin American Cinema proponents who 'stress the need for a cinema of lucidity', where 'what is at stake . . . is the yoking together of the cognitive and the emotive aspects of the cinema' (Willemen, 1989: 6). This is an affirmation of intellectuality without banishing the emotional, what Paul Willemen calls 'reversing the hierarchy between the cognitive and the emotive' in an industry 'adept at orchestrating emotionality while deliberately atrophying the desire for understanding and intellectuality' (*ibid*.: 13). This serves to reconstitute the pleasurable not just as a facile recognition of the known but as an engaged process of learning, and is a feature of the avant-garde (Kaplan, 1983: 138).

But the problem of film languages remains caught in the impasse of seeking invention while being constrained within an already mapped terrain of practices. There is, first, the point of cinematic languages being locked into the paradigm of Oedipus, often following a male trajectory of desire, disruption to order and restoration of (the male) order. Then there is the divide between avant-garde and mainstream practices, both established traditions which exemplify, in their extreme versions, the polarized positions of élite cultivated spectating and mass audience consumption. I would suggest two ways of negotiating this impasse. First, to reformulate desire from a lesbian standpoint, thereby reworking Oedipus as male narrative. And second, to go for a mix of avant-garde and mainstream practices, where the conjunction can create new syntheses of meaning production.

While developing this suggestion, I will briefly look at some of the issues concerning realism, because it is through this mode that ideology attempts to efface itself, and therefore to play with the codes of realism would be to offer the possibility of breaking out of certain codifications of the pleasurable.

Dyer makes the point that 'it is very hard for "realism" to do anything but reproduce dominant ideology' (Dyer, 1978: 291). Rather than reject realism on these grounds, we need to celebrate what realism can offer us while breaking down some of its operations. Gledhill makes the important point that realism 'embraces both hegemonic and radical aspirations', and that 'an assertion of realism is the first recourse of any oppressed group' (Gledhill, 1978a: 20). E. Ann Kaplan's analysis finds that realist films 'are far more heterogeneous and complex in their strategies than the theoretical critique can allow for' (Kaplan, 1983: 130). Kaplan points to a key paradox, that documentary can end up 'as much a "narrative" in a certain sense as an explicitly fiction film' (*ibid*.: 135). This I think is a clue toward the finding of new languages, with the mixing of forms, for instance as takes place in Michelle Citron's *Daughter-Rite*, where the apparent documentary is revealed as being scripted and as having actors (*ibid.*: 136).[3] This enables a stretching of the boundaries of realism in relation to spectatorial response.

Realism, of course, is most disrupted by the avant-garde tradition, which Kaplan characterizes as having practices that draw attention to the cinema as illusory, that position an active spectator through devices of distanciation, that refuse Oedipal pleasures around emotional manipulation and facile recognitions, and that mix the forms of documentary and fiction (*ibid.*: 138). I am completely in favour of the development of such practices in mainstream film, where new languages need not necessarily entail the elimination of narrative and realism but can involve their selective disruption.

Already established methods can achieve such disruption. For instance, intertexting can fuse different cinematic moments into a self-referential commentary. There is the reformulating of the narrative question in terms of whether a given text will stay within the realist mode or whether it will veer into anti-realism. There is lack of closure which denies plenitude and Oedipal pleasures in a fixed reading with a refusal of completion. There is subtexting, of course, whether in examining symptoms in the ideological cracks of a text, or in the suggestion of lesbian desire. And there is also intercutting, whether of parallel narrative threads sewed in or of distancing devices serving to break the narrative flow. There is also the use of 'merging and blurring', seen as techniques 'of a specifically feminine aesthetic' (Dyer, 1990: 176), and their congruence for lesbian imagings is apparent when we remember the mergence that can take place as two women mix and melt.

Given that we are confined within already established parameters, the only future languages immediately accessible to us are to play with new configurations. I myself think that intelligibility and extratexting are the way forward, insofar as audiences can enjoy making sense of images in a self-conscious way, as well as importing practices from other genres in new syntheses.

Given that the cinema functions on the fusion of the innovative with the traditional, and if we accept that the mapping of possible languages is already in place for the foreseeable future, we might find that it is through the lesbian subject that new frontiers are worked out in a reformulation of desire. The lesbian, as woman, as desirous subject, has come into a cinematic articulation of her own, and I do not think this is a transitory phenomenon. Current representations of us mark a welcome departure from the previous morbidification of our desires on-screen, which lesbians are happy to receive, and which can educate the general public about our identities and political positionings. Lesbians are here to stay.

It is not out of the blue that we have arrived at this position, but as the result of historical changes, including the recognition of sexuality as a significant social arena for women, and the creation of the social and economic conditions that enable some women to affirm a lesbian identity. If this articulation is taking place so prominently as we head into the new millennium, I think this significant historical moment has much to do with the contestation of the dominant order that is posed by the fact of dissident sexualities. Our challenge as a viable alternative to the heteropatriarchal order is an exemplary outcome of our contestation.

Ideology and discourse both depend on contestation. For Althusser, 'ideologies are set up in what are ultimately antagonistic relations' (Macdonell, 1986: 33). Diane Macdonell quotes Barthes on discourse as that which 'moves, in its historical impetus, by *clashes*' (Barthes, quoted by Macdonell, 1986: 3; original emphasis). From this inevitable fact of contestation have emerged many instances of resistance, whether of liberation struggles, fights for rights, or oppositional practices threatening to dismantle the dominant order. Concrete examples include struggles for independence from imperialism, black political movements and feminisms, and dissident sexualities. As contestation is of key importance, so most oppositional practices strive to keep up the pressure for transformation, not for the sake of change for itself, but for the sake of our survival.

I have indicated that I am in favour of experimental techniques within a framework of established mainstream practices, in a fusion of the politics of the avant-garde with the pleasures of the classical film text. Peter Wollen refers to 'an ambivalence between contravening legitimate codes and practices (a negative act) and exploring possibilities deliberately overlooked within the industry, or tightly contextualized (in contrast, a positive act)' (Wollen, 1980: 20). A key question is, of course, who is to decide which is which? Who would ever have the right to such a mandate?

Young reports that 'many black people still crave positive images' of ourselves (Young, 1996: 37). In the absence of imagings of lesbian desire between Asian women, *Fire* is a welcome departure in showing the evolving emergence of lesbian identities for two Indian women. Set in New Delhi, the film features the domestic arrangements of a household in the context of psychic claustrophobia and physical crowding, where every inch of space is a premium in a city known for its excessive overpopulation. The young woman Sita has just married Jatin, whom she is initially open to, only to discover that he is in love with someone else, a Chinese woman also resident in New Delhi. Sita meets Radha at her new home. Radha is married to Jatin's brother, Ashok. The family run a take-away and video rental business. The household is also composed of Biji, the elderly mother to the two brothers, and Mundu, the household servant.

Radha is childless and infertile, and her husband Ashok sees this as a confirmation that sexual desires are to be repressed. Radha is a devoted wife. She cooks, cares for Biji, and is completely self-sacrificial. Radha's dignity is a testimony to her having transcended the constraints of the prevalent social order, and though she is a woman who cannot produce sons in a society where that is the woman's main function, she inspires respect and admiration. Sita recognizes Radha's true subjectivity. She sees in her devotion a desire to give, share, exchange, and realizes that Radha's dignity and strength of character come from integrity and courage. The women are drawn together. Sita kisses Radha on the lips. 'I hadn't planned / any of this / and it was grand / to melt into a kiss of fire.'

Radha resists the first kiss, but when Sita comes to her again in bed, she is receptive. 'I closed my eyes / and drew in some air / instead of lies / we shared a share of fire.' The women's relationship is fraught with the danger of discovery, and Mundu witnesses their intimacy and tells Ashok. We do not hear the revelation nor any mention of the word lesbian. Ashok returns home and discovers Radha and Sita in bed. There is a confrontation and Radha's clothes accidentally catch on fire. Ashok saves his mother Biji, leaving Radha to save herself. By doing this he is affirming his support for an old order of values, as represented by the aged mother. Radha can no longer conform to the dictates of such an order, and as arranged, she rendezvouses with Sita so they can start a new life together. 'You fire my desire / my heart is aflame / and when you feel the fire / you feel the same.'

Although Sita does the initiating, it is Radha's awakening to lesbian desire that forms the film's central narrative interest. It is Radha who has to undergo the endurance test of a 'trial by fire'. There are several figurations of 'fire' in the narrative, including from the Hindu legend of Ram and Sita, where Sita survives a trial by fire but is still sent into exile. This episode from the legend is featured four times, in graduated narrative steps, on video and at a local performance by a theatrical troupe. In the same way, 'fire' itself is featured in graduated stages, from images of cooking, to a later scene which includes a shot of a naked flame while Radha is cooking, to the fire itself which nearly consumes her. She survives her trial by fire. But she is still compelled to go into exile, although this is for reasons of acting on an autonomous lesbian desire, and not because of loyalty and docile devotion to a social order signified by duty towards one's husband. As Radha reports, Sita thinks 'the concept of duty is overrated'.

Fire is also a potent image, additionally resonant for historical reasons, of suttee and dowry-bride burnings in the Indian context. This reminds us of the literal 'witch-hunts' against independent women in Western Europe during the fifteenth, sixteenth and seventeenth centuries, when many women were burned at the stake (Daly, 1978: 178–222). Fire also spells desire as a metaphor for danger but, equally, the danger in desire can reside in its not maintaining respect and responsibility. 'Walking on wire for your fire / walking on wire . . .'[4]

There is a suggestion in the film that when men are confronted with resistance from their wives, they can resort to violence and rape. Jatin even effectively says that using force can be a sexual turn-on for him. And when Ashok discovers Radha's involvement with Sita, his idea of her wanting passion is to impose a clumsy kiss on her. However, neither of the men persists with violent coercion, and this is their saving grace. When the two men refuse to resort to violence after all, there is in this decision not their emasculation but revelation that violence as aggression is damaging – it is deleterious to the self and destructive towards the other.

On the issue of intergender relations, when women protest at some men's behaviours, it is not their 'biological maleness' at stake (Combahee River Collective, 1978: 17). Rather, we resist certain enculturations of 'maleness' as macho and we promote the adoption of masculinities that are relational. It is not feminism that is the problem but the sexism that we seek to eliminate. However, to categorically state that all men are oppressors is too reductive. Susan Bordo makes the point that the oppressor/oppressed model is too simplistic, as many men are acutely uncomfortable with and may be 'tyrannised' by certain versions of masculinity (Bordo, 1994: 190). I agree that many 'New Men' are equally oppressed and delimited by patriarchal definitions of 'normal' masculine behaviours, such as aggression and a lack of affective expression. What is necessary is a space for dialogue between the genders, a mutual process of listening to and being listened to, for the purposes of relational contact and interpersonal exchange. We do not want Peeping Toms, Clever Dicks and Dirty Harrys. We want men who are aware of their personal and sexual politics, and who take responsibility in the form of changing behaviours that are infused with sexism.

One disturbing feature I found in the film was its device of having the servant Mundu watch porn videos while masturbating in the same room as the elderly Biji, the mute and disabled mother. Also disturbing was the conflation of pornography with lesbianism, with what was possibly an unconscious paralleling of the two activities, where the illicit pleasures of pornography are equated with the pleasures of lesbian desire. This reflects that, in public discourses unpoliticized around sexuality, there is a collapsing of the lesbian with the perverse, and she is also aligned with criminality, insanity, degeneracy and prostitution.

The choices open to the lesbian in India occur in the context of a history of having been colonized. First, there is some contention as to where lesbianism 'originated' from, as if its emergence should be located in a geographic specificity, rather than be seen as a cross-cultural phenomenon emerging transhistorically. Giti Thadani analyses the 'contradictions' between the prevalent myth in India 'that any form of lesbianism is a product of Western decadence', and the historical evidence of lesbian activity and its explicit outlawing in India (Thadani, 1996: 56–7). The second myth is that India's problems as a developing nation mean that issues of sexuality should be secondary, where a lesbian identity is 'the expression of only a few Westernized, individualistic and economically independent women', and 'lesbian feminist activity is seen as a privilege' available only to very few women in India (*ibid.*: 60).

Thadani reports that the contemporary feminist movement in India, which started in the early 1980s, has failed to take on board the fight for lesbian rights and recognition, seeing open declarations of a lesbian identity as damaging to the movement (*ibid.*: 64). Thadani finds that this lack of endorsement by the Indian feminist movement has served to maintain lesbian invisibility, leading 'to the perpetuation of a closeted lesbian culture', where to be out is seen as 'the prerogative of the "first world" but remains unsuitable for a "developing country"' (*ibid.*).

We have to see this in the context of the legacy of British colonialism, and I will offer a brief overview. 'Indian links with Europe go back 10,000 years' (Visram, 1986: 1). What we are more familiar with is the history of India's colonization by British rule, started for reasons of commerce by the East India Company from the beginning of the seventeenth century. By the middle of the eighteenth century, the East India Trade Company had started 'its expansionist forays into Indian territory' (*ibid.*: 3). Robert Clive's conquest of Bengal 'laid the foundation of the British Indian Empire' (*ibid.*: 4). The British presence became one of representing trading interests as well as maintaining administrative control. In 1813, the East India Company's trading monopoly was abolished as a result of free trade legislation in Britain. India was opened up to other British traders intent on capitalizing on this new market. The East India Company still maintained administrative control of the country, and this was extended to a policy of rule by conquest. British rule in India was established by the 1850s (*ibid.*: 5).

Traditionally seen as a vast reservoir of cheap labour, Indians were to become embroiled in a system of indentured labour, which Hugh Tinker refers to as a 'new system of slavery' (Tinker, 1974: 19). Indians were contracted to work abroad because of the demand for labour on plantations that could no longer draw on the slave trade. The terms under which Indians were imported to serve in the plantations 'included residual elements of the slave laws' (*ibid.*: 17). Emigrations reached a peak in 1858 and 1859 (*ibid.*: 97), over twenty-five years after the British abolition of slavery in 1833. The British interest in exploiting Indian labour through organizing the emigration of Indian subjects to other parts of the empire was, as usual, motivated by capital. With the additional exploitation of labour and resources within India, 'India's mixed economy was being transformed into a support system for British capitalism' (Hamilton, 1989: 2). Rozina Visram refers to the 'drain theory' that Britain was benefiting from India by £30 to £40 billion annually by the start of the twentieth century (Visram, 1986: 80).

The British public seemed resistant to confront the actualities of imperialism, and could not see the hypocritical doublethink of what was being perpetrated under the guise of 'reform' and in the name of 'civilization'. It took much agitation, from the Indian National Rising in 1857 to the massive drive for independence in the first half of the twentieth century, to make the British withdraw. India became independent in 1947, when the subcontinent was divided into India and East and West Pakistan, largely along religious lines of Hindu and Muslim communities. In 1971 West Pakistan became Pakistan and East Pakistan became Bangladesh.

The Indian women's movement had a long history of activism in the struggle for independence, with many hundreds of thousands of women participating in mass demonstrations. Many were harassed, attacked and arrested. Some were imprisoned, including Sarojini Naidu and Kamaladevi Chattopadhyaya, in their fight to free India (Jayawardena, 1986: 99–101). Indian women were also active in the areas of social reform. And yet there still persist some outdated notions of feminism in the Third World context. Jayawardena reports that many subjects still locate feminism as 'a product of "decadent" Western capitalism' that has no relevance to Third World Women. There is also the view that feminism is the province of middle-class women and should not divert women away from their religion, family, or support for revolutionary struggles (*ibid*.: 2). This is to suppose that the rights of women do not constitute a site for revolutionary practice.

Sujata Gothoskar and Vithubai Patel outline how the women's movement in India has 'to take a different trajectory from the movement in the West' (Gothoskar and Patel, 1982: 101). This is because of socio-economic and historical conditions which must include considerations such as

a) the extent of women's economic dependence on the man or the family – only thirteen percent of women are in the work force; b) that cultural values have confined and continue to confine women to their role within the family; c) that the huge reserve army of labour created by the historical development of capitalism in India makes a state social security system impossible, and d) the close relation to women's questions and class questions. (*ibid*.)

Edward Said has talked about the West's othering of the Orient for the purposes of containment and control, and he proposes a freeing up of Orientalism, an 'Orientalism reconsidered', which 'entails nothing less than the creation of new objects for a new kind of language' (Said, 1986: 212). I would venture to suggest that othering is permissible provided that what the other represents is seen as inhabiting the self who is doing the defining. For this we would need a system of sociality which can accommodate plural social and cultural specificities in a politics of inclusion.

To conclude with Kuhn's opening quotation, if 'theories of representation may have to come to terms with discursive formations of the social, cultural and textual', then this will involve a recognition of the need to engage in dialogue, to connect voices in a mutual interactive process. Social subjects, with positionings determined by culture and other specificities of gender, sexuality, race, class, age, ability, and so on, will have to negotiate the text on both their own terms and the terms of the text within an order where discourses compete on a terrain of shifting practices.

Amina Mama defines discourse as 'historically constructed regimes of knowledge', where subjects speak through a modality involving power relations, with domination and contestation locked in struggle (Mama, 1995: 98). Subjects take up different and sometimes contradictory sides in this arena of struggle. Rosalind Coward reminds us that 'identity is a discursive construction', and that subjectivities and the modes of their construction are multiple, so that 'any individual would be subject to the workings of any number of discursive constructions' (Coward, 1983: 283). As Leigh Gilmore states, 'the *I* is multiply coded in a range of discourses' (Gilmore, 1994: 42; original emphasis), so that the constitution of identity is founded on fracturations as well as contradictions.

For theories of representation to adequately reflect the complexity of the spectatorial process, some provision must be made for the spectator's pleasures in intelligibility, in making sense of the text in ways which make the act of spectating a self-conscious process of recognitions and resistances to prevailing discursive positions. We would have to be aware of the formal construction of cinematic practices as well as the inter-discursive constitution of our own subjectivities. Mayne refers to how the relationship is unresolved between the subject as a position and the viewer as a person (Mayne, 1993: 8). To go towards resolving this tension we would need texts that engage us as well as provoke us into examining our pleasures, in a play with positions of self-conscious spectating as well as merged identifications. In Nancy Miller's borrowing from Barthes, 'The pleasure of the text is also a critical politics' (Miller, 1986: 281). Ultimately, I think it is our political positionings that will determine how we extract the pleasure of a text.

Notes

1. Annette Kuhn (1992: 309).
2. As an example of extratexting I cite an instance from a play I wrote, between 1985 and 1987, about which I can retrospectively say that I am infinitely glad it was never accepted for production. However, I am pleased to have written it, and the example I cite is of a scene taking place on stage with an Asian woman and white woman kissing, while a screen overhead features images of hands in movement to convey the eroticism of the kiss. I was deliberately extratexting with the different media of theatre as stage space and the screen as visual space. One reader was surprised that I should want to incorporate another medium into the theatrical space, but it was precisely the extratexting outside genre-based conventions that I was exploring.
3. I first saw an example of playing with fiction and passing it off as documentary in an *Arena* programme on Graham Greene. This was so striking and worked so well that I was inspired to write several programme ideas where the supposedly spontaneously spoken words were in fact scripted. I think this is very beneficial for the purposes of structuring and editing, although it carries dangers of collapsing into controlling behaviours.
4. In case readers are wondering where the lines from this lyric have come from, they are taken from a song I wrote in 1989, appropriately called 'Fire'.

9

The Lesbian Subtext in Cinema

Resistant Readings: *Thelma and Louise*

It may be more fruitful to ask how lesbianism functions as a sign within the text.

Bonnie Zimmerman[1]

By venturing to link up diverse digressions on *Thelma and Louise*, on resistant readings, women and the law of the father, and issues of gender, space and control, I will suggest that we need nothing less than a new symbolic order, a new system of sociality for the subject.

First we begin with the concept of the subtext, those ulterior layerings of meaning that run through the text, whether these meanings are intentional or not, immediately ascertainable or not. Lesbians have been hooked on the concept of the subtext for years, when we longed for some hint of our desire for women, and had few images of ourselves as anything other than perverts. So we supplied oppositional readings wherever we could, by reimagining and reinventing meanings for ourselves. Edith Becker *et al.* say that for lesbian spectatorship, 'The most important viewing strategy has been to concentrate on the subtext, the "hidden" meaning, of commercial films' (Becker *et al.*, 1981: 301). Such subtexting can be a clarification: 'Such readings can be valuable and accurate. They can resolve ambiguities otherwise inexplicable in the film text. Or they can construct alternate explications' (*ibid.*: 302).

It is this latter point, that readings 'can construct alternate explications', that I wish to explore. Women as readers of fiction often read against the grain, and our capacity for oppositional and deconstructive readings enables us to reinvent ourselves. Black women, especially those of us who are lesbians, particularly have to do this in the absence of adequate models, because too many of us have been silenced and rendered invisible.

Oppositional readings have the effect of validating a counter-culture in opposition to the dominant culture, where we not only resist the received orthodoxies, but also reinvent the parameters of what is possible.

In 'Encoding/decoding', Stuart Hall writes an account of the production of meaning in relation to its reception. When readings are made that do not correspond to the ones intended, 'what are called "distortions" or "misunderstandings" arise precisely from the *lack of equivalence* between the two sides in the communicative exchange' (Hall, 1980: 131; original emphasis). I think this discrepancy between intention and response is due to the plurality of political positionalities, which determine the extent to which we resist passive readings. Hall outlines three hypothetical positions in reception. The first is the '*dominant-hegemonic position*', when the viewer accepts the material at face value, and '*is operating inside the dominant code*' (*ibid.*: 136; original emphases). The second position is that of the '*negotiated code*', which both adapts to the dominant code and is aware of resistant readings by being composed of 'adaptive and oppositional elements' (*ibid.*: 137; original emphasis). The third position offers the most potential, that of the '*oppositional code*', where the viewer is aware of the dominant meanings, but prefers to decode them with resistant readings (*ibid.*: 137–8; original emphasis). In the oppositional or resistant reading, 'he/she detotalizes the message in the preferred code in order to retotalize the message within some alternative framework of reference' (*ibid.*: 138).

While the 'negotiated' position merely accounts for other readings, the oppositional code actively supplies them. To read lesbian as I do in *Thelma and Louise* is to provide 'alternate explications', to operate 'within some alternative framework of reference', where we read beyond the male fantasy that structures many a text. By asking 'how lesbianism functions as a sign within the text' of the film, we see one suggestion of its presence in the transgression of (patriarchal) law. We will explore both law and the law of the father.

A contradictory set of impulses is at work in the film, which critiques the patriarchal controlling of women even while it endorses male pleasure in fantasies of punishing women. This punishment is done in the name of realism as a regime of representations that attempts to efface inevitable contradictions. Much work has been done in film theory on the way the classic realist Hollywood text depends on disguising its construction as a product of representation. Christine Gledhill refers to how 'the project of representation itself is said to be based on the denial of contradiction' (Gledhill, 1978b: 10). Rather than acknowledge the material features in the ways films are fabricated, from the technical to the institutional, the

Hollywood text attempts to represent itself as naturalized, where it faithfully reflects an out-there that is real, unmediated and innocent of ideological underpinning. Of course this is a myth, but one we may go along with for the duration of the film, all the more so if the continuity editing is seamless and our identifications are engaged, whereby we suspend our disbelief. But if we can retain our critical alertness, we will be aware of when the text comes up against the internal contradictions in its meaning, that is, when it reveals gaps, because by definition representation is mediated, it is not the thing itself, naturalized and real, but a refiguration involving absence. So quite logically the text will often have a subtext, seen in its symptomatic gaps and silences, its omissions and evasions, its contradictions and incohesions. These are the *structuring absences* (*Cahiers*, 1970: 496; original emphasis) that inform some texts, where the tension of the text is revealed through its subtext. Therefore 'to expose the contradiction it is the film's project to unify' becomes 'a kind of *aesthetic subversion*' (Gledhill, 1978b: 11; original emphasis). This suggests that we can both enjoy and engage with the text while being alert and contesting in our readings.

I find the lesbian subtext in the film is its point of *aporia*, that silent thread through the text that can serve to pull apart its pretensions towards cohesiveness.[2] In this I coincide with Lynda Hart's reading that '"lesbian" is the aporia in this narrative' (Hart, 1994: 78). To borrow from an analysis of another film, 'if one looks beyond its apparent formal coherence, one can see that it is riddled with cracks' (Comolli and Narboni, 1969: 27). We specifically see how the apparent heterosexuality of the film's overt content is really maintained through overdetermination, through a hetero-bias trying to assert male presence, whereas the central concerns in the film are really those of the two women for each other. As Hart states, 'response to this film is hovering anxiously around the threat of the lesbian as the unspeakable sign' (Hart, 1994: 74). An examination of detail reveals the contradictions of the apparent heterotext, and provides us with 'alternate explications' around lesbian desire.

Before proceeding, I would like to pose a question: 'A is the son of B, but B is not the father of A. What relation is B to A?' (The answer is after the notes to this chapter.)

The film is a female buddy movie that abounds with male stereotypes, sometimes seen in their worst manifestations, so that the woman-identifications operating in the film are not presented in separation, but in the context of a real world where male power and masculine privileges are the order of the day. The film shows how sexual politics and gender wars between women and men are not just isolated subjects, of exaggerated interest to the Western ethos, but of crucial relevance to the future re-enculturation of gendered subjectivities. It is a road movie that travels on the journey towards sexual liberation, that unravels the realities of patriarchal oppression against women, only to destroy these women because they are caught in a cycle of circumstance beyond their control, which can supposedly find a solution only in self-destruction. The film's ending presents a sombre message, one we must learn from to avoid the snares of a symbolic order that would like to see women entrapped and disempowered. I found the ending so very distressing and disappointing that I will attempt to 'rewrite' it, literally on paper, as a way of re-envisioning and reconstructing the demands of realism in film narrative. More on that later.

The film begins with Susan Sarandon and Geena Davis planning a weekend away together. There is no doubt for me that the women-bonding we see between them has a lesbian subtext despite all their connections with men. I base this reading on the discrepancy between what I see as the women's passion for each other and its lack of sexual expression. This absence of explicit lesbian desire is the gap I have to fill as I myself experience desire for desire. My reading of lesbian desire in the film's subtext is to work with alternative logics and re-envisioned possibilities. In reading the women as having desire for each other, I acknowledge that I am supplying meanings which may or may not have been deliberately intended, but of course intentionality can sometimes be irrelevant to the processes of reception.

The women drive through the American South. Davis is being raped by a man she had danced with at a nightclub. Sarandon shoots him dead, and they become fugitives, trying to make an escape to Mexico. Their on-the-road journey is intercut with the activity of their male partners and the police. Davis rejects her husband, but is soon seduced by another man who betrays her. Sarandon enlists the help of her partner, who brings her money. Harvey Keitel plays the sympathetic detective who offers us the false hope that the law can work for and not against the women. When their money is stolen, Davis commits armed robbery. There is no turning back and they continue their escape, but are eventually trapped by scores of armed policemen and squadrons of police cars. They decide to drive over a cliff edge rather than face the law, and there is a freezeframe of their car suspended over a drop. We do not see them die. Like their desire for each other, their death remains unrepresented in an explicitly visual way.

Many people can watch the film as entertainment, see it as fun and funny, with a regrettably sad ending. While I too enjoy it at this level of reception, I am conscious that the issues it raises make me uncomfortable, and the only way I can counter such discomfort is through supplying resistant readings. This involves taking well-rehearsed routes regarding how characterization functions to create meaning. Therefore I defend rather than apologize for my emphasis on character as it functions in the context of cultural meanings.

The most obvious feature of the women's characterization is to make Davis and Sarandon form a daughter–mother dynamic, in which Davis is vulnerable and in need of protection, and Sarandon alternates between phallic mother and equally vulnerable potential victim. When Davis hesitates about asking Darryl for permission to go away with Sarandon for the weekend, Sarandon asks her if Darryl is her husband or her father, and this suggests that Davis has child-like qualities. She is innocent. She does not share Sarandon's ability to read men accurately. When a man sits down uninvited at their table in a nightclub, she is friendly while Sarandon is unwelcoming. It is significant that Davis is forthcoming and volunteers that Sarandon has a boyfriend. Why does she feel compelled to tell this to a stranger? This detail serves to establish Sarandon (and herself) as heterosexual. When we look for the subtextual implications of such a statement, we can suspect a defensive need in Davis to clarify their heterosexuality. Why? Because Sarandon looks like a dyke with her short haircut and her style of dress, just as Davis could conceivably be her femme partner. The overdetermination around men runs concurrently with the lesbian subtext in the film, a compensatory device that takes the form of making women emphasize their interest in men even when their involvement with women is a far more valuable set of relations. Davis's volunteering of this detail about their heterosexuality is a reassurance to male concern over women's continued investment in men's interests. But it must be emphasized that this response from Davis is just being friendly, that she is forthcoming as a child would be, unaware of most male sexual practices, and completely unsuspecting.

When the stranger tries to rape her in a parking lot, Davis does what she can to resist, but it takes Sarandon's intervention to stop the attack going further. After the shooting, Davis wants to go to the police, but Sarandon knows their account will be challenged. It emerges intermittently that Sarandon herself is a rape victim, and this explains her wariness about men and their intentions. The rape of Davis shows up the psychology of some men. When Harlan the rapist ignores Davis's resistance, this is a clear indication that some men cannot accept that 'no' means 'no', that women have a right to assert their autonomy through a rejection of male advances. When he tells her she is gorgeous and expresses desire for her, this is not a desire for her as an autonomous subject who is desirous of him. On the contrary, this desire is formed in a culture of misogyny. It is a desire not to mutually enjoy sex together, but to subject and humiliate the woman. What is important to note here is that Harlan is not seen as a pervert in the usual sense, so we get a true exposure of one common aspect of the rape phenomenon. Here, the rapist is 'normal', indeed his normality is predicated on his being a masculine subject who asserts male privileges. Harlan is married, he is presentable, he is definitely not one's idea of the 'psycho' that Davis fears. The very fact that he is presented as Mr Average Guy says a lot about the common assumptions made by many men about their sexual 'rights' to women's bodies. He resorts to the ultimate cliché for rape perpetrators, that they are just having fun. Again, rape is not about desire for the woman but hatred, not about her pleasure but her humiliation.

The women do not approach the law to protect them, because they and we know that the law is a patriarchal-based system of control which has nothing to do with women, justice or reality, but with ancient legislation that penalizes women. This is a confirmation of the social order organized around male privilege, where the law of the father, seen as the precondition for social assimilation, coincides with a system of legislature not paternalistic in its protection, but disempowering in its treatment of women. The idea that law is chivalrous to women is easily refuted when we consider how legal judgements often pathologize the woman offender, so that those women who are convicted as criminals are stigmatized as unnatural because crime is not seen as an area for normal women's activity (H. Allen, 1987).

One response to patriarchal prohibition is to resist by bonding with women. The two women enter into an alliance that must evade the law because that law threatens and ruins women's lives. As Manohla Dargis says, 'Thelma and Louise become outlaws the moment they seize control of their bodies' (Dargis, 1993: 87). Their bonding together takes the delightful form of a mother–daughter dyad, where they sometimes take it in turns to support and sustain the other. But initially there is a deliberate infantilization of Davis, and part of the film's movement is to show how she evolves into an adult. During the course of their flight, Davis rejects Darryl and wants to go to Mexico with Sarandon, but she keeps getting diverted. Although she has rejected the infantile husband for the adult female friend, the presence of men is completely over-determined. There is literally no respite, as within seconds of rejecting Darryl, she collides with J. D., a young man who hitches a ride with them. As Hart says of this, 'the heroines' heterosexuality is guaranteed by the production of male lovers even in the most unlikely circumstances' (Hart, 1994: 69).

Once in Oklahoma City, they meet up with Jimmy, Sarandon's partner, and the four spend the night in a motel. Davis has a one-night stand with J. D., which Hart finds improbable after the previous stranger-rape (*ibid.*: 75). Davis discovers the pleasures of sex for the first time, and Sarandon is genuinely pleased for her. This for me does not detract from the lesbian subtext, but confirms the way heterosexism is overdetermined. That Davis discovers sex with a male partner is a history that many lesbians still share, and it can be an irrelevance when we remember that the object of desire is not fixed but fluctuating.

Davis's innocence and vulnerability are most evident in the way J. D. abuses her by stealing their money. Davis, empowered and betrayed at the same time, takes the initiative. They need money, so Davis robs a store. She is like a child who has been prematurely initiated into adulthood. She does the only thing she can think of, to imitate the man and take what she can get. This short-term thinking, characteristic of immature behaviour, shows her to be an incorrectly socialized subject, who demonstrates the adolescent lawlessness of the disaffected and dispossessed who have no stake in the system.

From now on Davis has a growing maturity in reading men. When she calls Darryl, she knows immediately from his forced hello that the police are there. When the women are nearly caught by a policeman who stops them for speeding, she again takes the initiative and enables their escape. She tells Sarandon that something in her has crossed over, she can't go back, she couldn't live that way. Sarandon understands. Both she and Davis have transgressed the parameters acceptable under patriarchy and the law. Davis's transgression is a source of transformation. She is initiated into living, having only nominally existed before. It is she who suggests they go over the edge, as being preferable to a living death of incarceration. She finds her identity, only to have her life cut off at the moment of discovery.

It seems appropriate here to digress from the film to a general consideration of women under law, specifically linking this in relation to the law of the father, thereby connecting the film's overt treatment of transgression with its subtextual content of lesbian desire. We need to remember that law is a system of judicial organization that has little to do with protecting women's interests. Helena Kennedy confirms the pathologization of women offenders, who are 'mad rather than bad', so that those who are seen as criminals are doubly morbidified as monsters (Kennedy, 1992: 23, 20). In her chapter on rape, Kennedy shows how 'blaming the victim is the classic courtroom response' and she reports that 'rape still has a lower conviction rate than any other serious crime' (*ibid.*: 106, 114).

Carol Smart also wants us to be alert to 'the "malevolence" of law and the depth of its resistance to women's concerns' (Smart, 1989: 2). In her chapter on rape, she demonstrates irrefutably the workings of the 'phallocentric culture', where the woman is blamed for sexual indiscretions, while the man is often acquitted despite the atrocity of the crime (*ibid.*: 26–49). Men's sexual 'rights' to women's bodies, regardless of pleasure or consent, is validated by the acquittal of rapists.

Although these commentators are reporting on the situation in Britain, we can assume from cultural commonalities that these findings on law and rape apply equally to America. No wonder then, that Thelma and Louise do not have any confidence in the law to safeguard their interests against those of a dead rapist. In their contravention of the law, they place themselves outside its jurisdiction, but of course they remain within its realm of power, so that their transgression liberates them but also constrains them. As fugitives they are free, but only within the confines of a possible entrapment.

But there is a further linkage between their transgression of law and of the law of the father, and it is here that I wish to reopen the subject of their lesbian desire. We begin with Lacan's formulation of how 'desire is the desire for desire, the desire of the Other and it is subject to the Law' (Lacan, quoted by Coward and Ellis, 1977: 120). According to Lacan, the law here is the law of the father, introduced through the phallus, the third term to intervene in the mother–child dyad, thereby causing the rupture through lack that precipitates the infant into an eventual acquisition of language and an attendant sociality. To expand further, the child must be subjected to the prohibition of its desire for the mother through the law of the father, who interdicts exclusive access to the mother. The boy as well as the girl suffers from the rupture that the father/phallus introduces, and I am indebted to Heather Price for confirming that the boy child also experiences lack as extremely as the girl. However, it is of course the female who is much more severely disadvantaged in the theoretical formulations of the Oedipus complex. For Freud, the woman could negotiate this complex by being 'normal' and attaining heterosexuality, or she could become frigid and inhibited, or she could become lesbian. So in fact one way out of the impasse of Oedipus for women is to bypass the phallus through adopting a revised lesbian identity, accepting our castration only in the symbolic sense, where we recognize that we are disempowered under phallocentrism, but where some of us can still attempt to function outside the domain of the phallus, while remaining coherent social subjects. If, as Lacan states, it is 'the assumption of castration which creates the lack through which desire is instituted' (Lacan, quoted by Coward and Ellis, 1977: 120), to disavow castration enables the female subject to rework definitions of desire, where we accept lack without attempting to compensate for it by instituting illusory notions of plenitude.

Luce Irigaray argues for the need for '*two* genealogies' coexisting, a matriarchy and a patriarchy (Whitford, 1992a: 23; original emphasis). She suggests that the fundamental position for women to their first love-object is primarily homosexual, because the girl child is usually first merged with her mother in a same-sex encounter. The boy child is from the start usually in a relation of heterosexuality with his mother, in that she is usually the primary caretaker and is therefore initially merged with him, yet she is other than him in being female. Therefore women usually first encounter same-gender relations, and have to switch allegiances to men with a gender-jolt missing from most men's heterosexual alliances (Irigaray, 1987: 44). So in theory the precedent or foundation for a future lesbian desire exists from the beginning for the female child.

What this confirms for me is the possibility of bypassing the phallus as a signifier of desire by adopting a lesbian identity and thereby reconstituting the ways desire itself is instituted. We would need to reread the mother through a valorization of her, and if the mother–child dyad could re-theorize and re-enact that primary bonding in the context of the mother's autonomous desire, the child's sociality would be dependent on the recognition and acceptance of this autonomous desire. We would have to accept that the prohibition against incest is a maternal prohibition as well, where the mother is an active subject of desire, where it is she who denies the infant's fantasy desire for her, and where it is she who retains autonomy through her desire for others besides the child. In the case of the lesbian mother, her desire for her female partner(s) can equally prohibit the child's desire in terms other than those involving the phallus as the third term. Lesbian desire can dismantle phallocentrism.

In transgressing the law, Thelma and Louise break through the same processes that have prohibited their desire for each other as women, a sexual lesbian desire that can undermine the very fabric of the patriarchy by its challenge to phallocentric formulations of female desire. That this remains a subtext that cannot be developed due to the film's phallocentric logic says more about the failures of that logic than it does about the fact of lesbian desire.

Sarandon's status as a phallic mother is necessarily undermined by her own vulnerabilities. But initially she is seen to have more power than

Davis, especially in her ability to read men. At the nightclub when Harlan first arrives uninvited, she is clear about her unapproachability. She says to the man's first empty question of what are they doing there that she is minding her own business. She blows smoke in his face in a fine gesture of her unsociability towards him, which is funny because she is open about her distrust of his advances. She gets rid of him but he hovers in the background. The women talk about their partners, whether Darryl and Jimmy are back yet, and it seems Sarandon has planned this weekend away to make Jimmy want to get her back. All this serves to do is again to emphasize the importance of men, but there is a breaking through to another attitude, through humour which allows the repressed to emerge, where the women jokingly ask each other why they don't just leave their male partners. They are not consciously serious about the suggestion, but because humour allows for the acknowledgement of material they would not usually consider, there is in this exchange some possibility of their breaking off from the men, which in fact they do by the end.

Meanwhile Harlan is still watching in the background. He indicates the dance floor from where he has been hovering, and Davis says to Sarandon, 'Let's dance.' The way Sarandon is seated means she cannot see Harlan, so obviously when she gets up she thinks she will be dancing with Davis. Given the heterosexual ambience of the nightclub, it is a bold statement of female solidarity for two women to dance together. Nevertheless this was Sarandon's clear intention, and when she sees Davis go to have a dance with Harlan, she does not follow them. Disappointed?

Sarandon is the unavailable adult woman with a dyke haircut and androgynous cowboy outfit. In the car park she saves Davis from further assault, and is provoked into killing Harlan. They make their escape. She knows the law will punish them, and it emerges that she has possibly been through this before. She decides to go to Mexico. She tells Davis this is not a game, much as a mother has to sometimes alert a child to the seriousness of a situation. She wants to know if Davis is up to this. Obviously she is asking if Davis will come with her to Mexico. Davis says she doesn't know what Sarandon is asking of her, and we are immediately alerted to the gap in her consciousness which signals a subtext. Sarandon says Davis is not to start flaking out on her, that Davis goes 'blank' or pleads 'insanity or some such shit' at a crisis. This is clearly a piece of projection, and serves to contextualize Sarandon's crime within a framework of an evacuation of the self that rape victims have described (Bal, 1992: 368). Is this why Sarandon pulled the trigger automatically? Because she had lost her sense of self and went 'blank', because she was catapulted into committing manslaughter by a deep relapse or flashback into an evacuated space in her consciousness, due to a previous rape and in this case akin to insanity?

Sarandon is virginal and phallic at the same time. She is vulnerable but strong, innocent but knowledgeable. She inspires sympathy and also immense respect. When Jimmy arrives in Oklahoma City and she denies that there is someone else, she is not lying, but she is repressing her involvement with Davis, not a sexual involvement but an intimate arrangement nevertheless. And she does not for a moment consider involving Jimmy more or asking him to join them in their flight. She wants to break clean, let go, and her reference to 'bad timing' is a delightful (intentional?) intertextual reference to Nicolas Roeg's *Bad Timing*, also featuring Harvey Keitel as a sympathetic detective trying to establish the facts on a woman's behalf. Compared to the irresponsible love-making going on between Davis and J. D., Sarandon spends the night at the motel trying to confront the gravity of lack and loss.

The next day Davis tells Sarandon she always wanted to travel, but never had the opportunity. Sarandon tells her she has it now. Travel can stand in for exploration, adventure, pleasure, all of which can be sexual. Davis is just starting out – she is at the crossroads of new beginnings. They are alive.

In fictional fact this will be their last night alive. For the first time the musical score reflects more appropriately than otherwise the emotional content of the scene. Marianne Faithfull's 'The Ballad of Lucy Jordan' plays to their driving in the night, the lyrics melancholically reworking themes of regret, loss, grief.

It is as if Sarandon is prescient about it being their last night. She stops the car, and gets out near a cliff edge. Is she contemplating suicide? Davis joins her, and asks her what's going on. Sarandon says 'Nothing.' Of course 'nothing' is a loaded word, but in being reductive and not expansive, nothing and not everything, this one exchange typifies for me how the film falls into a phallocentric mould of film-making. In the name of realism, these women must be stopped. They cannot have it all, but must lose their lives to serve narrative conventions of what constitutes the realistic. However, I think realism has a lot to answer for, not just by invoking a unitary subjecthood, but by being the standard in whose name violence and hatred are recycled.

The next day they continue their escape with some impressive driving from Sarandon. But of course escape is impossible under such a regime, and they are trapped on the edge of the Grand Canyon. They decide to commit suicide to avoid entrapment. They kiss on the lips, hold hands and drive off the edge into the canyon, with a freezeframe of their car suspended over the drop. (Compare the concluding freezeframe of the male buddy movie, *Butch Cassidy and the Sundance Kid*, where the moment of retribution and death is also frozen.)

The ending cuts off the woman spectator with a phallocentrically framed conclusion. Nothing in the fiction of the film necessitates this ending, beyond the demands of realism and censorship considerations. An alternative ending could be to follow an anti-realist tradition. I will suggest that the male director, Ridley Scott, should have sacrificed realism to the much more valuable objective of affirming women. He could have done this with a device as established as the *deus ex machina,* the god out of the machine, of ancient Greek drama, where endings had interventions, as in Euripides' *Medea.* In this case, we could have had a film-maker emerge out of the fabrication. For instance, on the freezeframe, we could have had Sarandon and Davis speaking as themselves, as actors who want to assert alternative logics, other endings, to those usually deployed under the demands of realism. They could have addressed Ridley Scott by name, saying let's benefit from the possibilities of fiction by inventing another ending. What? Not a dream. Not a trial that acquits the women. Not an escape to Mexico. But a deus/director out of the machine/machinery of the art-product, exposing that product as a fabrication. Davis could suggest that they rewind back to their kiss and freezeframe briefly on that, then to have the car move over the edge and fly across the canyon. Sarandon could suggest a future sex scene between the women. Anything could be possible to celebrate the plasticity of fiction. Rather than cut off the escape routes, and give realism an over-exaggerated respect, it could have been possible to envisage alternative endings. This could become a way of instituting new narrative questions. Not 'will they get together in a happy ending?' Not 'will it end in tragedy?' But 'will the film remain within the realist tradition?' Or 'will it use anti-realism as a self-reflexive strategy?' New narrative questions could establish revised cinematic languages.

If the ideas I have proposed seem too ludicrous for cinematic purposes, Ridley Scott could have opted for another conclusion, borrowing from the precedent of a cult film from 1971, *Vanishing Point*, where an on-the-road fugitive is pursued by police cars in what becomes a convoy, only to evade entrapment at the end in an explosive diappearance. If Thelma and Louise could have made their escape by literally disappearing, this ending would have exposed realism in cinema as a fabrication. Moreover, it would have given women spectators some idea of another 'space', an 'elsewhere' other than the allocation to the female of death, failure, destruction.

I am not proposing this idea for the sake of anti-realism for itself, because 'anti-realism is not necessarily more politically correct than realism' (Holmlund, 1991: 16). Rather, I think this option in this instance points to there having been a lack of imagination in operation, and a missed opportunity to allow women some sense of celebration. It was also a missed opportunity to refigure Oedipus, first by demonstrating the agency of female rather than male desire, second by refusing to confine the narrative within realist closure. From the point of view of making political interventions at the level of reception, certainly I believe the least we can do as spectators is to re-envision such endings by supplying subversive and resistant readings, especially when confronted with such an appalling cutting down of the women. They find themselves to lose their lives, they locate their identities at the point they must be wasted, and this tragedy is a serious reminder to women of our disenfranchisement under the symbolic order as it currently stands.

Let us now consider in more detail the issues of gender, space and control that are raised by the film's action. One dynamic of gendered subjectivities can revolve around male violence against female autonomy, and this is what we see in the rape. Such a dynamic maintains the inequality between the sexes, by perpetuating 'a relationship of dominance and subordinance' (Millett, 1970: 25). We know that positions of domination and subordination are the key to inequality. Sheila Jeffreys finds that it is this very inequality that is at the heart of male heterosexual desire, where 'under male supremacy, sex consists of the eroticising of women's subordination' (Jeffreys, 1990: 301). Forget a parity of pleasure, a mutuality of desire, an equity between partners. To be gendered female is to invite domination, just as under this phallocentric regime, to be gendered male is to exercise power as manifested in the subordination of the woman, where 'feminine means violable' (MacKinnon, 1987: 118). Such a regime must be challenged and dethroned if we are to rethink subjectivities in meaningful and positively productive ways.

When gender dictates and determines space, the location/position we occupy as women, and when that space has to be asserted constantly in the context of a phallocentric order that subjugates women, we see that attaining our autonomy as women is the most desirable objective we could achieve. This question of female space, operating under the threat to invade or curtail it, is enacted in the film from the rape by one man to the pursuit of the women by many other men, in the name of the law and carrying the threat of entrapment. At the end, the women have nowhere to go, they have no space beyond what is over the edge.[3] They are defeated, not by realism or reality, but by the phallocentrism of patriarchy.

Economically, anatomically, culturally, socially and politically, the woman is controlled by the phallocentric order. The masculine economy, one of exploitation, appropriates the labour of the woman. When she works for a formal wage she earns less because of unequal pay structures that privilege men, and she is often financially dependent. She is also oppressed for anatomical reasons which pervert her reproductive capacity by reducing her to a maternal function. Her body can be the site of abuse and medical experimentation, as well as fetishization and false worship. Culturally, the woman is objectified, marginalized, vilified, often persecuted and punished. She is humiliated in daily media representations and degraded in pornography. Socially, she is a sexual servicer and a domestic servant, who lives in a culture of male violence and a climate of compulsory heterosexuality. She is primarily responsible for child care in the context of a derogation of motherhood. Politically, the woman has inadequate representation and is not recognized as an equal subject in a jurisprudence determined by the male viewpoint. She has less power and privilege than men by virtue of her gender.

Having outlined patriarchy in some of its larger operations, we can see how it has historically held the woman in a position of subordination to men. Let us now look closely at the subject of rape again, as symptomatic of male violence under a patriarchy. The phenomenon of rape takes place as a logical correlative to the construction of gendered subjectivities as it exists in the current malestream. I argue that rapists can apparently be quite normal, insofar as their acts of sexual atrocity against women are symptomatic of a woman-hating culture, and signify an adoption of a version of masculinity as aggression. We will look in detail at how rape trials are conducted to demonstrate the phallocentric bias in this culture, where the rapist is normalized and the victim is pathologized. By locating gender as central, and by identifying a misogynist patriarchy as largely responsible, it becomes necessary to reformulate the construction of masculinities and femininities if we wish to achieve minimums of parity between men and women.

By arguing that the average rapist is a 'normal' man, I intend this as an indicting comment on the social construction of masculinities and femininities, where the gendered binary system accords agency and activity to the male, while the female is derogated on all fronts. By seeing many rapists as normal, I subscribe to the radical feminist position that locates patriarchy as an identifiably oppressive structure, rather than seeing the phenomenon of rape as isolated incidents expressing misogyny at an individual and not institutionalized level.

Rape involves sexual violation, where the woman's punishment is the man's pleasure. Sex becomes not an exchange of consensual pleasure, but an act of terrorization, humiliation and control, expressing hatred and frustration, and only coincidentally involving sex as a forum for that expression. It should not be considered normal. But given the present regime of gendered subjectivities, we find that the act of rape is normalized, in that many men who commit rape often do so with impunity, because of the readings made of masculinities as the right of men to have sexual access to women's bodies. The psychic make-up of the average rapist is therefore seen to be reflective of a predatory rather than pathological enculturation of masculinity, although I would want to challenge this reading, and see it rewritten, so that rape can be clearly identified as that which is not normal, by reconstructing gendered subjectivities. However, under the present regime of how masculinities are read, we find that rapists are quite normal and not pathological. Angela Davis reports:

> Most rapists are not psychopaths, as we are led to believe by typical media portrayals of men who commit crimes of sexual violence. On the contrary, the overwhelming majority would be considered 'normal' according to prevailing social standards of male normality. (Davis, 1984: 42)

Other feminists have also documented that studies find convicted rapists to be 'normal' men. Andrea Dworkin and Susan Griffin both cite Menachem Amir's study of 646 convicted rape cases in Philadelphia, where he states:

> Studies indicate that sex offenders do not constitute a unique clinical or psychopathological type; nor are they as a group invariably more disturbed than the control groups to which they are compared. (Amir, quoted by Dworkin, 1975: 34; by Griffin, 1986: 5)

Dworkin and Griffin also cite a California parole officer who worked with rapists, and who said of them, 'Those men were the most normal men there' (quoted by Dworkin, 1975: 34; by Griffin, 1986: 5). Dworkin takes this 'normality' a step further, by asserting the social presentability of some rapists. 'Remember, rape is not committed by psychopaths or deviants from our social norms – rape is committed by *exemplars* of our social norms' (Dworkin, 1975: 45; original emphasis).

Although media accounts publicize the stereotypes of the so-called 'ideal' and the 'perfect' rape, where the rapist and victims are strangers to each other, more like over 85 per cent of alleged rapists are known to women as acquaintances or more, 'such as colleagues, neighbours, friends, or those who have more intimate relationships, such as relatives, husbands and fathers' (Lees).[4] Clearly then, men who are presentable, employed, married, apparently well adjusted, are committing rape. As Sue Lees states, 'Rapists are not psychotic or psychologically disturbed, but perfectly normal men who are at the more sexist end of the spectrum of sexist attitudes' (Lees, 1996: 221).

Because men's sexual urges are seen as naturally uncontrollable, the responsibility is shifted from the man's lack of self-control to the woman's so-called provocation. Hence in rape trials, the issue is often reduced to whether the woman really consented, which Smart sees as a gross simplification of the complexity of women's experience (Smart, 1989: 33).

The Heilbron Commission which was set up to examine rape came up with a report on some of the procedural flaws in the courtroom treatment of rape. The resulting Heilbron Report recommended that the woman's sexual history be largely inadmissible as evidence, on the obvious logic of its irrelevance. However, the Sexual Offences (Amendment) Act of 1976 does not allow for an adequate reflection of this recommendation in practice. Although women's previous sexual history rarely has any relevance to the evidence, and is supposed to be allowed only in exceptional circumstances, it is frequently introduced, subject to an application by the defence and dependent on judicial discretion. A judge can allow a cross-examination of the rape victim about her sexual history if he thinks not to do so would be 'unfair' to the defendant. As there are no guide-lines on the admission of this evidence, it has depended on the decision of individual judges. The bias is clear. In Zsuzsanna Adler's study of rape trials, 'evidence relating to the sexual past of 96 per cent of the victims was introduced some way in the trial' (Adler, 1987: 100).

The evidence of previous sexual history is used to challenge the woman's credibility as a witness and any suggestion of promiscuity is eagerly seized on as a way to discredit the charge of rape. Some judges clearly flout the law by allowing the introduction of such evidence when it is nearly always completely irrelevant, and by making outrageous interventions and interpretations on the defendant's behalf. The woman's trauma is exacerbated because she is 'not allowed to meet the Prosecution who is preparing her case beforehand' (Lees). Unlike in the USA, 'the rape complainant in Britain is not allowed to consult the Prosecution Counsel', while the defendant has legal representation including consultation and a preparation of the defence, 'and can converse during the trial' (Lees; cf. Lees, 1996: 108). This is clearly a procedural fault in need of reform. Rape victims who go to court frequently find that they are the ones on trial, and the court appearance is sometimes as humiliating as the original violation. The woman's interrogation in court can involve how many sexual partners she has had, her use of contraceptives, her gynaecological history. If by chance the victim has had previous sexual contact with the defendant, he will almost invariably be acquitted. The woman will have to repeat, over and over, how the rape took place, what was done to which body part, all a salacious reworking of the original rape for the benefit of a male audience. The woman is made to speak the unspeakable, where being a subject speaking of sexual atrocity in detail serves to sexualize her and make her seem complicit in the crime (Smart, 1989: 40).

When evidence of the victim's previous sexual history is not allowed to be introduced directly, then there is the use of indirect evidence and suggestion (Adler, 1987: 99). The defence seizes on alcohol and drug abuse, on previous convictions, on psychiatric treatment, as a way of pathologizing the victim (*ibid*.: 103–5). Rather than holding the man accountable for his sexual actions, his sexual urges are seen as normal by blaming the victim. This holds the woman responsible for being attractive, out to have a good time, alone at night, drinking, using strong language, wearing 'seductive' clothing (*ibid*.: 107–10). The assumption is that if a woman flirts with a man, or kisses him, she has to have sexual intercourse with him (*ibid*.: 112; Smart, 1989: 34). Adler finds the same assumption of the woman's sexual consent being made by the defence who impute provocation for minor sexual contact (Adler, 1987: 130–1).

In addition to the first violation and the second humiliation, where violation and humiliation are interchangeable terms, women may well find themselves suffering from rape trauma syndrome (Temkin, 1986: 276). They may feel fearful and guilty, ashamed and anxious. When the man is acquitted because the jury believes his testimony rather than the woman's, this confirms that it is the rapist who has been normalized and the woman who has been pathologized. This is of course a gross injustice, and the Home Office Statistics for the conviction rates show a drop from 37 per cent in 1980 to 8.6 per cent in 1994 in the UK, indicating a decline when in fact the incidence of violent crime is on the increase.[5] When rapists walk free, despite some of them having a history of committing similar offences, this is because the woman's sexual history is on trial.

How can we address this injustice? The phallocentric bias of the court systems cannot be addressed solely at the level of legal reform, although clearly this is a start. More importantly, we need a wider sea-change of attitude, by problematizing and challenging the construction of masculinities and femininities. bell hooks, for instance, has pointed out that feminists have realized it has been a mistake not to address the issue of masculinity more (hooks, 1989: 127). This view is reaching a larger circulation.

R. W. Connell finds that 'masculinity, like femininity, is always liable to internal contradiction and historical disruption' (Connell, 1995: 73). He refers to 'hegemonic masculinity' where 'the successful claim to authority, more than direct violence', is 'the mark of hegemony' (ibid.: 77). It is primarily through the realm of finance that men maintain their control. 'In the rich capitalist countries, men's average incomes are approximately *double* women's average incomes' (ibid.: 82; original emphasis). However, it is violence that holds together such 'a massive dispossession of social resources' (ibid.: 83). Although much violence is manifested against women, Connell makes the point that 'most episodes of major violence (counting military combat, homicide and armed assault) are transactions among men' (ibid.). What is evident is that male violence damages all subjects, of whichever gender.

Jane Caputi cites a grim anecdote from Margaret Atwood, that men feel threatened by women because 'they are afraid women will laugh at them', while women feel threatened by men because 'We're afraid of being killed' (quoted by Caputi, 1987: 1). This shocking contrast reminds us how our subjectivities are engaged in very fragile and precarious processes, and that, in this instance, the fragility of men's egos and their obsession with castration can become a serious threat to disrupt the autonomy of the other through their imposition of violence in a false bid for agency. One prototype of masculinity sees the real man as the man who has taken life, just as one prototype of femininity sees the woman as only a real woman if she becomes a mother and gives birth to life.

A reconstruction of masculinity would involve a rereading of mutuality and co-dependence not as anathema, but as ways of enabling emotional growth and relational contact. Beatrix Campbell reports how 'the very idea of dependency is incompatible with masculinity' (Campbell, 1984: 22). Campbell finds that 'masculinity has remained relatively unreconstructed' despite the experience of unemployment for many men, whose 'tragedy is that unemployment makes them feel unmanned' (ibid.: 190).

It is evident that dominant definitions of masculinity assume a position of financial solvency, and this has led to a crisis in some men's adoptions of a masculine identity. This crisis is to be welcomed if it can challenge 'hegemonic masculinity', but the too frequently realized danger is that many men can adopt macho behaviour as a defensive compensation for any threat to their status as men. But masculinity as aggression, whether competitive, corporate or overtly violent, can only serve the destructive ends of a death-dealing order.

One way of reconstructing masculinity is at the level of representations. Adler states that newspapers sell more copies when they report sordid sex crimes because of the pornographic content of such reporting (Adler, 1987: 63). Clearly, some men enjoy the representations and reports of their violence against women. If we cannot stop the supply of this material, we must try to problematize it, so as to have it interpreted differently. In an ideal and equitable system of sociality there would be a more self-conscious and critical awareness of the material being consumed, and of the implications of such consumption. Rather than being seen as a source of pleasure, if this violent and woman-hating material could be seen as disturbing and dangerous, it might help change these men's perceptions of their masculine privileges, where to be normal would be precisely *not* to want to rape, terrorize and humiliate.

In order to problematize masculinity through representations, we would also need to demystify some of the myths around the rapist, for instance that it is black men who are predominantly the rapists of white women. Davis has documented how this charge against black men was a 'distinctly political invention' which was fabricated at the time of the American Civil War to justify the lynching of black men (Davis, 1981: 184–5). She points out the statistical facts that white men rape black women more frequently than black men rape white women (Davis, 1984: 43). Historically as well, it was white men who raped black women as a matter of course under slavery, not for reasons of desire but of domination.

Although the phenomenon of rape is on the increase, it is helpful to see it in a wider context, where the use of rape as a tool of terrorization and subjugation has probably been in operation since prehistory. Its occurrence in times of modern warfare also has a long tradition, and soldiers have routinely raped women out of a militaristic policy functioning in the mode of conquest and domination, where rape is a normal practice for subjugating the vanquished in the name of victory, and can involve brutal violations of the woman's body. The phenomenon of corrupt police officers who commit rape has also been reported widely, from the Indian subcontinent to the Americas.

What is at issue here is the adoption of a masculinity characterized by a desire to express power through aggressiveness. Diana Russell cites Nicholas Groth, who has categorized different types of rapists, and who finds 'the power rapist, who asserts his masculinity by coercing and subduing his victim, is by far the most typical' (Groth, quoted by Russell, 1990: 143). Masculinity becomes the enculturation of a gendered subjectivity based on domination and control, power and conquest. 'It is a combination of force, skill and the irresistible occupation of space as an expression of power which constitutes adult masculinity' (Collier, 1995: 167). What is termed 'the irresistible occupation of space as an expression of power' could be a euphemism for rape itself, where the violation of the woman's physical space is metaphorically matched by the violation of her subjectivity, all in the name of the man's masculinity and its assertion. I understand from the phenomenon of rape that male subjects who assert an aggressive masculinity are denying their relational capacities, and are choosing to abuse women because of their derogation of us. This abuse takes many forms, of which rape as a phenomenon is a significant index that male violence against women is commonplace. It is worth re-emphasizing that rape is about hatred and violence, not sex and desire. There is some speculation that only one in eight or one in ten cases are reported, so the scale of the phenomenon is widespread. What this demonstrates are the problematics of a system of sociality where subjects take on gendered positionings that are rooted in power politics and domination models.

Just as 'normal' masculinity has to be problematized, so too 'normal' femininity has to be refigured, because 'femininity' as it has been socially constructed is certainly not healthy either. Conventional femininity makes the woman masochistic, objectified, powerless. Under such a regime, the woman is seen to invite her domination, sexual exploitation, subjugation. We need to rewrite femininity by embracing the pluralism of difference, so that we account for 'femininities' much as has been done with masculinities. Above all, we would endorse that which grants us agency and autonomy without aggression, so that all gendered subjects could appropriate what is relationally productive.

In another context, Michele Wallace sees 'the problem as one of representation' (Wallace, 1992: xix). Representations could allow for a reformulation of femininities. Helen Birch states that there is no language to represent female transgression, beyond the terms of the female criminal as monster, and in this gap we see a double standard at work (Birch, 1993: 61). Christine Holmlund also alerts us to this in her examination of *Thelma and Louise*, where the men's violent and aggressive behaviour was merely their 'sexism', while the women's justifiable lawlessness caused an outrage (Holmlund, 1993: 146). The film's depiction of the women adopting 'masculine' behaviours exposes the 'performativity' of gender, but it also reinforces masculinity as agency and aggression. The men are emasculated while the women are masculinized. Although this involves a renegotiation of gender in a non-biological framework, I have difficulties with seeing women adopting the deleterious characteristics of masculinities, especially when this involves imitating aggressive behaviours.

Susan Jeffords reports that 1991, the year of *Thelma and Louise*'s release, 'was the year of the transformed U.S. man' (Jeffords, 1993: 197). She finds that the warriors of the 1980s, with their invincible bodies and violent posturings, have now become family men, no longer alienated but happily relating to women and children (*ibid*.: 198–200). As Jeffords points out, 'the transformations undergone by white male characters do nothing to address the consequences of the privileges associated with white U.S. masculinities' (*ibid*.: 207). She argues that in this logic, it is seen to be enough for these men to change, and that they do not accept responsibility for their previous behaviours, nor do their futures promise social or political action to address the inequities of the system of sociality that gives them so much privilege (*ibid*.). The 'new' masculinity being endorsed is that of the family man. Although this could be seen as a progressive development, the potential for its reactionary status can also be easily realized, especially as the child/ren can become the focus of oppressive and even abusive behaviours.

Although I have taken a radical feminist position in relation to this argument, I hope it has been informed by my Asian lesbian identity, the multiple locations of which allow me to see culture as constructed, and therefore open to transformation through contestation. Such contestation of course takes place on multiple fronts, but I do believe that global concerns, to be prioritized along with the rewriting of the black subject, must address the reconstruction of masculinities and femininities, where we would pathologize aggression and celebrate the relational.

As long as rapists are normalized by their acquittal in the courts, as long as women are pathologized for asserting their sexual autonomy, including their right to say no and have it understood and respected as a refusal, the cultural and socio-sexual regime we live under will remain one of aggression and destructiveness. Such a regime must be challenged and dethroned if we are to rethink subjectivities in meaningful and beneficial ways. We are strikingly reminded of our disempowerment when we consider the statistics from a 1980 United Nations report, which calculate that women constitute half of the population and are responsible for nearly two-thirds of the world's labour, but that we only earn one-tenth of the world's income and possess less than one-hundredth of the world's property (M. Evans, 1994: 2). How can we begin to address the enormity of such inequality?

I have suggested that we need a new way of structuring the symbolic order, and in this I follow Irigaray's thesis, that 'the whole of our western culture is based upon the murder of the mother' (Irigaray, 1992: 47). She reverses Freud's positing of a primordial murder of the father and argues that the mother has been unrepresented, that relations between her and her daughters remain unsymbolized, because desire is framed within a phallocentric model. As a result, the female is devalued, often reduced solely to 'the *maternal function*' (Whitford, 1990: 112; original emphasis).

A new symbolic order would therefore necessarily involve a re-evaluation of the woman within a non-phallocentric framework. One possibility is to celebrate the mother, but in ways that do not reduce her to a maternal function. We would have to renounce our fantasy of her as the phallic woman with omnipotent power, just as we would have to see her not as symbolically castrated, but as an autonomous subject who *herself* prohibits the child's desire for her exclusive attention. Through sharing the mother's divided attentions, through the recognition that this attention *must* be divided and not exclusive, we can see the workings of separation, of alterity, of autonomy and other needs.

We see that in the phallocentric formulations of Lacan's account, the name of the father is the law of the father, where *le nom du père* is *le non du père*, his name is the no to the child's desire for the mother, the paternal prohibition that introduces lack and the symbolization through sociality that follows. If these relationships were to be symbolized or represented differently, in a non-phallocentric frame that no longer murders the mother, we could glimpse the workings of the maternal *non/nom*, and we could expose the present 'no-name' of the mother by insisting on the mother's own no and on her own name. We need to recognize the mother as an autonomous subject, and 'We must refuse to let her desire be annihilated by the law of the father' (Irigaray, 1987: 43).

This is to recognize the woman as a subject of her own separate desires. We can see the suggestion that when this desire is for another woman, the supremacy of the phallic model can be challenged and supplanted through a celebration of female desire, where the child can learn to accept the mother's name/no as equally a prohibition against the child's desire for exclusive attention, where it is not the phallus that introduces desire, but desire as mediated by the mother. Rather than meeting the demands for unconditional love, the mother can let her love be conditional on the child's ability to accept the mother as having separate desires that do not always include the child. Here, by valorizing the female, by seeing the mother not as a maternal function but as an active subject of desire, it would be she who prohibits desire. That is, not the father/phallus as the third term, but the mother's autonomous desire would enable the child to acquire its individuation and alterity in a non-phallocentric order, all the more so if this desire were clearly for a female partner.

This is one way forward, but the project is not possible without concerted action that involves a complete revolution of sexual practices as they are currently maintained in the mainstream. For one thing, lesbian desire and lesbian identity would have to be valorized for what they are, potent vehicles for social transformation, just as the fraudulence of the phallus would have to be exposed and accepted as the fiction it is.

I think that instead of banding under a single banner, we would need to embrace the principle of the plural, not in the liberal sense where anything goes, but in an inclusive sense which privileges previously silenced voices. Nothing less than our sanity, if not our survival, is at stake. 'In order to survive in this world we must make a commitment to change it; not reform it – revolutionize it' (Parker, 1980: 242). If we do not alter the terms of the symbolic order as it currently stands, with its racist heteropatriarchy and its exploitative, abusive and aggressive set of relations, we will find not a release from but a re-imprisoning within a sick social system fuelled by destructive drives and death-dealing values. Do we really want that? Surely the time is long overdue for a transfiguration of sociality itself.

To return to the phallocentric terms of *Thelma and Louise*, its lesbian subtext reveals that heterosexual desire has to be maintained by overdetermination, whereas lesbian desire is the unspoken, the unspeakable, between the women. This subtext or point of *aporia* shows the film's internal tensions, and it is through some of its contradictions that we get glimpses of other potential meanings. Because the apparently heterosexual content is in fact heavily underlaid with the thread of lesbian desire, it is through this possibility of lesbian desire that we go beyond shared meanings, to mixed readings, and then to resistant readings. This last position is to supply subversive or oppositional readings.

As a black subject who is marginalized under white supremacism, as a woman operating in a patriarchy, and as an out lesbian despite heterosexism and homophobia, my identity predisposes me towards making oppositional as well as split readings. I am therefore drawn to the contradictions in texts, especially when they allow for the possibility of alternative logics. If my resistant readings favour an anti-realist method, it is because I think contradictions should not be denied or suppressed, but seized as a way of destabilizing conventional practices. Rather than deny contradictions, representations can draw on them to show their own status as mediated and manufactured. I also find that the demands of realism need to be tempered so long as realism is used to justify the disempowerment of women. We want celebration, not suppression. And we clearly need a revised system of representing the female, where we celebrate non-phallocentric possibilities that accord the woman her equality *and* her difference, that account for men *and* women in a new symbolic order, in an-other structuration of sociality.

Notes

1. Bonnie Zimmerman (1981:195).

2. I am indebted to Malcolm Evans for first introducing me to the concept of *aporia* in a text, during literary criticism classes at the Polytechnic of North London, now the University of North London, 1983–86.

3. A similar point was made by Pam Cook in *Reel Women*, a documentary on women film directors shown on 19 February 1995 as part of Channel Four's *Cinephile* series.

4. Undated quotations from Professor Sue Lees were made as a response to an essay I wrote on the phenomenon of rape for a Women's Studies Unit in 'Gender, Violence and Social Control' at the University of North London, 1996, which was taught by Sue. They are quoted here with her permission.

5. Home Office Statistics supplied by Sue Lees.

Answer to the question on page 210: B is A's mother.

Bibliography

Note: The original date of publication for books and articles has been given here, wherever possible, and used in the text. If a later edition has been published, details of that edition are also given.

Adams, Parveen (1983) 'Mothering', in Parveen Adams and Elizabeth Cowie (eds), *The Woman in Question*. London: Verso, 1990.

Adams, Parveen (1996) *The Emptiness of the Image: Psychoanalysis and Sexual Differences*. London: Routledge.

Adams, Parveen and Cowie, Elizabeth (eds) (1990) *The Woman in Question*. London: Verso.

Adler, Zsuzsanna (1987) *Rape on Trial*. London: Routledge and Kegan Paul.

Afshar, Haleh and Maynard, Mary (eds) (1994) *The Dynamics of 'Race' and Gender: Some Feminist Interventions*. London: Taylor and Francis.

Ainley, Rosa (1995) *What Is She Like?: Lesbian Identities from the 1950s to the 1990s*. London: Cassell.

Alexander, Karen (1991) 'Fatal beauties: Black women in Hollywood', in Christine Gledhill (ed.), *Stardom: Industry of Desire*. London: Routledge.

Alexander, Karen (1993) 'Julie Dash: "Daughters of the Dust" and a black aesthetic', in Pam Cook and Philip Dodd (eds), *Women and Film: A Sight and Sound Reader*. London: Scarlet Press.

Allen, Hilary (1986) 'Psychiatry and the construction of the feminine', in Peter Miller and Nikolas Rose (eds), *The Power of Psychiatry*. Cambridge: Polity Press.

Allen, Hilary (1987) *Justice Unbalanced: Gender, Psychiatry and Judicial Decisions*. Milton Keynes: Open University Press.

Allen, Louise (1995) '*Salmonberries*: consuming k.d. lang', in Tamsin Wilton (ed.), *Immortal, Invisible: Lesbians and the Moving Image*. London: Routledge.

Allen, Paula Gunn (1986) 'Lesbians in American Indian cultures', in Martin Bauml Duberman, Martha Vicinus and George Chauncey Jr (eds), *Hidden from History: Reclaiming the Gay and Lesbian Past*. Harmondsworth: Penguin, 1991.

Amos, Valerie and Parmar, Pratibha (1984) 'Challenging imperial feminism', in *Many Voices, One Chant: Black Feminist Perspectives*. London: Feminist Review.

Apter, Emily (1991) *Feminizing the Fetish: Psychoanalysis and Narrative Obsession in Turn-of-the-Century France*. Ithaca, NY: Cornell University Press.

Apter, Emily and Pietz, William (eds) (1993) *Fetishism as Cultural Discourse*. Ithaca, NY: Cornell University Press.

Armstrong, Louise (1994) *Rocking the Cradle of Sexual Politics: What Happened When Women Said Incest*. London: The Women's Press, 1996.

Auchmuty, Rosemary (1992) *A World of Girls: The Appeal of the Girls' School Story*. London: The Women's Press.

Backett, Kathryn (1987) 'The negotiation of fatherhood', in Charlie Lewis and Margaret O'Brien (eds), *Reassessing Fatherhood: New Observations on*

Fathers and the Modern Family. London: Sage Publications.

Bal, Mieke (1992) 'Rape: problems of intention', in Elizabeth Wright (ed.), *Feminism and Psychoanalysis: A Critical Dictionary.* Oxford: Blackwell.

Barker, Francis, Hulme, Peter, Iversen, Margaret and Loxley, Diana (eds) (1986) *Literature, Politics and Theory: Papers from the Essex Conference 1976–84.* London: Methuen.

Barrett, Michèle (1980) *Women's Oppression Today: Problems in Marxist Feminist Analysis.* London: Verso.

Barrett, Michèle and McIntosh, Mary (1982) *The Anti-Social Family.* London: Verso, 1994.

Barthes, Roland (1977) *Image – Music – Text.* Glasgow: Collins.

Becker, Edith, Citron, Michelle, Lesage, Julia and Rich, B. Ruby (1981) 'Lesbians and film', in Peter Steven (ed.), *Jump Cut: Hollywood, Politics and Counter Cinema.* New York: Praeger Publishers, 1985.

Belsey, Catherine and Moore, Jane (eds) (1989) *The Feminist Reader: Essays in Gender and the Politics of Literary Criticism.* London: Macmillan.

Benjamin, Jessica (1988) *The Bonds of Love: Psychoanalysis, Feminism, and the Problem of Domination.* London: Virago.

Bethel, Lorraine (1982) '"This infinity of conscious pain": Zora Neale Hurston and the black female literary tradition', in Gloria T. Hull, Patricia Bell Scott and Barbara Smith (eds), *All the Women Are White, All the Blacks Are Men, But Some of Us Are Brave: Black Women's Studies.* New York: The Feminist Press.

Bhabha, Homi K. (1983) 'The other question: the stereotype and colonial discourse', in *The Sexual Subject: A Screen Reader in Sexuality.* London: Routledge, 1995.

Bhabha, Homi K. (1994) *The Location of Culture.* London: Routledge.

Birch, Helen (1993a) 'If looks could kill: Myra Hindley and the iconography of evil', in Helen Birch (ed.), *Moving Targets: Women, Murder and Representation.* London: Virago.

Birch, Helen (ed.) (1993b) *Moving Targets: Women, Murder and Representation.* London: Virago.

Bland, Lucy (1983) 'Purity, motherhood, pleasure or threat? Definitions of female sexuality 1900–1970s', in Sue Cartledge and Joanna Ryan (eds), *Sex and Love: New Thoughts on Old Contradictions.* London: The Women's Press.

Bobo, Jacqueline (1990) '*The Color Purple*: Black women as cultural readers', in E. Deidre Pribram (ed.), *Female Spectators: Looking at Film and Television.* London: Verso.

Bobo, Jacqueline (1992) 'The politics of interpretation: black critics, filmmakers, audiences', in Gina Dent (ed.), *Black Popular Culture.* Seattle: Bay Press.

Bordo, Susan (1994) 'Feminism, Foucault and the politics of the body', in Caroline Ramazanoğlu (ed.), *Up Against Foucault: Explorations of Some Tensions between Foucault and Feminism.* London: Routledge.

Brah, Avtar (1993) 'Women of South Asian origin in Britain: issues and concerns', in Peter Braham, Ali Rattansi and Richard Skellington (eds), *Racism and Antiracism: Inequalities, Opportunities and Policies.* London: Sage Publications.

Braham, Peter, Rattansi, Ali and Skellington, Richard (eds) (1993) *Racism and Antiracism: Inequalities, Opportunities and Policies.* London: Sage Publications.

Brennan, Teresa (1990) 'Introduction', in Teresa Brennan (ed.), *Between Feminism and Psychoanalysis.* London: Routledge.

Bronfen, Elisabeth (1992) 'Castration complex', in Elizabeth Wright (ed.), *Feminism and Psychoanalysis: A Critical Dictionary.* Oxford: Blackwell.

Brunsdon, Charlotte (1987) 'Introductions', in Charlotte Brunsdon (ed.), *Films for Women.* London: BFI.

Bryan, Beverley, Dadzie, Stella and Scafe, Suzanne (1985) *The Heart of the Race: Black Women's Lives in Britain.* London: Virago, 1988.

Bulkin, Elly (1984) 'Hard ground: Jewish identity, racism and anti-Semitism', in Elly Bulkin, Minnie Bruce Pratt and Barbara Smith (eds), *Yours in Struggle: Three Feminist Perspectives on Anti-Semitism and Racism.* Ithaca, NY: Firebrand Books, 1988.

Bulkin, Elly, Pratt, Minnie Bruce and Smith, Barbara (eds) (1984) *Yours in Struggle: Three Feminist Perspectives on Anti-Semitism and Racism.* Ithaca, NY: Firebrand Books, 1988.

Burke, Aggrey W. (1986) 'Racism, prejudice and mental illness', in John L. Cox (ed.), *Transcultural Psychiatry*. London: Croom Helm.

Burston, Paul and Richardson, Colin (eds) (1995) *A Queer Romance: Lesbians, Gay Men and Popular Culture*. London: Routledge.

Butler, Judith (1993) *Bodies That Matter: On the Discursive Limits of 'Sex'*. London: Routledge.

Cade, Toni (1970) 'On the issue of roles', in Toni Cade (ed.), *The Black Woman: An Anthology*. New York: Signet.

Cahiers du Cinéma (1970) 'John Ford's *Young Mr. Lincoln*', in Bill Nichols (ed.), *Movies and Methods*. Berkeley: University of California Press, 1976.

Cameron, Deborah (1985) *Feminism and Linguistic Theory*. London: Macmillan.

Campbell, Beatrix (1984) *Wigan Pier Revisited: Poverty and Politics in the Eighties*. London: Virago.

Caputi, Jane (1987) *The Age of Sex Crime*. London: The Women's Press, 1988.

Carby, Hazel V. (1982) 'White woman listen! Black feminism and the boundaries of sisterhood', in *The Empire Strikes Back: Race and Racism in 70s Britain*. Centre for Contemporary Cultural Studies, University of Birmingham/ London: Hutchinson, 1988.

Carby, Hazel V. (1992) 'The multicultural wars', in Gina Dent (ed.), *Black Popular Culture*. Seattle: Bay Press.

Cartledge, Sue and Ryan, Joanna (eds) (1983) *Sex and Love: New Thoughts on Old Contradictions*. London: The Women's Press.

Chodorow, Nancy (1978) *The Reproduction of Mothering: Psychoanalysis and the Sociology of Gender*. Berkeley: University of California Press, 1979.

Chodorow, Nancy (1989) *Feminism and Psychoanalytic Theory*. New Haven: Yale University Press.

Clarke, Cheryl (1983a) 'Lesbianism: an act of resistance', in Cherríe Moraga and Gloria Anzaldúa (eds), *This Bridge Called My Back: Writings by Radical Women of Color*. New York: Kitchen Table/Women of Color Press.

Clarke, Cheryl (1983b) 'The failure to transform: homophobia in the black community', in Barbara Smith (ed.), *Home Girls: A Black Feminist Anthology*. New York: Kitchen Table/ Women of Color Press.

Collier, Richard (1995) *Masculinity, Law and the Family*. London: Routledge.

Collins, Jim, Radner, Hilary and Collins, Ava Preacher (eds) (1993) *Film Theory Goes to the Movies*. London: Routledge.

Collins, Patricia Hill (1990) *Black Feminist Thought: Knowledge, Consciousness, and the Politics of Empowerment*. London: Routledge.

Combahee River Collective, The (1978) 'A black feminist statement', in Gloria T. Hull, Patricia Bell Scott and Barbara Smith (eds), *All the Women Are White, All the Blacks Are Men, But Some of Us Are Brave: Black Women's Studies*. New York: The Feminist Press, 1982.

Comolli, Jean-Luc and Narboni, Jean (1969) 'Cinema/ideology/criticism', in Bill Nichols (ed.), *Movies and Methods*. Berkeley: University of California Press, 1976.

Connell, R. W. (1995) *Masculinities*. Cambridge: Polity Press.

Cook, Pam (1993) 'Border crossings: women and film in context', in Pam Cook and Philip Dodd (eds), *Women and Film: A Sight and Sound Reader*. London: Scarlet Press.

Cook, Pam and Dodd, Philip (eds) (1993) *Women and Film: A Sight and Sound Reader*. London: Scarlet Press.

Coward, Rosalind (1983) *Patriarchal Precedents: Sexuality and Social Relations*. London: Routledge and Kegan Paul.

Coward, Rosalind and Ellis, John (1977) *Language and Materialism: Developments in Semiology and the Theory of the Subject*. London: Routledge and Kegan Paul.

Cowie, Elizabeth (1978) 'Woman as sign', in Parveen Adams and Elizabeth Cowie (eds), *The Woman in Question*. London: Verso, 1990.

Cowie, Elizabeth (1979), 'The popular film as a progressive text – a discussion of *Coma* – Part 1', in Constance Penley (ed.), *Feminism and Film Theory*, London: Routledge and BFI, 1988.

Cowie, Elizabeth (1980) 'The popular film as a progressive text – a discussion of *Coma* – Part 2', in Constance Penley (ed.), *Feminism and Film Theory*, London: Routledge and BFI, 1988.

Cox, John L. (ed.) (1986) *Transcultural Psychiatry*. London: Croom Helm.

Creed, Barbara (1992) 'Introductions', in *The Sexual Subject: A Screen Reader in Sexuality*. London: Routledge, 1995.

Creed, Barbara (1993) *The Monstrous-Feminine: Film, Feminism, Psychoanalysis*. London: Routledge.

Curb, Rosemary and Manahan, Nancy (eds) (1985) *Lesbian Nuns: Breaking Silence*. London: The Women's Press, 1993.

Curtis, Liz (1984) *Nothing But the Same Old Story: The Roots of Anti-Irish Racism*. London: Information on Ireland.

Daly, Mary (1978) *Gyn/Ecology: The Metaethics of Radical Feminism*. London: The Women's Press, 1984.

Dargis, Manohla (1993) '"Thelma and Louise" and the tradition of the male road movie', in Pam Cook and Philip Dodd (eds), *Women and Film: A Sight and Sound Reader*. London: Scarlet Press.

Davies, Kath, Dickey, Julienne and Stratford, Teresa (eds) (1987) *Out of Focus: Writings on Women and the Media*. London: The Women's Press.

Davis, Angela (1981) *Women, Race and Class*. London: The Women's Press, 1988.

Davis, Angela Y. (1984) *Women, Culture, and Politics*. London: The Women's Press, 1990.

de Beauvoir, Simone (1949) *The Second Sex*. Harmondsworth: Penguin, 1976.

de Lauretis, Teresa (1984) *Alice Doesn't: Feminism, Semiotics, Cinema*. London: Macmillan, 1994.

de Lauretis, Teresa (1987) *Technologies of Gender: Essays on Theory, Film, and Fiction*. Bloomington: Indiana University Press.

de Lauretis, Teresa (1994) *The Practice of Love: Lesbian Sexuality and Perverse Desire*. Bloomington: Indiana University Press.

de Lauretis, Teresa and Heath, Stephen (eds) (1980) *The Cinematic Apparatus*. New York: St. Martin's Press.

D'Emilio, John (1984) 'Capitalism and gay identity', in Ann Snitow, Christine Stansell and Sharon Thompson (eds), *Desire: The Politics of Sexuality*. London: Virago.

Dent, Gina (ed.) (1992) *Black Popular Culture*. Seattle: Bay Press.

Doane, Mary Ann (1991) *Femmes Fatales: Feminism, Film Theory, Psychoanalysis*. London: Routledge.

Doane, Mary Ann, Mellencamp, Patricia and Williams, Linda (1984) 'Feminist film criticism: an introduction', in Mary Ann Doane, Patricia Mellencamp and Linda Williams (eds), *Re-Vision: Essays in Feminist Film Criticism*. Los Angeles: American Film Institute/Frederick, MD: University Publications of America.

Donald, James and Rattansi, Ali (eds) (1993) *'Race', Culture and Difference*. London: Sage Publications.

Duberman, Martin Bauml, Vicinus, Martha and Chauncey, George Jr (eds) (1991) *Hidden from History: Reclaiming the Gay and Lesbian Past*. Harmondsworth: Penguin.

Dworkin, Andrea (1975) *Our Blood: Prophecies and Discourses on Sexual Politics*. London: The Women's Press, 1982.

Dyer, Richard (1977) 'Introduction', in Richard Dyer (ed.), *Gays and Film*. London: BFI.

Dyer, Richard (1978) 'Rejecting straight ideals: gays in film', in Peter Steven (ed.), *Jump Cut: Hollywood, Politics and Counter Cinema*. New York: Praeger Publishers, 1985.

Dyer, Richard (1990) *Now You See It: Studies on Lesbian and Gay Film*. London: Routledge, 1991.

Dyer, Richard (1993) *The Matter of Images: Essays on Representations*. London: Routledge.

Ellis, John (1982) *Visible Fictions: Cinema, Television, Video*. London: Routledge 1988.

Ellsworth, Elizabeth (1986) 'Illicit pleasures: feminist spectators and *Personal Best*', in Patricia Erens (ed.), *Issues in Feminist Film Criticism*. Bloomington: Indiana University Press, 1990.

Erens, Patricia (1990) 'Introduction', in Patricia Erens (ed.), *Issues in Feminist Film Criticism*. Bloomington: Indiana University Press.

Evans, Caroline and Gamman, Lorraine (1995) 'The gaze revisited, or reviewing queer viewing', in Paul Burston and Colin Richardson (eds), *A Queer Romance: Lesbians, Gay Men and Popular Culture*. London: Routledge.

Evans, Judith (1995) *Feminist Theory Today: An Introduction to Second-*

Wave Feminism. London: Sage Publications.

Evans, Mary (1994) 'Introduction', in Mary Evans (ed.), *The Woman Question*, 2nd edition. London: Sage Publications.

Faderman, Lillian (1981) *Surpassing the Love of Men: Romantic Friendship and Love between Women from the Renaissance to the Present*. London: The Women's Press, 1985.

Fanon, Frantz (1952) 'The fact of blackness', in James Donald and Ali Rattansi (eds), *'Race', Culture and Difference*. London: Sage Publications, 1993.

Feldstein, Richard and Roof, Judith (eds) (1989) *Feminism and Psychoanalysis*. Ithaca, NY: Cornell University Press.

Felski, Rita (1989) *Beyond Feminist Aesthetics: Feminist Literature and Social Change*. London: Hutchinson Radius.

Fernando, Suman (1986) 'Depression in ethnic minorities', in John L. Cox (ed.), *Transcultural Psychiatry*. London: Croom Helm.

Fernando, Suman (1988) *Race and Culture in Psychiatry*. London: Croom Helm.

Fischer, Lucy (1989) *Shot/Countershot: Film Tradition and Women's Cinema*. London: Macmillan.

Flagg, Fannie (1987) *Fried Green Tomatoes at the Whistle Stop Café*. London: Vintage, 1992.

Fraser, Nancy and Bartky, Sandra Lee (eds) (1992) *Revaluing French Feminism: Critical Essays on Difference, Agency, and Culture*. Bloomington: Indiana University Press.

Fraser, Nancy and Nicholson, Linda J. (1990) 'Social criticism without philosophy: an encounter between feminism and postmodernism', in Linda J. Nicholson (ed.), *Feminism/Postmodernism*. London: Routledge.

Freedman, Estelle B., Gelpi, Barbara C., Johnson, Susan L. and Weston, Kathleen M. (eds) (1985) *The Lesbian Issue: Essays from Signs*. Chicago: University of Chicago Press.

Freud, Sigmund (1900) *The Interpretation of Dreams*. Harmondsworth: Pelican, 1980.

Friedberg, Anne (1990) 'A denial of difference: theories of cinematic identification', in E. Ann Kaplan (ed.),

Psychoanalysis and Cinema. London: Routledge.

Gaines, Jane (1984) 'Women and representation: can we enjoy alternative pleasure?', in Patricia Erens (ed.), *Issues in Feminist Film Criticism*. Bloomington: Indiana University Press, 1990.

Gaines, Jane (1986) 'White privilege and looking relations: Race and gender in feminist film theory', in Patricia Erens (ed.), *Issues in Feminist Film Criticism*. Bloomington: Indiana University Press, 1990.

Gallop, Jane (1982) *Feminism and Psychoanalysis: The Daughter's Seduction*. London: Macmillan.

Gallop, Jane (1988) *Thinking through the Body*. New York: Columbia University Press.

Gamman, Lorraine and Marshment, Margaret (eds) (1988) *The Female Gaze: Women as Viewers of Popular Culture*. London: The Women's Press, 1994.

Gever, Martha, Greyson, John and Parmar, Pratibha (eds) (1993) *Queer Looks: Perspectives on Lesbian and Gay Film and Video*. London: Routledge.

Gibbs, Liz (ed.) (1994) *Daring to Dissent: Lesbian Culture from Margin to Mainstream*. London: Cassell.

Giddings, Paula (1984) *When and Where I Enter: The Impact of Black Women on Race and Sex in America*. New York: William Morrow.

Gilbert, Sandra M. and Gubar, Susan (1989) 'Sexual linguistics: gender, language, sexuality', in Catherine Belsey and Jane Moore (eds), *The Feminist Reader: Essays in Gender and the Politics of Literary Criticism*. London: Macmillan.

Gilman, Sander L. (1985) *Difference and Pathology: Stereotypes of Sexuality, Race and Madness*. Ithaca, NY: Cornell University Press.

Gilman, Sander L. (1987) 'Black bodies, white bodies: toward an iconography of female sexuality in late nineteenth-century art, medicine and literature', in James Donald and Ali Rattansi (eds), *'Race', Culture and Difference*. London: Sage Publications, 1993.

Gilman, Sander L. (1993) *Freud, Race, and Gender*. Princeton, NJ: Princeton University Press.

Gilmore, Leigh (1994) *Autobiographics: A Feminist Theory of Women's Self-Representation*. Ithaca, NY: Cornell University Press.

Gittins, Diana (1985) *The Family in Question: Changing Households and Familiar Ideologies*. London: Macmillan.

Gledhill, Christine (1978a) 'Developments in feminist film criticism', reprinted in Mary Ann Doane, Patricia Mellencamp and Linda Williams (eds), *Re-Vision: Essays in Feminist Film Criticism*. Los Angeles: American, Film Institute/Frederick, MD: University Publications of America, 1984.

Gledhill, Christine (1978b) '*Klute* 1: A contemporary film noir and feminist criticism', reprinted in E. Ann Kaplan (ed.), *Women in Film Noir*. London: BFI, 1981.

Gledhill, Christine (1990) 'Pleasurable negotiations', in E. Deidre Pribram (ed.), *Female Spectators: Looking at Film and Television*. London: Verso.

Gledhill, Christine (ed.) (1991) *Stardom: Industry of Desire*. London: Routledge.

Gomez, Jewelle and Smith, Barbara (1990) 'Talking about it: homophobia in the black community', *Perverse Politics: Lesbian Issues*. London: Feminist Review.

Gothoskar, Sujata and Patel, Vithubai (1982) 'Documents from the Indian women's movement', *Feminist Review*.

Green, Gayle and Kahn, Coppélia (eds) (1985) *Making a Difference: Feminist Literary Criticism*. London: Routledge 1988.

Griffin, Susan (1986) *Rape: The Politics of Consciousness*. Revised edition of *Rape: The Power of Consciousness* (1979). London: Harper and Row.

Grosz, Elizabeth (1990) *Jacques Lacan: A Feminist Introduction*. London: Routledge, 1995.

Grosz, Elizabeth (1993) 'Lesbian fetishism?', in Emily Apter and William Pietz (eds), *Fetishism as Cultural Discourse*. Ithaca, NY: Cornell University Press.

Hall, Stuart (1980) 'Encoding/decoding', in Stuart Hall, Dorothy Hobson, Andrew Lowe and Paul Willis (eds), *Culture, Media, Language: Working Papers in Cultural Studies 1972–1979*. Centre for Contemporary Cultural Studies: University of Birmingham/London: Hutchinson.

Hall, Stuart (1993) 'New ethnicities', in James Donald and Ali Rattansi (eds), '*Race', Culture and Difference*. London: Sage Publications.

Hall, Stuart, Hobson, Dorothy, Lowe, Andrew and Willis, Paul (eds) (1980) *Culture, Media, Language: Working Papers in Cultural Studies 1972–79*. Centre for Contemporary Cultural Studies: University of Birmingham/London: Hutchinson.

Hamilton, Florence (1989) *British Women and the British Empire in India, 1915–1947*. CNAA thesis: Polytechnic of North London, now the University of North London.

Hammer, Barbara (1993) 'The politics of abstraction', in Martha Gever, John Greyson and Pratibha Parmar (eds), *Queer Looks: Perspectives on Lesbian and Gay Film and Video*. London: Routledge.

Hart, Lynda (1994) *Fatal Women: Lesbian Sexuality and the Mark of Aggression*. London: Routledge.

Hartsock, Nancy (1990) 'Foucault on power: a theory for women?', in Linda J. Nicholson (ed.), *Feminism/Postmodernism*. London: Routledge.

Haskell, Molly (1974) *From Reverence to Rape: The Treatment of Women in the Movies*. Second edition. Chicago: University of Chicago Press, 1987.

Heath, Stephen (1978) 'Difference', in *The Sexual Subject: A Screen Reader in Sexuality*. London: Routledge, 1995.

Hensman, Savitri (1995) 'A retrospective: Black together under one banner', in Valerie Mason-John (ed.), *Talking Black: Lesbians of African and Asian Descent Speak Out*. London: Cassell.

Hirsch, Marianne (1981) 'Mothers and daughters', *Signs*, 7(1).

Hirsch, Marianne (1989) *The Mother/Daughter Plot: Narrative, Psychoanalysis, Feminism*. Bloomington: Indiana University Press.

Holmlund, Christine Anne (1991) 'Displacing limits of difference: gender, race, and colonialism in Edward Said and Homi Bhabha's theoretical models and Marguerite Duras's experimental films', in Hamid Naficy and Teshome H. Gabriel (eds), *Discourse of the Other: Postcoloniality, Positionality, and Subjectivity*. Quarterly Review of

Film and Video, Reading: Harwood Academic Publishers.

Holmlund, Christine (1993) 'A decade of deadly dolls: Hollywood and the woman killer', in Helen Birch (ed.), *Moving Targets: Women, Murder and Representation*. London: Virago.

hooks, bell (1984) *Feminist Theory: From Margin to Center*. Boston: South End Press.

hooks, bell (1989) *Talking Back: Thinking Feminist, Thinking Black*. London: Sheba.

hooks, bell (1990) *Yearning: Race, Gender, and Cultural Politics*. Boston: South End Press.

hooks, bell (1992) *Black Looks: Race and Representation*. Boston: South End Press.

Hull, Gloria T., Scott, Patricia Bell and Smith, Barbara (eds) (1982) *All the Women Are White, All the Blacks Are Men, But Some of Us Are Brave: Black Women's Studies*. New York: The Feminist Press.

Iginla, Biodun (1992) 'Black feminist critique of psychoanalysis', in Elizabeth Wright (ed.), *Feminism and Psychoanalysis: A Critical Dictionary*. Oxford: Blackwell.

Irigaray, Luce (1987) 'The bodily encounter with the mother', in Margaret Whitford (ed.), *The Irigaray Reader*. Oxford: Blackwell, 1992.

Irigaray, Luce (1992) 'Women-Mothers, the silent substratum of the social order', in Margaret Whitford (ed.), *The Irigaray Reader*. Oxford: Blackwell.

Jacobus, Mary (ed.) (1979) *Women Writing and Writing about Women*. London: Croom Helm.

Jayawardena, Kumari (1986) *Feminism and Nationalism in the Third World*. London: Zed Books, 1989.

Jefferson, Ann (1984) 'Russian formalism', in Ann Jefferson and David Robey (eds), *Modern Literary Theory: A Comparative Introduction*. London: Batsford.

Jeffords, Susan (1993) 'The big switch: Hollywood masculinity in the nineties', in Jim Collins, Hilary Radner and Ava Preacher Collins (eds), *Film Theory Goes to the Movies*. London: Routledge.

Jeffreys, Sheila (1989) 'Does it matter if they did it?', in Lesbian History Group (eds), *Not a Passing Phase: Reclaiming Lesbians in History 1840–1985*. London: The Women's Press.

Jeffreys, Sheila (1990) *Anticlimax: A Feminist Perspective on the Sexual Revolution*. London: The Women's Press.

Jeffreys, Sheila (1993) *The Lesbian Heresy: A Feminist Perspective on the Lesbian Sexual Revolution*. London: The Women's Press, 1994.

Jeffries, John (1992) 'Toward a redefinition of the urban: the collision of culture', in Gina Dent (ed.), *Black Popular Culture*. Seattle: Bay Press.

Johnston, Claire (1973) 'Women's cinema as counter-cinema', in Bill Nichols (ed.), *Movies and Methods*. Berkeley: University of California Press, 1976.

Johnston, Claire (1975) 'Dorothy Arzner: Critical strategies', in Constance Penley (ed.), *Feminism and Film Theory*. London: Routledge and BFI, 1988.

Johnston, Claire (1985) 'Femininity and the masquerade: *Anne of the Indies*', in E. Ann Kaplan (ed.), *Psychoanalysis and Cinema*. London: Routledge, 1990.

Jordan, June (1989) *Moving Towards Home: Political Essays*. London: Virago.

Kaplan, E. Ann (ed.) (1978) *Women in Film Noir*. London: BFI, 1981.

Kaplan, E. Ann (1983) *Women and Film: Both Sides of the Camera*. London: Routledge, 1990.

Kaplan, E. Ann (1984) 'Is the gaze male?', in Ann Snitow, Christine Stansell and Sharon Thompson (eds), *Desire: The Politics of Sexuality*. London: Virago.

Kaplan, E. Ann (ed.) (1990) *Psychoanalysis and Cinema*. London: Routledge.

Kaplan, E. Ann (1992) *Motherhood and Representation: The Mother in Popular Culture and Melodrama*. London: Routledge.

Kaye/Kantrowitz, Melanie (1992) *The Issue Is Power: Essays on Women, Jews, Violence and Resistance*. San Francisco: Aunt Lute Books.

Kennedy, Helena (1992) *Eve Was Framed: Women and British Justice*. London: Vintage Books, 1993.

Kitzinger, Celia (1987) *The Social Construction of Lesbianism*. London: Sage Publications, 1995.

Kristeva, Julia (1981) 'Women's time', in Catherine Belsey and Jane Moore (eds), *The Feminist Reader: Essays in Gender*

and the Politics of Literary Criticism.
London: Macmillan, 1989.

Kuhn, Annette (1982) *Women's Pictures: Feminism and Cinema.* London: Verso, 1993.

Kuhn, Annette (1985) *The Power of the Image: Essays on Representation and Sexuality.* London: Routledge, 1992.

Kuhn, Annette (1988) *Cinema, Censorship and Sexuality 1909–1925.* London: Routledge.

Kuhn, Annette (1992) 'Women's genres', in *The Sexual Subject: A Screen Reader in Sexuality.* London: Routledge, 1995.

Lawrence, Errol (1982) 'Just plain common sense: the "roots" of racism', in *The Empire Strikes Back: Race and Racism in 70s Britain.* Centre for Contemporary Cultural Studies, University of Birmingham/London: Hutchinson, 1988.

Lees, Sue (1996) *Carnal Knowledge: Rape on Trial.* London: Hamish Hamilton.

Leland, Dorothy (1989) 'Lacanian psychoanalysis and French feminism: toward an adequate political psychology', in Nancy Fraser and Sandra Lee Bartky (eds), *Revaluing French Feminism: Critical Essays on Difference, Agency and Culture.* Bloomington: Indiana University Press, 1992.

Lesbian History Group (eds) (1989) *Not a Passing Phase: Reclaiming Lesbians in History 1840–1985.* London: The Women's Press.

Lewis, Charlie and O'Brien, Margaret (eds) (1987) *Reassessing Fatherhood: New Observations on Fathers and the Modern Family.* London: Sage Publications.

Lindsey, Kay (1970) 'The black woman as a woman', in Toni Cade (ed.), *The Black Woman: An Anthology.* New York: Signet.

Lorde, Audre (1984) *Sister Outsider: Essays and Speeches.* Freedom, CA: The Crossing Press.

Lovell, Terry (ed.) (1990) *British Feminist Thought: A Reader.* Oxford: Blackwell.

McClintock, Anne (1995) *Imperial Leather: Race, Gender and Sexuality in the Colonial Contest.* London: Routledge.

Macdonell, Diane (1986) *Theories of Discourse: An Introduction.* Oxford: Blackwell 1993.

MacKinnon, Catharine A. (1987) *Feminism Unmodified: Discourses on Life and Law.* Cambridge, MA: Harvard University Press.

Mama, Amina (1984) 'Black women, the economic crisis and the British state', in *Many Voices, One Chant: Black Feminist Perspectives.* London: Feminist Review.

Mama, Amina (1995) *Beyond the Masks: Race, Gender and Subjectivity.* London: Routledge.

Mason-John, Valerie (1995) 'Herstoric moments', in Valerie Mason-John (ed.), *Talking Black: Lesbians of African and Asian Descent Speak Out.* London: Cassell.

Mason-John, Valerie and Khambatta, Ann (1993) *Lesbians Talk: Making Black Waves.* London: Scarlet Press.

Mason-John, Valerie and Okorrowa, Adowa (1995) 'A minefield in the garden: Black lesbian sexuality', in Valerie Mason-John (ed.), *Talking Black: Lesbians of African and Asian Descent Speak Out.* London: Cassell.

Mayne, Judith (1990) *The Woman at the Keyhole: Feminism and Women's Cinema.* Bloomington: Indiana University Press.

Mayne, Judith (1993) *Cinema and Spectatorship.* London: Routledge, 1995.

Memmi, Albert (1957) *The Colonizer and the Colonized.* London: Earthscan Publications, 1990.

Mercer, Kobena (1986) 'Racism and transcultural psychiatry', in Peter Miller and Nikolas Rose (eds), *The Power of Psychiatry.* Cambridge: Polity Press.

Merck, Mandy (1987) '"Lianna" and the lesbians of art cinema', in Charlotte Brunsdon (ed.) *Films for Women.* London: BFI.

Metz, Christian (1982) *Psychoanalysis and Cinema: The Imaginary Signifier.* London: Macmillan, 1983.

Meyers, Diana T. (1992) 'The subversion of women's agency in psychoanalytic feminism: Chodorow, Flax, Kristeva', in Nancy Fraser and Sandra Lee Bartky (eds), *Revaluing French Feminism: Critical Essays on Difference, Agency and Culture.* Bloomington: Indiana University Press.

Miller, Nancy K. (1986) 'Arachnologies: the woman, the text, and the critic', in Nancy K. Miller (ed.), *The Poetics of*

Gender. New York: Columbia University Press.

Miller, Peter and Rose, Nikolas (eds) (1986) *The Power of Psychiatry.* Cambridge: Polity Press.

Millett, Kate (1970) *Sexual Politics.* London: Virago, 1979.

Minh-ha, Trinh T. (1989) *Woman, Native, Other: Writing Postcoloniality and Feminism.* Bloomington: Indiana University Press.

Mitchell, Juliet (1974) *Psychoanalysis and Feminism.* Harmondsworth: Penguin 1979.

Mitchell, Juliet (1982) 'Introduction – I', in Juliet Mitchell and Jacqueline Rose (eds), *Jacques Lacan and the École Freudienne: Feminine Sexuality.* London: Macmillan.

Modleski, Tania (1991) *Feminism Without Women: Culture and Criticism in a 'Postfeminist' Age.* London: Routledge.

Moi, Toril (1989) 'Feminist, female, feminine', in Catherine Belsey and Jane Moore (eds), *The Feminist Reader: Essays in Gender and the Politics of Literary Criticism.* London: Macmillan.

Moraga, Cherríe and Anzaldúa, Gloria (1983) 'The roots of our radicalism', in Cherríe Moraga and Gloria Anzaldúa (eds), *This Bridge Called My Back: Writings by Radical Women of Color.* New York: Kitchen Table/Women of Color Press.

Mulvey, Laura (1975) 'Visual pleasure and narrative cinema', in Constance Penley (ed.), *Feminism and Film Theory.* London: Routledge and BFI, 1988.

Mulvey, Laura (1979) 'Feminism, film and the *Avant-Garde*', in Mary Jacobus (ed.), *Women Writing and Writing about Women.* London: Croom Helm.

Mulvey, Laura (1981) 'Afterthoughts on "Visual pleasure and narrative cinema" inspired by *Duel in the Sun*', in Constance Penley (ed.), *Feminism and Film Theory.* London: Routledge and BFI, 1988.

Naficy, Hamid and Gabriel, Teshome H. (eds) (1991) *Discourse of the Other: Postcoloniality, Positionality, and Subjectivity.* Quarterly Review of Film and Video, Reading: Harwood Academic Publishers.

Nataf, Z. Isiling (1995) 'Black lesbian spectatorship and pleasure in popular cinema', in Paul Burston and Colin Richardson (eds), *A Queer Romance:*

Lesbians, Gay Men and Popular Culture. London: Routledge.

Neale, Stephen (1980) *Genre.* London: BFI, 1987.

Newton, Esther (1984) 'The mythic mannish lesbian: Radclyffe Hall and the new woman', reprinted in Martin Bauml Duberman, Martha Vicinus and George Chauncey Jr (eds), *Hidden from History: Reclaiming the Gay and Lesbian Past.* Harmondsworth: Penguin, 1991.

Nichols, Bill (ed.) (1976) *Movies and Methods.* Berkeley: University of California Press.

Nicholson, Linda J. (1986) *Gender and History: The Limits of Social Theory in the Age of the Family.* New York: Columbia University Press.

Nicholson, Linda J. (ed.) (1990) *Feminism/Postmodernism.* London: Routledge.

Nye, Robert A. (1993) 'The medical origins of sexual fetishism', in Emily Apter and William Pietz (eds), *Fetishism as Cultural Discourse.* Ithaca, NY: Cornell University Press.

O'Dowd, Liam (1990) 'New introduction', to Albert Memmi, *The Colonizer and the Colonized.* Earthscan Publications: London, 1957.

Onodera, Midi (1995) 'Locating the displaced view', in Laura Pietropaolo and Ada Testaferri (eds), *Feminisms in the Cinema.* Bloomington: Indiana University Press.

Pajaczkowska, Claire and Young, Lola (1993) 'Racism, representation, psychoanalysis', in James Donald and Ali Rattansi (eds), *'Race', Culture and Difference.* London: Sage Publications.

Parker, Pat (1978a) *Womanslaughter.* Oakland, CA: Diana Press.

Parker, Pat (1978b) 'Where will you be?', in Barbara Smith (ed.), *Home Girls: A Black Feminist Anthology.* New York: Kitchen Table/Women of Color Press, 1983.

Parker, Pat (1980) 'Revolution: it's not neat or pretty or quick', reprinted in Cherríe Moraga and Gloria Anzaldúa (eds), *This Bridge Called My Back: Writings by Radical Women of Color.* New York: Kitchen Table/Women of Color Press, 1983.

Parmar, Pratibha (1982) 'Gender, race and class: Asian women in resistance', in *The Empire Strikes Back: Race and*

Racism in 70s Britain. Centre for Contemporary Cultural Studies: University of Birmingham/London: Hutchinson, 1988.

Peary, Gerald and Shatzkin, Roger (1977) 'Introduction', in Gerald Peary and Roger Shatzkin (eds), *The Classic American Novel and the Movies: Exploring the Link between Literature and Film.* New York: Frederick Ungar Publishing.

Pence, Ellen (1978) 'Racism – a white issue', reprinted in Gloria T. Hull, Patricia Bell Scott and Barbara Smith (eds), *All the Women Are White, All the Blacks Are Men, But Some of Us Are Brave: Black Women's Studies.* New York: The Feminist Press, 1982.

Penley, Constance (1988) 'Introduction. The lady doesn't vanish: feminism and film theory', in Constance Penley (ed.), *Feminism and Film Theory.* London: Routledge and BFI.

Penley, Constance (1989) *The Future of an Illusion: Film, Feminism, and Psychoanalysis.* London: Routledge.

Phillips, Anne (1987) *Divided Loyalties: Dilemmas of Sex and Class.* London: Virago.

Phoenix, Ann (1990) 'Theories of gender and black families', in Terry Lovell (ed.), *British Feminist Thought: A Reader.* Oxford: Blackwell.

Pietropaolo, Laura and Testaferri, Ada (eds) (1995) *Feminisms in the Cinema.* Bloomington: Indiana University Press.

Pines, Jim and Willemen, Paul (eds) (1989) *Questions of Third Cinema.* London: BFI.

Poster, Mark (1978) *Critical Theory of the Family.* London: Pluto Press.

Pratibha (1984) 'Becoming visible: Black lesbian discussions', in Carmen, Gail, Shaila and Pratibha, *Many Voices, One Chant: Black Feminist Perspectives.* London: Feminist Review.

Pribram, E. Deidre (1990) 'Introduction', in E. Deidre Pribram (ed.), *Female Spectators: Looking at Film and Television.* London: Verso.

Rack, Philip (1982) *Race, Culture, and Mental Disorder.* London: Routledge, 1991.

Ragland-Sullivan, Ellie (1986) *Jacques Lacan and the Philosophy of Psychoanalysis.* London: Croom Helm.

Ragland-Sullivan, Ellie (1989) 'Seeking the third term: desire, the phallus, and the materiality of language', in Richard Feldstein and Judith Roof (eds), *Feminism and Psychoanalysis.* Ithaca, NY: Cornell University Press.

Ragland-Sullivan, Ellie (1992) 'Narcissism', in Elizabeth Wright (ed.), *Feminism and Psychoanalysis: A Critical Dictionary.* Oxford: Blackwell.

Ramazanoğlu, Caroline (ed.) (1994) *Up Against Foucault: Explorations of Some Tensions between Foucault and Feminism.* London: Routledge.

Reinfelder, Monika (ed.) (1996) *Amazon to Zami: Towards a Global Lesbian Feminism.* London: Cassell.

Rich, Adrienne (1976) *Of Woman Born: Motherhood as Experience and Institution.* London: Virago, 1986.

Rich, Adrienne (1979) *On Lies, Secrets, and Silence.* London: Virago, 1980.

Rich, Adrienne (1980) 'Compulsory heterosexuality and lesbian existence', reprinted in Ann Snitow, Christine Stansell and Sharon Thompson (eds), *Desire: The Politics of Sexuality.* London: Virago, 1984.

Rich, B. Ruby (1978) 'In the name of feminist film criticism', reprinted in Patricia Erens (ed.), *Issues in Feminist Film Criticism.* Bloomington: Indiana University Press, 1990.

Rich, B. Ruby (1981) 'From repressive tolerance to erotic liberation: *Maedchen in Uniform*', reprinted in Mary Ann Doane, Patricia Mellencamp and Linda Williams (eds), *Re-Vision: Essays in Feminist Film Criticism.* Los Angeles: American Film Institute/Frederick, MD: University Publications of America, 1984.

Rich, B. Ruby (1993) 'When difference is (more than) skin deep', in Martha Gever, John Greyson and Pratibha Parmar (eds), *Queer Looks: Perspectives on Lesbian and Gay Film and Video.* London: Routledge.

Roof, Judith (1991) *A Lure of Knowledge: Lesbian Sexuality and Theory.* New York: Columbia University Press.

Rose, Jacqueline (1982) 'Introduction – II', in Juliet Mitchell and Jacqueline Rose (eds), *Jacques Lacan and the École Freudienne: Feminine Sexuality.* London: Macmillan.

Rose, Jacqueline (1986) *Sexuality in the Field of Vision.* London: Verso.

Russell, Diana E. H. (1990) *Rape in Marriage* (1982). Revised edition. Bloomington: Indiana University Press.

Russo, Vito (1987) *The Celluloid Closet: Homosexuality in the Movies* (1981). Revised edition. London: Harper and Row.

Said, Edward W. (1986) 'Orientalism reconsidered', in Francis Barker, Peter Hulme, Margaret Iversen and Diana Loxley (eds), *Literature, Politics and Theory: Papers from the Essex Conference 1976–84*. London: Methuen.

Sayers, Janet (1986) *Sexual Contradictions: Psychology, Psychoanalysis, and Feminism*. London: Tavistock Publications.

Schor, Naomi (1992) 'Fetishism', in Elizabeth Wright (ed.), *Feminism and Psychoanalysis: A Critical Dictionary*. Oxford: Blackwell.

Segal, Naomi (1992) 'Motherhood', in Elizabeth Wright (ed.), *Feminism and Psychoanalysis: A Critical Dictionary*. Oxford: Blackwell.

Shaila (1984) 'Becoming visible: black lesbian discussions', in Carmen, Gail, Shaila and Pratibha, *Many Voices, One Chant: Black Feminist Perspectives*. London: Feminist Review.

Sharma, Ursula (1986) *Women's Work, Class, and the Urban Household: A Study of Shimla, North India*. London: Tavistock Publications.

Sheldon, Caroline (1977) 'Lesbians and film: some thoughts', reprinted in Richard Dyer (ed.), *Gays and Film*. London: BFI, 1980.

Sheldon, Caroline (1987) 'Lesbians in film', in Kath Davies, Julienne Dickey and Teresa Stratford (eds), *Out of Focus: Writings on Women and the Media*. London: The Women's Press.

Sherman, Charlotte Watson (ed.) (1995) *Sisterfire: Black Womanist Fiction and Poetry*. London: The Women's Press.

Shockley, Ann Allen (1979) 'The black lesbian in American literature: an overview', reprinted in Barbara Smith (ed.), *Home Girls: A Black Feminist Anthology*. New York: Kitchen Table/Women of Color Press, 1983.

Showalter, Elaine (1985) *The Female Malady: Women, Madness and English Culture, 1830–1980*. London: Virago, 1988.

Sidney, Philip (1595) *A Defence of Poetry*. London: Oxford University Press, 1973.

Silverman, Kaja (1988) *The Acoustic Mirror: The Female Voice in Psychoanalysis and Cinema*. Bloomington: Indiana University Press.

Silverman, Kaja (1990) 'Historical trauma and male subjectivity', in E. Ann Kaplan (ed.), *Psychoanalysis and Cinema*. London: Routledge.

Sivanandan, A. (1991) *A Different Hunger: Writings on Black Resistance*. London: Pluto Press.

Smart, Carol (1989) *Feminism and the Power of Law*. London: Routledge.

Smith, Barbara (1977) 'Toward a black feminist criticism', reprinted in Gloria T. Hull, Patricia Bell Scott and Barbara Smith (eds), *All the Women Are White, All the Blacks Are Men, But Some of Us Are Brave: Black Women's Studies*. New York: The Feminist Press, 1982.

Smith, Barbara (1979) 'Racism and women's studies', reprinted in Gloria T. Hull, Patricia Bell Scott and Barbara Smith (eds), *All the Women Are White, All the Blacks Are Men, But Some of Us Are Brave: Black Women's Studies*. New York: The Feminist Press, 1982.

Smith, Barbara (ed.) (1983) *Home Girls: A Black Feminist Anthology*. New York: Kitchen Table/Women of Color Press.

Smith, Barbara (1984) 'Between a rock and a hard place: relationships between black and Jewish women', reprinted in Elly Bulkin, Minnie Bruce Pratt and Barbara Smith (eds), *Yours in Struggle: Three Feminist Perspectives on Anti-Semitism and Racism*. Ithaca, NY: Firebrand Books, 1988.

Smith, Beverly (1982) 'Black women's health: notes for a course', in Gloria T. Hull, Patricia Bell Scott and Barbara Smith (eds), *All the Women Are White, All the Blacks Are Men, But Some of Us Are Brave: Black Women's Studies*. New York: The Feminist Press.

Smith-Rosenberg, Carroll (1985) 'Discourses of sexuality and subjectivity: the new woman, 1870–1936', reprinted in Martin Bauml Duberman, Martha Vicinus and George Chauncey Jr (eds), *Hidden from History: Reclaiming the Gay and Lesbian Past*. Harmondsworth: Penguin, 1991.

Smyth, Cherry (1992) *Lesbians Talk: Queer Notions*. London: Scarlet Press.

Smyth, Cherry (1995) 'The transgressive sexual subject', in Paul Burston and Colin Richardson (eds), *A Queer Romance: Lesbians, Gay Men and Popular Culture*. London: Routledge.

Snitow, Ann; Stansell, Christine and Thompson, Sharon (eds) (1984) *Desire: The Politics of Sexuality*. London: Virago.

Stacey, Jackie (1988) 'Desperately seeking difference', reprinted in Lorraine Gamman and Margaret Marshment (eds), *The Female Gaze: Women as Viewers of Popular Culture*. London: The Women's Press, 1994.

Stacey, Jackie (1991) 'Feminine fascinations: forms of identification in star–audience relations', in Christine Gledhill (ed.), *Stardom: Industry of Desire*. London: Routledge.

Stacey, Jackie (1994) *Star Gazing: Hollywood Cinema and Female Spectatorship*. London: Routledge.

Stacey, Judith (1992) 'Backward toward the postmodern family: reflections on gender, kinship, and class in the Silicon Valley', in Barrie Thorne and Marilyn Yalom (eds), *Rethinking the Family: Some Feminist Questions*. Boston: Northeastern University Press.

Stam, Robert (1991) 'Eurocentrism, Afrocentrism, polycentrism: theories of third cinema', in Hamid Naficy and Teshome H. Gabriel (eds), *Discourse of the Other: Postcoloniality, Positionality, and Subjectivity*. Quarterly Review of Film and Video, Reading: Harwood Academic Publishers.

Stanton, Martin (1992) 'Oedipus complex', in Elizabeth Wright (ed.), *Feminism and Psychoanalysis: A Critical Dictionary*. Oxford: Blackwell.

Stetson, Erlene (1982) 'Studying slavery: some literary and pedagogical considerations on the black female slave', in Gloria T. Hull, Patricia Bell Scott and Barbara Smith (eds), *All the Women Are White, All the Blacks Are Men, But Some of Us Are Brave: Black Women's Studies*. New York: The Feminist Press.

Steven, Peter (ed.) (1985) *Jump Cut: Hollywood, Politics and Counter Cinema*. New York: Praeger Publishers.

Still, Judith (1992) 'Feminine economy', in Elizabeth Wright (ed.), *Feminism and Psychoanalysis: A Critical Dictionary*. Oxford: Blackwell.

Stuart, Andrea (1988) '*The Color Purple*: in defence of happy endings', reprinted in Lorraine Gamman and Margaret Marshment (eds), *The Female Gaze: Women as Viewers of Popular Culture*. London: The Women's Press, 1994.

Temkin, Jennifer (1986) 'Women, rape and law reform', reprinted in Mary Evans (ed.), *The Woman Question*. London: Sage Publications, 1994.

Testaferri, Ada (1995) 'Introduction', in Laura Pietropaolo and Ada Testaferri (eds), *Feminisms in the Cinema*. Bloomington: Indiana University Press.

Thadani, Giti (1996) 'Jami or lesbian?', in Monika Reinfelder (ed.), *Amazon to Zami: Towards a Global Lesbian Feminism*. London: Cassell.

Thorne, Barrie and Yalom, Marilyn (eds) (1992) *Rethinking the Family: Some Feminist Questions*. Boston: Northeastern University Press.

Tinker, Hugh (1974) *A New System of Slavery: The Export of Indian Labour Overseas 1830–1920*. London: Institute of Race Relations/Oxford: Oxford University Press.

Trivedi, Parita (1984) 'To deny our fullness: Asian women in the making of history', in *Many Voices, One Chant: Black Feminist Perspectives*. London: Feminist Review.

Vance, Carole S. (1980) 'Gender systems, ideology, and sex research', reprinted in Ann Snitow, Christine Stansell and Sharon Thompson (eds), *Desire: The Politics of Sexuality*. London: Virago, 1984.

Vicinus, Martha (1985) 'Distance and desire: English boarding-school friendships', in Estelle B. Freedman, Barbara C. Gelpi, Susan L. Johnson and Kathleen M. Weston (eds), *The Lesbian Issue: Essays from Signs*. Chicago: University of Chicago Press.

Visram, Rozina (1986) *Ayahs, Lascars and Princes: The Story of Indians in Britain 1700–1947*. London: Pluto Press.

Visram, Rozina (1992) *Women in India and Pakistan: The Struggle for Independence from British Rule*. Cambridge: Cambridge University Press.

Walby, Sylvia (1990) *Theorizing Patriarchy*. Oxford: Blackwell 1991.

Walker, Alice (1983a) *The Color Purple*. London: The Women's Press, 1994.

Walker, Alice (1983b) *In Search of Our Mothers' Gardens: Womanist Prose.* London: The Women's Press, 1995.

Walker, Alice (1995) 'The right to life: what can the white man say to the black woman?', in Charlotte Watson Sherman (ed.), *Sisterfire: Black Womanist Fiction and Poetry.* London: The Women's Press.

Walker, Alice (1996) *The Same River Twice: Honoring the Difficult.* London: The Women's Press.

Wallace, Michele (1992) *Black Macho and the Myth of the Superwoman* (1978). Revised edition. London: Verso.

Weeks, Jeffrey (1977) *Coming Out: Homosexual Politics in Britain from the Nineteenth Century to the Present.* London: Quartet Books, 1990.

Weeks, Jeffrey (1985) *Sexuality and Its Discontents: Meanings, Myths and Modern Sexualities.* London: Routledge and Kegan Paul.

Weir, Allison (1996) *Sacrificial Logics: Feminist Theory and the Critique of Identity.* London: Routledge.

Weiss, Andrea (1992) *Vampires and Violets: Lesbians in the Cinema.* London: Jonathan Cape.

Wheeler, Erica (1994) 'Doing black mental health research: observations and experiences', in Haleh Afshar and Mary Maynard (eds), *The Dynamics of 'Race' and Gender: Some Feminist Interventions.* London: Taylor and Francis.

Whitaker, Claire (1981) 'Hollywood transformed: interviews with lesbian viewers', in Peter Steven (ed.), *Jump Cut: Hollywood, Politics and Counter Cinema.* New York: Praeger Publishers, 1985.

White, Patricia (1995) 'Governing lesbian desire: *Nocturne*'s Oedipal fantasy', in Laura Pietropaolo and Ada Testaferri (eds), *Feminisms in the Cinema.* Bloomington: Indiana University Press.

Whitford, Margaret (1990) 'Rereading Irigaray', in Teresa Brennan (ed.), *Between Feminism and Psychoanalysis.* London: Routledge.

Whitford, Margaret (ed.) (1992a) *The Irigaray Reader.* Oxford: Blackwell.

Whitford, Margaret (1992b) 'Mother–daughter relationship', in Elizabeth Wright (ed.), *Feminism and Psychoanalysis: A Critical Dictionary.* Oxford: Blackwell.

Willemen, Paul (1989) 'The third cinema question: notes and reflections', in Jim Pines and Paul Willemen (eds), *Questions of Third Cinema.* London: BFI.

Williams, Linda (1982) '"Personal Best": women in love', reprinted in Charlotte Brunsdon (ed.), *Films for Women.* London: BFI, 1987.

Williams, Linda (1984) '"Something else besides a mother": *Stella Dallas* and the maternal melodrama', reprinted in Patricia Erens (ed.), *Issues in Feminist Film Criticism.* Bloomington: Indiana University Press, 1990.

Wilson, Amrit (1978) *Finding a Voice: Asian Women in Britain.* London: Virago.

Wilson, Elizabeth (1981) 'Psychoanalysis: psychic law and order?', in *Sexuality: A Reader.* London: Virago, 1988.

Wilton, Tamsin (ed.) (1995) *Immortal, Invisible: Lesbians and the Moving Image.* London: Routledge.

Wings, Mary (1994) 'Rebecca redux: tears on a lesbian pillow', in Liz Gibbs (ed.), *Daring to Dissent: Lesbian Culture from Margin to Mainstream.* London: Cassell.

Wollen, Peter (1980) 'Cinema and technology: a historical overview', in Teresa de Lauretis and Stephen Heath (eds), *The Cinematic Apparatus.* New York: St. Martin's Press, 1985.

Wright, Elizabeth (1990) 'Thoroughly postmodern feminist criticism', in Teresa Brennan (ed.), *Between Feminism and Psychoanalysis.* London: Routledge.

Wright, Elizabeth (ed.) (1992) *Feminism and Psychoanalysis: A Critical Dictionary.* Oxford: Blackwell.

Young, Lola (1996) *Fear of the Dark: 'Race', Gender and Sexuality in the Cinema.* London: Routledge.

Zhana (ed.) (1988) *Sojourn.* London: Methuen.

Zimmerman, Bonnie (1981) 'What has never been: an overview of lesbian feminist criticism', in Gayle Greene and Coppélia Kahn (eds), *Making A Difference: Feminist Literary Criticism.* London: Routledge, 1988.

Index